Urban Worrier:
Making Politics Personal

Urban Worrier:

Making Politics Personal

Frank J. Gruber

The City Image Press

City Image Press
Santa Monica, CA

Published 2009
Printed in the United States of America

Gruber, Frank J.
Urban Worrier: Making Politics Personal /
Frank J. Gruber

2 4 6 8 9 7 5 3 1

To Janet
Always my first reader

CONTENTS

Preface

When political strategist and longtime Santa Monica resident Bruce Cameron—fondly known around the newsroom as "the source"—suggested having Frank Gruber write a column for the *Lookout*, we weren't sure what to make of the idea. We knew Frank as an articulate and thoughtful member of the Planning Commission and enjoyed his common-sense observations during the often long and technical deliberations. But could he write?

That week, we met with Frank, told him how much we loved Mike Royko and how Santa Monica needed a columnist of its own who reflected the sensibilities of its politically active residents, asked him to assure us he wouldn't use the platform to run for City Council, and requested a few writing samples.

So how good a columnist did Frank turn out to be? If Royko was the gritty, street-smart voice of a tough, blustery, often corrupt Midwestern city, Frank turned out to be his urbane, sophisticated counterpart in a trendy town at the edge of the Pacific that cherishes its gourmet restaurants, high-minded civic debate, and cutting-edge urbanism.

Highly educated and opinionated, Frank mirrors the general population of Santa Monica. He can spot the perfect cappuccino or espresso, can debate the merits of the latest architecture, and peppers his writing with foreign phrases readers in other towns might mistake for exotic dishes.

He can write articulately about everything from the placement of a pedestrian crosswalk to a parent's search for meaning in the wake of a child's death. Frank's prose shines a light on some of the dark urban corners we tend to ignore. His writing can make the intricacies of a bureaucrat's zoning decision sound like it really can have a lasting effect on our lives.

The following pages reprint many of the writings the *Lookout* has been proud to publish since Frank Gruber's column "What I Say" was launched in October 2000. They were written week after week, year after year, during heavy workloads, long vacations, natural disasters, and the interruptions of life in general.

They are what Frank Gruber has to say. They also happen to reflect what Santa Monica and its residents have been doing and saying during the early years of a new century.

Jorge Casuso
The Lookout News, Santa Monica

Introduction

I love cities, and I love local politics, and I love Santa Monica, the blesséd little city that sits inside the western edge of the megalopolis of "L.A." into which I casually moved almost twenty-five years ago. I didn't know then that ten years later I would be spending much of my life fretting about my new town and arguing for its future and about its past with others who thought they loved Santa Monica even more than I did. I found myself defending urbanness, defending the meaning of one of those threatened, if resilient, places we call cities. I became an urban worrier.

"All politics is local," in the late House Speaker Tip O'Neill's famous words. But not unless you want to read about it. Of all the political books published each year, few pay any attention to what matters most to Americans on a day-in, day-out basis.

The same goes for the columns that fill the opinion pages and for radio and television commentary. It is as if the average American cares more about who is the president of France than who is on the school board—a farfetched notion.

On a regional level, newspapers and local television cannot cover all the local political news for every city or town. Nor are many readers and viewers interested in the news in someone else's town. To sell papers and attract viewers, regional news outlets cover negative stories about politics gone wrong, or crime stories that have always been the bread and butter of tabloids and TV news. Little coverage can be given to the long-term stories in every jurisdiction about land use and zoning or school funding or capital improvements that have a sustained impact on the way people live and their attitudes toward government—attitudes that ultimately affect how they vote in statewide and national elections.

The job of reporting these stories has fallen on the least heralded, but perhaps hardest working, of all journalists—those who work for the various local papers, many of them throwaway advertisers and the like, that nearly every town has. They cover the city council and planning commission and school board meetings, not to mention local sports and spelling bees. In so doing, they provide the fodder for millions of conversations every day that take place while parents wait to pick their kids up at school, in the supermarket parking lot, or at the park while watching a soccer or little league game.

Recently, with the rise of the Internet, there are new outlets for local news—news websites that focus on particular localities or particular stories. I was lucky to start writing for one of the first. But before that I had to become *involved*.

* * *

In the early 1990s I was an ordinary resident of Santa Monica. Then a local development issue—plans to rebuild our Civic Center—caught my attention. I wrote a memo suggesting how the City might plan a better Civic Center. The memo circulated, I attended some meetings, and, what do you know, I became an activist. I joined the local neighborhood association and ultimately became the treasurer of a successful campaign to get voter approval, against no-growth opposition, for the new Civic Center plan. I came to know members of our city council, and the council appointed me to the Planning Commission in 1995. But later, after four years on the commission, when the slate I backed in a city council election lost, the new council declined to reappoint me, and I suddenly became a "former planning commissioner."

I was out of the "corridors of power," but I wanted to stay involved. Fortunately for me, in 1999 I met some people who were interested in the same topics I was, although for different reasons. The *Outlook*, the newspaper that had covered Santa Monica for 123 years—since the birth of the city—ended its publication in 1998, but reporters there were concerned that the city no longer had a paper, and they decided to try to keep the residents informed. The *Lookout News* was born. Accessed through www.surfsantamonica.com, the news website was a pioneer: the first local media outlet not affiliated with an existing print media publication. It was homegrown and optimistic.

I met the two main partners, publisher Jorge Casuso and technologist Iris Oliveras. Jorge had been an investigative reporter for the *Outlook* and former West Coast bureau chief for the *Chicago Tribune*. Iris had recently completed her master's degree at MIT, where she had researched visualization technologies and virtual environments as public tools for community involvement in the design and planning process.

I approached them about writing a weekly opinion column for the *Lookout* about Santa Monica and its politics. They bought into the idea—provided that I would first read a collection of columns by Mike Royko (Jorge worships Royko). Just before the 2000 election I began writing a column we called "What I Say." More than eight years later, I have written over 400 columns, and with the support of Jorge and Iris, and with help from the *Lookout's* great staff, I am still doing it.

My purpose in writing "What I Say" was to treat the politics of Santa Monica and the issues that confronted Santa Monica with the same seriousness that the Paul Krugmans and Thomas Friedmans of the world applied to national and international news. I brought to the subject the knowledge I had gained from community service, a cosmopolitan outlook derived from a career outside politics (as an entertainment lawyer and erstwhile movie producer), a sense of humor and a love for my subject—Santa Monica.

Santa Monica is a writer's dream: a fascinating microcosm of the twenty-first century, post-sprawl, American city, with a lot of ideological politics thrown in. The "Peoples' Republic of Santa Monica" is a place famous for both its beaches and its political scene.

But Santa Monica is not what people think it is. It's not a rich suburb of Los Angeles, a "Brentwood West" or Beverly Hills, and it's not a sleepy beach town or resort either. While it has always had elements of both suburb and tourist trap, for most of the twentieth century Santa Monica was a blue-collar industrial town famous for building Douglas aircraft like the DC-3. It had a large minority population, although much of it had to disperse when a freeway ripped the town in half in the '60s. Urban renewal followed that, and by the '70s, the city was in bad shape. Santa Monica revived, however, and not coincidentally because after decades of being run by a close-knit group of local power brokers, politics in Santa Monica got "hot" when left-wing idealists found a pocketbook issue—rent control—and took over.

Ultimately, what I have tried to do with "What I Say" is write about civic virtue in the modern age; about what it means to be a good citizen; about how one struggles to juggle compassion and pragmatism; about what liberalism means and what it doesn't mean. I have tried to take local issues and use them to shine a light on national issues and, above all, human issues. I have hoped that my passionate involvement in one local community could be an example not only of something that is very American, recalling our oldest traditions, but also of something that people today tend to forget or, worse, disparage as meaningless in a complicated and connected world.

When you read these columns, I hope they give you a good picture of Santa Monica. But even more, I hope they give you a lens for observing your own city, town, or neighborhood.

* * *

Acknowledgments

In the introduction I acknowledged my debt to Jorge Casuso and Iris Oliveras, the founders and publishers of the *Lookout*. I cannot write another word without thanking all of the reporters who have been writing for the website since I started writing my column. Besides Jorge's own reporting, I have been able to rely on the ever-reliable reporting of Teresa Rochester, Olin Ericksen, Ann K. Williams, Gene Williams, Oliver Lukacs, Mark McGuigan, Erica Williams, Elizabeth Schneider, Ed Moosbrugger, Constance Tillotson, Blair Clarkson, and Susan Reines. I also have to acknowledge my sources, whose names are too numerous to recount here.

For a city with such contentious politics, Santa Monicans are remarkably cordial and helpful. The City's staff is professional and courteous, and I could not have written my columns without the help I received from them in finding the information I needed. The same goes for the politicians and the members of citizen groups, even, or especially, those with whom I have had disagreements. I want to specially mention the members of the City Council, a uniformly intelligent bunch. Often while writing a column I will find myself "arguing" with one council member or another—imagining what holes he or she would poke in my reasoning. I also have loyal readers to thank, many of whom send me emails with criticism, encomiums, and, best of all, information.

I also want to thank Lori Stassi, a former editor and reporter at the *Santa Monica Outlook,* for proofreading the book.

I have my family to thank. I am fortunate to be married to a philosophy professor and, as mentioned in the dedication of this book, my wife Janet Levin read nearly every column before I sent it off to Jorge, and her criticism has been invaluable. My son and his friends have been the inspiration for many columns. Most of all I want to thank Janet and Henry for tolerating my obsession with all things local.

Finally—my most sincere thanks go out to all the people of Santa Monica. You are fun to write about.

2000

After the 2000 election, the country was in turmoil over the Florida debacle, but the returns were business as usual in Santa Monica: Our dominant political organization, Santa Monicans for Renters Rights (SMRR) reelected its three incumbents: Ken Genser, Michael Feinstein, and Pam O'Connor. Also on the ballot was an initiative, Measure KK, which would have preempted the right of the City Council to pass a living wage ordinance. Voters rejected KK decisively.

NOVEMBER 10, 2000

Why is it that during every election in Santa Monica, the most left-wing jurisdiction south of the Tehachapis and west of the Hudson, the opposition to the ruling center-left party takes the form of aliens from Orange County 1957? (Revenge of the not-so-long-departed [former Congressman] Robert Dornan?)

The opposition to Santa Monicans for Renters Rights must either seek professional counseling or open a branch of the Hemlock Society.

What glimmering flame attracts not normally delusional people like Herb Katz, Donna Block, or David Cole to align themselves with a train-wreck like KK, a measure that from the beginning was so out of sync with the politics of the city?

The SMRR opposition is blinded by primal hatreds. Like an old boxer with blood in his eyes, the opposition thrashes about, landing few blows on SMRR, but cutting itself rather deeply on the ropes. Meanwhile the spectators in the front rows—the electorate—either flee the spray of blood and sweat in disgust, or watch the carnage, transfixed with glee.

I write from experience. Two years ago, after years of voting the SMRR slate, I found myself on the other side, supporting the opposition candidates. We thought we were going to run a thoughtful campaign consistent with Santa Monica's liberal ethos, but in

---

the end our consultants created mail pieces just as bad as those clunkers the Santa Monica Hospitality Industry Coalition mailed last week on behalf of their hapless candidates.

"The Santa Monica Hospitality Industry Coalition" (SMHIC). What a name to engender confidence and trust. With friends like these, the opposition candidates didn't need enemies.

Fortunately for the opposition, SMRR has a sense of *noblesse oblige* and left a seat open.

Nonetheless, one can sympathize. It is hard to run against SMRR because the city is in good shape and they are the incumbents. Notwithstanding the incessant whining, people who live in Santa Monica know they've got a good thing going. If traffic, crime, the homeless were truly such problems, if our schools were in real crisis, then why would everyone in the world want to live here?

* * *

It is hard not to admire Santa Monicans for Renters Rights. SMRR is a grassroots organization. It is open to anyone who wants to join. Its nominating conventions are open. SMRR does what it says it is going to do and its success is daily proof of "the logic of collective action."

Yet, even as SMRR's candidates have swept all before them in this election, one must wonder if there are pitfalls in its path. For one thing, SMRR so dominates Santa Monica politics, including the school board, that if for any reason residents become seriously disenchanted, as they did in the early 1990s, SMRR could be in trouble.

SMRR dodged a bullet last year during the school district's budget crisis. By putting themselves in at least the rhetorical forefront of efforts to get more money from the City for the school district, SMRR leaders and council members were able to avoid blame, not only for the budget problems, but also for myriad other complaints that surfaced during the crisis, notwithstanding that they had elected most of the school board.

SMRR has the uncanny ability to adapt to circumstances by co-opting the issues of its opponents. But it is no secret that as the organization has done so, many of SMRR's old leftie stalwarts have either left the party or no longer actively participate. Still, new members are attracted to the organization by the power it has, and SMRR rolls merrily along.

Of course it doesn't hurt that each election year the opposition manages to find an issue to tie itself to that is so outrageous that SMRR can rally Santa Monica's liberal majority to its side, even though SMRR's positions, or those of its candidates, often resemble those of a homeowners' association in the San Fernando Valley more than those of a radical political group seeking to empower the powerless.

Then there was, of course, that other election in 2000, which had a particular resonance in Santa Monica. Two members of the Santa Monica City Council, including our new mayor (chosen by the council) Michael Feinstein, along with Kevin McKeown, were prominent members of the Green Party. Some of us Democrats were angry.

NOVEMBER 17, 2000

"If you voted for Nader, don't feel guilty or conflicted for one minute." From Tim Wise, "Why Nader is Not to Blame" (accessed from the Green Party Elections website: http://www.greens.org/elections)

Well, that's a relief. I was concerned all through the election that Nader voters would feel guilty—or conflicted. Now I don't have to worry. Not for one minute.

I mean I would hate for Mike Feinstein and Kevin McKeown to feel guilty—or conflicted—a couple of years from now when Hotel Employees and Restaurant Employees. Local 814 appears before the National Labor Relations Board to protest Loews' use of Darth Vader to intimidate its workers and faces an NLRB majority appointed by George W. Bush.

"And don't mourn, organize!" Ibid.

For an organization that espouses small-*d* democracy, the Greens have a surprisingly top-down attitude toward organizing. Around the country they have elected just a few score local officials, but they ran someone for president.

Sorry, but America as a whole is a conservative place. The most unproductive and self-defeating effort for the Left is to try to elect a radical president, yet the Left has always made progress under moderate Democrats.

But I am not sure the Greens care. Practical politics—getting things done—is not their thing.

I might be more generous to the Greens if I had not witnessed Green Party "organizing" firsthand here in Santa Monica, which began when Mike Feinstein arrived in the early '90s.

One has to ask, why should the Greens organize in Santa Monica in the first place?

Without help from the Green Party the westside of L.A. established some of the strongest grassroots environmental organizations around, such as Heal the Bay, the Santa Monica Mountains Conservancy, Coalition for Clean Air, and Tree People. Santa Monica already had Santa Monicans for Renters Rights, perhaps the most successful local left-

3

c. 2,000 B.C.E. - 700
Uto-Aztecans arrive in Southern California, including Tongva people
(a.k.a. "Gabrielinos") who settle along Santa Monica Bay, and along
the coast from Malibu to Orange County.

Possible Tongva names for Santa Monica: Kecheekvet or Koruuanga.

---

wing political organization in the country. We have active neighborhood organizations and homegrown social service organizations like Ocean Park Community Center and Community Corporation.

What was left to organize?

When Mike Feinstein arrived his idea of "organizing" was to join with hard-line "neighborhood protectionists" to take over the Ocean Park Community Organization. OPCO at the time was the progressive organization that had spearheaded the revitalization of Ocean Park.

Mike chose to join a faction that was so no-growth they had opposed construction of the new Los Amigos elementary school campus. Too much traffic.

Mike and his friends got themselves elected to the OPCO Board of Directors, which was easy to do at the time because there were not enough candidates to create competitive elections. Driven by Mike and these other ideologues, OPCO abandoned the mix of social justice and sustainable development that had always been at its core and came to be like a typical no-growth homeowners association, opposed to everything. It is now a shadow of its former self.

The most outrageous example of OPCO's transformation was its opposition to Project New Hope, the affordable apartment complex on Ocean Avenue for people with HIV. I will never forget the City Council hearing where Mike, appearing as OPCO's representative, went toe-to-toe with Council Member Ken Genser, arguing that the City, which owned the land, should develop it for a "higher use."

Having now "organized" Ocean Park, Mike moved on. His next target was SMRR. Specifically, he wanted to run for the City Council and he wanted SMRR's endorsement. Mike tried packing the 1994 SMRR convention with Green Party members, but the tactic failed. He came back in 1996 and succeeded. Further "organizing" led to SMRR's endorsement of fellow Green Kevin McKeown in 1998.

That is the extent of Green Party organizing in Santa Monica. It has not been quite as bloody as the Homestead Strike, but, by golly, someone had to do it.

Feinstein and the Green Party have received far more in benefits from their association with SMRR, and with Local 814 and SMART, than these local organizations have received back. Feinstein has become an important figure in the international Green network. He's often quoted in the national media. Santa Monica is a well known city, and having two Greens on the City Council has added considerably to Green Party USA's legitimacy. Feinstein has never run as a Green in Santa Monica, but when it is his turn to become mayor, you can be sure the Green Party will take credit.

1542
Juan Cabrillo sails three ships into "Bay of Smokes" — either Santa
Monica Bay or San Pedro. Cabrillo claims California for Spain.

Oh yes, one more thing. When construction began on Project New Hope in 1997, Feinstein, by now a member of the City Council, appeared at the groundbreaking to accept the people's gratitude. Now that's organizing.

* * *

Are we still fighting the Civil War? Look at the electoral map. The old Confederacy and the West vote one way, the Union (at least most of it) votes the other.

We hope politics will be about issues. We fear it will be about personalities. But in a close election it becomes apparent that politics comes down to an American version of tribalism. Race, ethnicity, and religion have been crucial in the creation of our political culture.

The states whose electorates are largely the product of nineteenth century and later immigration (including internal migration by African-Americans) vote for the Democrat. States dominated by "real Amurcans" vote Republican. It is not just a matter of prejudice or affinity, but also different attitudes arising from different experiences.

As we all know, the swing state is Florida, which used to vote like Georgia but which is now "immigrant."

In the long term, this trend bodes well for the Democrats. Since the Civil War the majority party has never been for long the party of the South, although for a time Democrats in the South were part of the New Deal coalition.

But Ralph Nader says the closeness of the vote between the Democrats and the Republicans means that they are the same. If this is the case, does that mean three percent of the voters are progressive and the rest not? I sure don't think so.

It's true that national elections have to be won in the center, and the mixed-up views of the "undecideds" can drive everyone crazy.

But the convergence of the parties and the compromises real politicians have to make to move their programs forward should not hide the progress that has been made in this sometimes strange and unpredictable democracy.

The fact is that the Left should be proud that decades of activism have changed the political dialogue. Even lip service is important as an expression of normative values. Civil rights, the environment—no politician can win without at least saying the right things. Talk is no substitute for action, but good talk is better than bad talk. This is good convergence, and if Nader is upset with this, then he's got a problem.

I hope he is conflicted. At least.

Around the time of Thanksgiving 2000, President Clinton visited Vietnam. Subsequent events have made me nostalgic for what now seems to have been a brief decade of innocence.

NOVEMBER 22, 2000

In the midst of a civil war of unequalled magnitude and severity, which has sometimes seemed to foreign States to invite and to provoke their aggression, peace has been preserved with all nations, order has been maintained, the laws have been respected and obeyed, and harmony has prevailed everywhere except in the theatre of military conflict; while that theatre has been greatly contracted by the advancing armies and navies of the Union. —Excerpt from Abraham Lincoln's Thanksgiving proclamation of 1863.

That was equanimity. In the midst of a terrible civil war, Lincoln had the aplomb to offer thanks.

I suppose it is the Biblical tradition of sacrificing the fatted calf, but it always seems presumptuous to offer thanks by stuffing ourselves with the bounty for which we are grateful.

Yet, like all right-thinking Americans, I hold Thanksgiving to be the best holiday. Few things have remained so true to their essentials.

When I was a kid we drove over the river and through the suburbs of Philadelphia—not to grandmother's house, because my grandmothers lived in far corners of the country, Houston and Los Angeles—but to the big, old-fashioned house of family friends, Negley and Ruth Teeters. They were an older couple. Neg taught at Temple University and he and Ruth more or less adopted my parents when they were young and Temple hired my father and they moved to Philadelphia.

This made Neg and Ruth foster-grandparents for me and my sister and brother, and they could have been grandparents from Central Casting. White hair, clear skin, blue eyes. Neg played ragtime on the piano, and Ruth had this upper Midwest accent that has always been my benchmark for reasonableness and rationality.

But by the mid-'60s, when I was a teenager, Neg Teeters had retired, and he and Ruth had moved away. Our Thanksgivings entered the Vietnam era. In the Vietnam era any large gathering of friends and relatives resulted in an argument about Vietnam, and it didn't hurt that my father was a Humphrey Democrat and my mother and her friends belonged to the Women's International League for Peace and Freedom.

1769
Portolá expedition stops near present day Veterans Adminstration
facility four miles east of Santa Monica beach.

One Thanksgiving my parents hosted both my cousin David who was at West Point and my cousin Bob who, having dodged the draft, was attending college in Philadelphia. Wow.

One thing about the '60s, there was always something to talk about.

Last week after looking at the electoral map I wondered in this column if we were still fighting the Civil War. Certainly, we still disagree about Vietnam. There is no consensus. My guess is that if you put your average Bush supporter in a room with your average Gore supporter, gave them some drinks to loosen up, and casually mentioned Vietnam, they'd be arguing in a minute.

So over the weekend, in between the talking heads from Tallahassee, I tried to catch a glimpse of President Clinton in Vietnam. I'm not complaining about the coverage—I understand that actual history rates over merely momentous news. But still .... Maybe it's just a baby boomer thing, but my heart beats faster when I remember.

Resolving our relationship with Vietnam means more than selling more widgets to China.

My son was born on the last day of 1989, that *annus mirabilis*. I have tried to explain to him what it was like growing up worrying about atomic annihilation. I have tried to explain why the Vietnam War was different from all those other wars he's obsessed with in his ten-year-old way.

There is a lot of shouting going on in Florida now. We do not know who our president will be. But "peace has been preserved with all nations, order has been maintained, the laws have been respected and obeyed."

That's something to be thankful about.

L and-use issues are the bread and butter of local politics, and the biggest issue the first year I wrote my column was whether the City of Santa Monica should allow Target to build a store downtown. My first (of many) columns on Target focused on the misconceptions Santa Monicans have about who they are.

DECEMBER 6, 2000

"I wonder where those workers are going to come from in Santa Monica, which has become more and more and more an affluent community. So hiring locally may well not be as important an aspect of this as we would like to think." —Commissioner Julie Lopez Dad, at the Planning Commission's October 30, 2000, hearing on the proposed Target store at Fifth Street and Santa Monica Boulevard, speaking on whether the 400 jobs Target would create should be considered a significant factor in the store's favor.

No matter who becomes our next president, the next big land-use issue in Santa Monica will be the proposed Target department store at Fifth and Broadway.

Wolf Blitzer will not cover the story, but, by the time the City Council debates the matter next year, much will have been written about it here in Santa Monica.

A Target store downtown would be an excellent thing for Santa Monica. Not only that, but it would be a model for how current mass-market retailing can be adapted for the post-sprawl era of American cities.

Back on October 30, the Planning Commission denied the approvals necessary to build the store. The vote was 5-2.

The reason the majority gave for disapproval was their concern about traffic congestion. These concerns outweighed the benefits a Target store would provide by way of affordable shopping, resident-serving retail, and more jobs.

The commission conducted an extensive public hearing over two nights. Many people from the public spoke including, I might add, myself, in my last public utterance before joining the Fourth Estate.

While the store's impact on traffic congestion, a technical issue that requires considerable technical analysis, will no doubt be the primary substantive issue [when the City Council makes the final decision], for me the most dramatic impact of the hearing was rhetorical and ideological.

What I saw and heard confirmed that the line between "no-growth" development policies and right-wing indifference to other peoples' problems is thin at best.

As quoted above, Commissioner Julie Lopez Dad stated that the four hundred jobs Target would create were not important. She did not believe that in an "affluent community" like Santa Monica people would care about those jobs.

Leaving aside the snobbery inherent in the attitude that jobs at Target would not interest the affluent, Ms. Dad's assessment of who lives in Santa Monica is wrong.

According to the City of Santa Monica's Community Profile, prepared for the city by Rand and published this past March, many Santa Monicans, particularly our youth, live in poverty. For instance:

• As of 1998, 12.7 percent of the people in Santa Monica live in poverty by the federal standard. In the 90404 zip code, 22 percent live in poverty, a percentage higher than the national rate.

• High numbers of our children and young adults live in poverty: 16.7 percent of those under five; 19.3 percent of those five to fourteen, 21.3 percent of those fifteen to nineteen, and 24.7 percent of those twenty to twenty-four. In total, 19 percent of our children under age eighteen live in poverty—virtually identical to the national childhood poverty rate of 18.9 percent

• 26 percent of Santa Monica public school students are eligible for free or reduced price school lunches.

Of course, the federal poverty standard is notoriously low—in 1998 the cutoff was $16,530 annual income for a family of four with two children under eighteen. More relevant, perhaps, to the question whether Santa Monica is "affluent"—or so affluent that no Santa Monican would want to work at Target—is that 38 percent of our households have incomes less than $35,000 per year and 53 percent have incomes less than $50,000.

Nor do these figures take into account the income levels of Venice, West L.A., Palms and Mar Vista, communities that are tied to Santa Monica whether some people like it or not.

Notwithstanding what the Planning Commission says, or what the City Council candidates yapped about this year, traffic congestion is not the number one problem in Santa Monica.

What is the number one problem? I do not know. There are a number of problems, however, that even at first glance are more important than traffic congestion.

1827
First official mention of the "place called Santa Monica"—in a grazing permit. Origins of the name are a mystery.

Consider one: the fact that out of an incomprehensible combination of despair and anger, some of our teenagers and young adults feel compelled, from time to time, to shoot each other. The most recent shooting occurred in the wee hours of November 11, when, as reported in the *Lookout*, two men were shot in an alley near the 2000 block of Twentieth Street. In July, another young man was shot in a driveway about three blocks away.

Is it surprising that in the 90404 zip code, where these shootings occurred, 37 percent of children and young adults aged fifteen to twenty-four live in poverty?

Two years ago during a spate of shootings there was much wringing of hands and other anguish that we needed to do more to help our young people—like help them find good jobs. During one evening vigil I, along with several members of the City Council, and council candidates, heard Tom Hayden make an inspired speech saying exactly that.

But that was then and this is now.

Not every young person graduates from college and finds a high-tech, $50,000 job.

When the City Council holds its public hearing on the Target store there will be many speakers complaining about traffic. These people already have cars, houses, and good incomes.

The City Council will also hear from property owners and business interests in downtown that do not want competition from Target. These people already have cars, houses, and good businesses.

I doubt that many sixteen year-old kids who in a few years might get their first job at Target will appear before the council.

But they live here, too.

The City Council will have to take a moment, between the other speakers, to listen.

After the Supreme Court based its egregious decision in *Bush v. Gore,* on the Equal Protection Clause, I came to the defense of the Fourteenth Amendment.

DECEMBER 21, 2000

"... nor shall any State ... deny to any person within its jurisdiction the equal protection of the law." —the Equal Protection Clause of the Fourteenth Amendment.

Last week's tease by the Supreme Court's conservatives —applying the Equal Protection Clause, then proscribing a remedy—reminded me of the elderly Classics professor who was teaching *Antigone.* Some smart aleck in the class was going on about how the title character of the play was in fact no heroine but rather a moralizing prig. The professor, indignant, cut the whippersnapper short with, "You are speaking of the woman I love."

When I read the Supreme Court's opinion in *Bush v. Gore,* I thought, equally indignant, "You are speaking of the words I love."

My favorite words are not a poem, or a prayer, or a lyric from a song, but rather the Equal Protection Clause.

For this, my post-decision and pre-holiday column, I will not rehash all you have read elsewhere about how the conservatives' decision ran counter to their prior holdings or about how Rehnquist and O'Connor are now free to retire. No, this column is about how a few radical words, just a fragment of a sentence, are at the heart of America's greatness. Those words, quoted above, gave political effect to the most revolutionary idea, that all are equal.

Originally "equality" as a political idea developed as the answer of the economically empowered but politically challenged seventeenth and eighteenth century bourgeoisie to aristocratic political systems justified by the divine right of kings. The narrow purpose of our Declaration of Independence was to sever the colonies from just such a political system, but the Declaration, by its sweeping self-evident truth that all men are created equal, let "equality" out of the box.

The Constitution put it back in. As originally written, the Constitution does not contain the word "equality," and it accommodated slavery. The Bill of Rights, wonderful as it is, describes rights of an individual against government but does nothing to create a just society as a whole. The French Revolution's Declaration of the Rights of Man did contain a clause akin to equal protection, but, between the guillotine and Napoleon, it never had much practical effect.

1828
Grazing rights awarded by Mexican Government to land between
Santa Monica and Topanga Canyons to Francisco Javier Alvarado and
Antonio Ignacio Machado.

It took the horrible sacrifices of the Civil War to turn the idea of equality into political reality. A U.S. Representative from Ohio, John A. Bingham, an abolitionist, wrote the first section of the Fourteenth Amendment, which includes the Equal Protection Clause. Someone should build Bingham a monument, or put him on a stamp.

But that is unlikely. Most of the credit, at least lately and no doubt rightly, for the Equal Protection Clause goes to Abraham Lincoln. Garry Wills in his 1992 book *Lincoln at Gettysburg,* made the argument that Lincoln in the Gettysburg Address "remade America" by explaining that the purpose of the Civil War was to create a "new birth of freedom." Freedom that harkened back to the Declaration of Independence—promulgated "four score and seven years" previous.

The beauty of the Equal Protection Clause resides, however, not only in the general concept, but also in the details.

First, it applies to any "person." Use of this expansive word to describe the protected set was not random. Consider the other Civil War amendments. The Thirteenth specifically prohibits slavery. The Fifteenth protects the right to vote only with regard to "race, color, or previous condition of servitude." Even the Privileges and Immunities Clause of section one of the Fourteenth Amendment applies only to "citizens."

Only the Equal Protection Clause and the Due Process Clause contained in the same sentence apply so broadly to "any person."

Second, the words "equal protection of the laws" were revolutionary themselves. They bespeak the idea that law, that government, exists for a positive good. The law is not merely a series of prohibitions. Justice is not only the right to be free from governmental excess, but also to have equal access to the benefits that come from living in a civil society.

We are a nation of immigrants. We are a nation of strongly held beliefs. We are a nation of people striving for advantage. Yet we are a nation.

Around the world people kill over cultural and ethnic differences that we embrace. In Denmark and Germany and other enlightened countries they squabble about citizenship. In Italy and the Czech Republic they persecute gypsies. Etc., etc.

The battle for mutual respect is ongoing and the field of tolerance has no boundary. The list of martyrs, from Lincoln himself, to the multitude of the lynched, to the four girls in Birmingham, to Martin Luther King Jr., to Matthew Shepard, is long.

Yet "these honored dead" have not "died in vain." That America's strength derives from its diversity has never been more apparent.

Let's hope that someday America's greatest cultural export—greater than Coca Cola or McDonald's or Hollywood movies—will be the Equal Protection Clause.

2001

It may have been unfair to them, but it was inevitable that I would include my family in my columns.

JANUARY 5, 2001

"Learn from me, if not by my precepts, at least by my example, how dangerous is the acquirement of knowledge and how much happier that man is who believes his native town to be the world, than he who aspires to become greater than his nature will allow."
—Victor Frankenstein, from *Frankenstein*, by Mary Shelley.

I think the world of Santa Monica, but I like to travel, and I take the "travel broadens the mind" view over "a little knowledge is a dangerous thing."

Especially when I travel with my son, who just turned eleven.

Last week Henry and I kicked around New York like a couple of sailors on liberty while my wife attended a convention at a big midtown hotel.

What did we do? You name it. The Museum of Natural History, including the new Rose Planetarium. The Statue of Liberty and Ellis Island. The aircraft carrier *Intrepid* and the destroyer *Edson*. The Met (but only the arms and armor and the Temple of Dendur). Central Park and the Central Park Zoo—in the snow (the sea lions and the polar bears were happy). And a Broadway show, *Annie Get Your Gun*.

We took taxis, buses, subways, ferries. I had to reload my MetroCard twice. We walked miles.

It was cold, in the 20's. Then it snowed. The blizzard was timed perfectly to cancel our return flight on December 31, and we spent New Year's Eve—which happens to be Henry's birthday—in New York. We skipped Times Square but watched the fireworks over Central Park. A friend baked Henry a cake.

What a week.

1828
Mexico grants Francisco Sepúlveda "Rancho San Vicente," later
renamed "Rancho San Vicente y Santa Monica."

I was lucky to have Henry in tow. Alone, I might have skipped the Statue of Liberty and the Ellis Island Museum. I certainly would not have toured the *Intrepid* and the *Edson* on what must have been the coldest day of the year.

New York is a monument to human achievement, but I know what Dr. Frankenstein meant. All that achievement causes us mortals to resent our chains.

At the Museum of Natural History I wondered why I wasn't smarter.

Looking in the shop windows on Fifth Avenue, I wondered why my life wasn't more glamorous.

At *Annie Get Your Gun*, I wondered why I couldn't sing and dance—even just a little.

At the Statue of Liberty, and in the aircraft carrier, I wondered why I hadn't accomplished something noble or important.

At Ellis Island, I wondered why I hadn't spent more time with my grandmother.

Oh well. I will not aspire to be greater than my nature will allow. But what now, now that I have returned to the world—I mean, to Santa Monica?

Ever since Jane Jacobs wrote about them so well, New York's streets have been holy ground to urbanists. Since long before that New York itself has been the *bete noire* of suburbanists.

Both views are unhelpful. New York is unique.

No matter how much density urbanists dream about, no American city will ever see so many people commute by transit as in New York.

No matter how much density the suburbanists fear, no American city will ever have so many apartments in so many tall buildings on so little land.

In that sense, this "acquirement of knowledge" about New York by both urbanists and suburbanists has been dangerous in just the way Mary Shelley predicted. Like Frankenstein, both kinds of planners have used this knowledge to construct monsters: "urban-renewed" wastelands of apartment towers with no urban context, on one hand, and suburban sprawl on the other.

Oh well.

Did I acquire any knowledge in New York? Any knowledge relevant to my world?

Yes. I learned:

That people like people. The crowds were immense, but the people in the crowds were happy and unexpectedly courteous. I thought of a photograph of a Santa Monica park that recently appeared in one of our local papers under the caption, "Perfection." But the park was empty—not a soul appeared in the picture. The people in Central Park enhanced its perfection.

That the value of good design and quality construction is impossible to quantify. Whenever I admired a well-proportioned facade of brownstone or brick, limestone or granite, I wondered how our stucco-on-sticks construction, "faux this and faux that," will stand the decades.

That numerous small streets can move traffic as well as a few big ones, but sometimes it's better to walk. I wish our planners had broken up the super-blocks of Colorado Place, the Arboretum, and the Water Garden, so that people would have streets to walk on and traffic would flow through those developments, rather than clog the boulevards that surround them.

That an eleven-year-old will happily walk forty blocks if he can throw snowballs along the way. How that applies to Santa Monica I will leave to you.

A column also depends on personal history, and after a few months I started to tell readers who I am.

JANUARY 12, 2001

I try to resist sentimentality, but two recent events have touched my mystic chords. One was Paul Rosenstein's retirement from the City Council. The other was the start of the process for redesigning the Santa Monica Civic Center.

I connect the two events because my involvement with public life in Santa Monica began with the original Civic Center Specific Plan and continued because of Rosenstein.

In 1993 a City task force, after four or five years of meetings, released its recommendations for developing the Civic Center. The two biggest landowners were the City itself and the Rand Corporation.

The planning department sought comments to the plan from the public, and I wrote a memorandum with my suggestions.

Until then, I had not participated in Santa Monica politics beyond largely passive memberships in the Ocean Park Community Organization (OPCO), my neighborhood association, and Santa Monicans for Renters Rights.

I didn't realize it at the time, but I had irrevocably "gone public."

People read the memo, and one thing led to another. I joined an OPCO committee that was reviewing the Civic Center Plan. We drafted a "Vision Statement" and submitted it to the Planning Commission.

The Planning Commission recommended that the City Council authorize a new process to focus on design. The City Council agreed and the City hired ROMA Design Group, the same firm that had completed the design work on the Third Street Promenade, to conduct a series of public meetings and workshops and ultimately formulate an "urban design plan."

The public process, which ROMA led in conjunction with a "Design Working Group" of council members and planning commissioners, was open, challenging, and, for me, very rewarding. It was like a year of urban design school. The City Council approved the resulting plan on a 7-0 vote, something no one would have predicted when the process began.

When anti-Rand and anti-growth interests placed the plan on the ballot, it passed with 60 percent of the vote in a June 1994 referendum.

Ysidro Reyes, a grape-grower, constructs a ranch house at the present location of the corner of Seventh Street and Adelaide Drive.

Since then, however, the plan and the Civic Center have gone almost nowhere. Financing most of the public improvements depended on Rand's developing its property, but the recession of the mid-1990s, the bankruptcy of Rand's developer, and rising costs put the kibosh on that.

The City went ahead with the public safety building, which includes building one-half of Olympic Drive, an important street that will connect Ocean Avenue with Fourth Street and the freeway, but as we all know construction of the facility is mired in cost overruns.

Rand decided to throw in the towel on the real estate and last year sold the City most of its land. It kept enough to build a new headquarters, but one that is about the same size as their current facility, about 300,000 square feet, forgoing the right under the plan to build another 200,000 square feet for its own use.

A few weeks ago the City issued a request for proposals for preparation of a new specific plan that will take into account the new realities.

A planning process that began in the boom of the late '80s, and which produced a plan just in time for the recession of the mid-'90s, is now beginning again—once more in boom times. Let's hope something gets built before the Bush recession.

Paul Rosenstein was one of the council members on the Civic Center Design Working Group, and I came to know him and to appreciate his good sense during the design process.

But I owe a special favor to Rosenstein because he encouraged me to stay "public" after the Civic Center process concluded. He persuaded me to join the Housing Commission, then encouraged me to seek appointment to the Planning Commission when a vacancy opened.

Rosenstein set a good example for me as well—as a pragmatic man of principle. He is a man of the Left—the Left being so much a part of his character that he has never had to worry about whether he is "left enough." His history, and his family's history (his father fought in Spain as a member of the Abraham Lincoln Brigade), is so full of victories and defeats, that he always sees the big picture in a practical way.

Rosenstein knows that people will always need jobs, housing, education, and a clean environment. He also knows that achieving these goals in a system where everyone is supposedly out for themselves is not a matter of rhetoric, but instead, hard work.

Now he is going to continue that work as the political director of his union local, Local 11 of the International Brotherhood of Electrical Workers.

It is easy to ridicule local activists. We all roll our eyes from time to time. But the joke is on the cynics, because the participants all know they are getting the best part of the bargain, the satisfaction that comes from trying to make a difference. True, sometimes this good feeling takes the form of self-satisfaction, but what is worse, a little pride for being an oversized fish, or the smug arrogance of complaining about the pond?

Get involved. It's not that hard. If you don't like what the busybodies do, become a busybody yourself. One of the blessings we Santa Monicans have is that our town is big enough for decisions to count, but small enough that individuals can have a real impact.

I wish Paul Rosenstein good luck, but I regret that during the next round of the Civic Center process, he won't be there to encourage someone else to go public.

B ush was inaugurated. Protesters planned a big demonstration and march in downtown L.A., which I decided both to attend and cover. (I'm lax about journalistic ethics outside of Santa Monica.) Then it turned out the Green Party was there, which made it something of a local issue, too. Talk about bad taste.

JANUARY 26, 2001

"Re-Elect Gore in 2004"—my new bumper sticker, acquired at the Pershing Square counter-inaugural demonstration.

My wife asked, "Where's the outrage?" On Saturday we set out to find it.

We located the outrage at Pershing Square, but I am not much happier for the experience.

First the good news. It was a beautiful day for a demonstration. We met friends and had a good breakfast at the Biltmore, across the street. When the speeches started at eleven o'clock, I was well-fortified and ready to be inspired.

There were only a few police, which was nice. I would hate for my son to think that dissent was only barely tolerated in this country.

(The last time I was in Pershing Square was during the Democratic Convention, when I was there, somewhat improbably, as a "faith-based observer" interposed between demonstrators and the police. Funny, isn't it, that during the convention a massive police presence faced demonstrators protesting everything from building subways to the Iraqi embargo, but on Saturday only a few police were needed to protect the city from demonstrators protesting the theft of the presidency.)

Ed Asner was the MC. That was good. He started off by assuring everyone that he was alive. That was very good.

Maxine Waters, Tom Hayden, and Sheila Kuehl were among the speakers. They spoke with fervor and righteous indignation. Kuehl was especially good, reminding us, with characteristic charm, that we had to work harder and think harder.

So how come I left after two hours and skipped the march to the Federal Building?

Look—I didn't expect to be happy Saturday afternoon even after locating the outrage. George W. Bush would still be president. I am happy someone organized a group I could join to be angry about it. But I started to get grumpy when I realized that the Green Party was there. Wasn't that in bad taste? Sort of like one of those Mafia funerals where the deceased's heartbroken "friends" send elaborate floral arrangements?

1839
Marquez and Reyes obtain title from the Mexican government to
Rancho Boca de Santa Monica, consisting of 6,657 acres extending
south as far as present-day Montana Avenue.

Then there was a comedy group called "Billionaires for Bush and Gore." Ha-ha-ha.

I left after a speaker denounced Al Gore for going along with disenfranchising black voters in Florida.

Guys, listen up: there is a difference.

I hesitate to criticize the organizers of the demonstration. After all, it is tough to organize a rally to protest an election you actually won. The real problem is that this election should never have been close enough for butterfly ballots in Palm Beach to be decisive.

And not because Al Gore ran a less than perfect campaign. I wish he hadn't sighed in the first debate, but, after all, he won, everyone knows that, and he did it fighting a two-front campaign, with the great Bubba, world's greatest unifier of Republicans, on his back.

No, the reason Gore should have won big is because Democrats should win every national election big, but somehow the Left has managed to turn off the working class middle. Not the working class Left: the union vote and minority vote were stronger than ever. But something is wrong when truckers making $40,000 identify more with Republicans than Democrats.

Look at it another way. Democrats have not polled 51 percent of the presidential vote since 1964 (Jimmy Carter got 50.06 percent), even though culturally the country is more liberal than ever. More liberal than ever? What, heresy! With the Supreme Court and Ashcroft running around? The Religious Right, and the WTO, and the LAPD, and Mumia on death row, and ...

The struggle continues, but the Left has won all the big cultural issues: civil rights, women's rights, abortion, gay rights, censorship, the environment. Notwithstanding Antonin Scalia, national values have changed completely from forty years ago.

Why can't the culture winners elect presidents on something like a regular basis?

The Left has become politically fragmented and therefore weak.

Why it has become fragmented has a lot to do with issue-oriented politics, and that's about all I heard Saturday.

I know it's hard to contemplate catering to white males in Georgia, whose fathers, after all, might have been in the Klan, who usually own guns, and who don't care about abortion or gay rights too much, but that's where the votes are. Not all the votes, but the ones the Left is not getting that the Left should get. And we don't need that many to add to the base we have.

The Left needs a strategy to convince Joe Six-pack that his fears about social change are irrational and what he really should worry about is that he—and his wife—are working harder and longer for less and less, while others get more and more.

1839
Litigation ensues between Marquez and Reyes and Sepúlveda over
conflicting land grants; the litigation is not resolved until the 1880's.

I didn't hear anything like that Saturday, but perhaps it wasn't the time or place. Outrage and self-reflection do not easily mix.

On February 23, 2001, David Attias, a student at UC-Santa Barbara, ran his car down a street crowded with young people out for fun on a Friday night; four of them died, and a fifth was seriously injured. David Attias grew up in Santa Monica, and he and his family are close friends of mine.

MARCH 2, 2001

"Thus his father wept for him." Genesis 37:35

A few years before I became a father, one of my friends came to my office. He brought with him his son, who was about two, or maybe even younger, and soon the little boy was exploring the floor of my work place.

I remember my friend picking up a spent staple from the carpet and handing it to me so that I could drop it in my trash basket.

"This is what you do when you're a father," he said—laughing at himself.

Four or five years later my Henry was born, and since then I have often thought about the staple.

In our family my wife is in charge of worrying about unseen forces—such as electromagnetic radiation or mad cow disease. My fears relate more to physical dangers—black diamond ski runs, for example, or systemic child rearing practices, such as whether Henry's bedtime is too late.

My wife worries whether Henry is learning enough math facts, while I harangue him to practice his music. At any given time one of us thinks Henry is eating too much and the other thinks he is not eating enough.

But we gang up on him if there is a behavior problem, such as those times Henry has tried to strangle a friend. Our greatest anxiety, of course, is that Henry will not be liked, or, even worse, be mean or a bully. Parents pound moral precepts into their children from the earliest age—"share," "use your words," "say you're sorry"—but I have never met a parent who could do much about a child's personality.

Henry is now eleven, and both he and his parents recently crossed a point of no return. A school friend invited him to go skiing with his family at Yosemite over Presidents' Day weekend, and we said yes.

Up until then Henry had never been away from both of us for longer than a sleepover.

1839
Mexico grants to brothers José Augustin and Ignacio Machado, and
brothers Felipe and Tomás Talamantes, Rancho La Ballona, consisting of 13,920 acres and including the southern portion of what is
now Santa Monica.

The parents of Henry's friend are also our friends, and we knew that they are responsible people. They went out of their way to assure us that they would take all safety measures.

Yet Presidents' Weekend was only a few days after a rapidly surfacing submarine sank a Japanese fishing boat, drowning nine people, including four high school students. I thought of those parents trying to comprehend the inexplicable. In the middle of the ocean, how can one submarine find one fishing boat with your child on it?

When I was seventeen my parents let me hitchhike through Europe. Were they crazy?

Although I always wanted to be a father, I never have thought people need to be parents to be complete or fully realized or whatever you want to call it. People do not deserve medals for being parents. It is usually a voluntary condition.

Yet I believe one uniquely learns one thing from being a parent, and that is how much your parents loved you.

A humbling realization. Perhaps a less self-obsessed person might figure this out for himself, but I never understood what my parents felt for me until I felt what I feel for my son.

Yet, as any parent will tell you—your children don't have a clue. Your love for your child is like the background radiation from the big bang: always humming, but who cares.

This is the stuff, of course, of every Jewish mother joke—"so he can't lift up the phone?" But kids don't ask to be born—we parents can't complain when they turn up the volume on the headphones. They didn't ask to be who they are, either.

Some children are not happy. Sometimes they don't have the molecules to be happy, no matter what their parents wish for or what their parents do.

When two adults fall in love, the underlying concept is that they are going to try to stay together. But the love of a parent for a child is different. The underlying concept is that someday the little boy or girl will grow up and walk out the door.

This love thing, this absolute obsession with the welfare of your children, at some point tolerates seemingly antithetical developments, such as allowing them to cross the street without holding hands, or even to ride their bicycles in the street or go away for skiing weekends or hitchhike through Europe or learn to drive or go away to college or join the army or whatever.

As much as you fear, you rejoice in each independent step.

The parent's job is to pick up the staples. At a certain point, you can't pick them all up.

Last Friday night the fears of many parents crossed paths with tragedy when a car plowed through a crowded street in Isla Vista.

Two weeks ago, when my editor suggested I write about what it was like to have my son away for the weekend for the first time, I recalled the story of my friend and the staple and decided that would be a good start for the column. I thought it would be a good column to write and hold for Father's Day.

When I heard the news about Isla Vista, I recalled the story again. The little boy on the carpet in my office grew up, was loved by his parents as much as life itself, yet found the world an incomprehensible place, and drove his car down the crowded street.

After a public hearing that extended over two nights, the City Council rejected the downtown Target on a 5-2 vote. The two votes in favor came from Pam O'Connor and Ken Genser; Genser was a surprise, because he is usually in the anti-growth camp. The bigger surprise was that the two council members supported by the business community, Herb Katz and Robert Holbrook, voted against the project, assuring its defeat.

MARCH 9, 2001

All the world's a stage, and that includes the dais of the Santa Monica City Council. Two weeks ago most of the council members chewed the scenery with empathy for the working and middle class and their shopping needs, and waxed poetic about the idea of a downtown that served all demographics. Nonetheless, a majority of five council members voted to kill the Target department store, and thus consigned downtown to an upscale and exclusive future.

The plot was too obvious to generate much suspense. But there were great roles for the council members to play.

Herb Katz, whose architectural firm has by my rough calculation designed more square footage downtown than the total square footage of Target, played the Yogi Berra role. That is the Yogi Berra of "nobody goes there anymore because it's too crowded."

Katz voted down Target because, as he said without apparent irony, the traffic it generated would be so great that people would stop coming downtown. This argument might be delusional, it could be cynical, but in any case it is as illogical as Yogi's famous quote. Yet just as meaningful.

The clear meaning from what Katz said, and in this all the other council members who voted no joined him to some extent, was that the interests of the property owners on the Promenade and their tenants take precedence over the needs of Target's potential shoppers and any other downtown uses.

The existing downtown business interests do not want competition from Target and its customers: not on price, not on quality, not on selection, and not on the use of the public infrastructure of streets, sidewalks, parking, and transit.

Property owners are now charging so much rent that even expensive restaurants, like Remi, are being driven off the Promenade by high-end retailers willing to pay for what amounts to billboard space on a world famous street. Meanwhile, chains like Benihana, P.F. Chang's, Hooters, and Buca di Beppo are replacing these restaurants and lower-priced foot outlets such as the Food Court.

1850s
First mention of tourism in Santa Monica, in the form of camping
excursions to Santa Monica Canyon.

Katz and colleagues repeatedly called the situation on the Promenade "fragile." Their attitude toward downtown businesses is like that of the Bush administration to the oil and gas industry. The City has made the property owners downtown rich: at what point can these self-reliant capitalists take care of themselves?

One hopes that Katz has the good taste to decline any commissions to design buildings that will replace Target.

If Katz was Yogi Berra, then Kevin McKeown was Yogi Bear. His contribution to the debate consisted of, "It's the traffic, stupid." Such a nuanced view of the state of civilization at the beginning of the twenty-first century demands more thoughtful analysis than this format allows, but one question worth asking is, to whom was McKeown addressing his question?

Was "stupid" merely rhetorical, or was McKeown trying to explain the situation to the large numbers of benighted fools who testified and wrote letters and signed petitions to the effect that there are in fact issues of convenience and price that are just as important as traffic?

To give the drama more historical weight, Richard Bloom played Marie Antoinette, as in: *Let them shop at Robinsons-May!* Many opponents of the Target store took pains to identify themselves as Target shoppers, but not Bloom, who did not like their service or selection.

Target was not Bloom's shopping "ideal," and he thought potential downtown Target shoppers should be happy with what they would find at Robinsons-May, at least during their sales. He assured Target shoppers that these sales occurred frequently.

Taking Katz's protectionist argument even further, Bloom said that the "chains are taking over" and that we need to protect Robinsons-May (a division of May Department Stores Company, a $14 billion retailer operating eight chains of regional department stores) and Macy's (a division of Federated Department Stores, Inc., the largest operator of department stores in the U.S., with 1999 sales of $17.7 billion) from Target.

At least Bloom is consistent. A few years ago he sued to stop Ralph's from building a supermarket that would serve the Pico Neighborhood. In an era when politicians say one thing on Monday and something else on Tuesday, it is somehow comforting that Bloom thinks poor people should be just as inconvenienced buying household goods as they are groceries.

Robert Holbrook played the Sphinx. He said little, and what he said was enigmatic. He began by describing the troubles he would have with his wife if he voted against Target. Then he voted against the store, but committed himself to bringing a Target to Santa Monica. Holbrook gave just one reason for voting no: that traffic in and out of the store's underground parking would back up onto Fifth Street.

Ken Genser pointed out that we survive the impacts of bigger parking structures, which have less room inside for queuing, on busier streets, but that did not persuade Holbrook to change his mind.

Last to speak was Mayor Michael Feinstein, who played the role he has been rehearsing for years: Ralph Nader. The mixture of unctuous concern for the downtrodden, unrealistic utopian solutions, and utter disregard for real-world consequences, can only be described as Naderesque.

You had to be there. Our leading "environmentalist" argued that the way to fix traffic downtown is to fly another on-ramp from Fifth Street onto the freeway, proving what many have suggested, that Feinstein's head is firmly in the '60s.

Briefly put, Feinstein's vision is that if we keep Target out of downtown, the growing number of people living there will cause the building of charming mom and pop shops to serve them. Just like in Europe, he said. Of course everyone in Europe hates the high prices those stores charge and goes to the *supermercato* whenever possible.

When Pam O'Connor pointed out that the European downtowns Feinstein loves all have department stores, he said that kind of urbanism would not be possible here until we had a "civilized transit system" and got beyond the "automobile culture."

There is no transit system I have traveled on, and I have traveled on many, more civilized than the [Santa Monica] Big Blue Bus. Feinstein owes an apology to its employees and its patrons.

It is also ridiculous to think we will transcend "automobile culture." However, if we stop building freeways and on-ramps to "solve" our traffic problems, and invest the money in transit, then perhaps we would have a bus system that was civilized even to Green Party standards.

Of course, if more people take transit, the beneficiaries will be all those people who "must" drive, because there would be fewer other drivers. But to make transit work we need to look at land-use, and it is politically easier to suggest spending $50 million on another traffic-generating freeway ramp.

In the end Feinstein wants the same tony downtown that Herb Katz's clients want. Except that his ideal consumers wear Birkenstocks, not Kenneth Cole.

Bad traffic never killed a downtown, but many were murdered in the name of fixing traffic. What killed our urban centers and our small town Main Streets were all the cures for traffic—all the freeways, overpasses, street-widenings, one-way streets, left-turn signals, right-turn lanes, etc., that made downtowns inhospitable to their users, and at the same time facilitated the flight of the bedrock middle- and working-class shopper to the malls and the sprawls. Target had a plan to bring them back.

Another big issue in Santa Monica was the living wage. Labor activists who were locked in a unionizing struggle with Santa Monica's big resort hotels made one of the first proposals for a municipal living wage ordinance applicable to private sector workers.

MARCH 23, 2001

"Caught in the labyrinth of modern industrialism and dwarfed by the size of corporate enterprise, [the employee] can attain freedom and dignity only by cooperation with others of his group." —From remarks of Senator Robert Wagner on the floor of the Senate in support of the 1935 National Labor Relations Act (also known as the "Wagner Act"), as quoted in Charles Morris, *The Developing Labor Law* (1971).

The plight of the working poor is the most dire crisis affecting our region.

As pointed out by the Southern California Studies Center at USC in *Sprawl Hits the Wall: Confronting the Realities of Metropolitan Los Angeles*, the Center's recent report on the state of the region, the numbers of working poor are rising faster than both the population as a whole and the numbers of non-working poor: "Between 1990 and 1998, the number of people living in working poor households ... grew from 1.6 million to 2.5 million, a 51 percent increase. During this period, the population grew 16 percent and the number of people living in non-working poor households grew by 24 percent."

The difficulties low-wage workers face worsened during the recent boom. There are more jobs, but wages at the low end increased only slightly, while the costs of many essentials, most notably housing, increased dramatically.

Santa Monica is, at the moment, grappling with this issue in its own way. Labor and political activists have proposed that the City adopt its own minimum wage for at least some businesses (those of at least a certain size), in one portion of the city (the "Coastal Zone"). This "living wage" would about double the national and state minimums.

In 1999 the City Council expressed general support for a living wage ordinance and commissioned an economic study of what effects it might have. Business interests commissioned their own study, and the City also hired two economists to review its study.

The economists did not agree on much.

Businesses, principally the big hotels near the beach, then spent more than a million dollars on Measure KK, a politically suicidal attempt to abort the living wage. Presumably, the hotels are prepared to spend equivalent amounts to challenge in court any ordinance the council passes.

Next Tuesday staff will ask the City Council for more direction, not on an ordinance to draft, but on what further research and public process the council believes necessary before it can stop cutting bait.

I am not surprised staff believes further study is required. The issue is complex. Drafting an ordinance will be even more complex, as there are many variables—economic, geographic, demographic, legal—to consider.

At this moment, I am as confused as anyone else. I have read the reports. I know a little about the law. I generally respect expertise, but in this case I believe neither that economists can predict what will happen nor that lawyers can predict what will survive judicial scrutiny.

Consequently, I have no views at the moment on any specific ordinance.

But I believe more than anything that this dispute is about unions. Specifically, it is about management's aversion to unions and is caused by, more than anything else, the disintegration, in the face of constant attack from the right wing, of the American system of industrial relations.

This system, which since the passage of the Wagner Act in 1935 has played a crucial role in America's amazing prosperity and our political liberty, is based on the fundamental principle that workers themselves have the right to decide whether to organize.

The genius of the Wagner Act was that, while the rest of the industrialized world resorted to top down bureaucracies (whether fascist, socialist, or communist, whether democratic or totalitarian) to deal with the social dislocations of industrialization, America chose a pluralistic and democratic model that relied on labor and capital resolving their differences over the bargaining table. Concurrently, under the vision of Senator Wagner, unions and management would solve other problems created by modernization, such as the delivery of medical care and the financial needs of retirees.

The key is worker choice. Many workers may not want to join unions, and unions have lost many certification elections, but if workers do not have choice free from employer interference, there is no brake on the employer's power over workers.

Ever since Ronald Reagan packed the National Labor Relations Board with anti-union zealots, this principle of worker self-determination has been under attack. It has become harder and harder for unions to organize workers. When unions cannot protect the interests of working people, our social system is in danger. Union contracts not only benefit union workers, but also set the standard for everyone else.

On the micro level, workers at our non-union hotels can thank union activists for their recent raises. On the macro level, every white-collar worker with medical benefits or a retirement plan can thank organized labor for establishing health insurance and pensions as routine perquisites of employment. Beyond even that, higher union wages turned workers into consumers, to the benefit of shareholders, and, of course, labor unions

c. 1870s
The Lucas family begins farming 861 acres obtained from Rancho La
Ballona in what is now Ocean Park.

---

have been key players in social legislation running the gamut from child labor laws to Medicare.

The hotels that have fought the proposed living wage ordinance have themselves to blame for it. The labor scene was quiet in Santa Monica until the owners of what was the Miramar Sheraton sought to decertify the union there. This action awakened two sleeping giants, the community's social conscience and the union itself, Local 814 of the Hotel Employees and Restaurant Employees Union. The social conscience manifested itself in the organization of Santa Monicans Allied for Responsible Tourism (SMART), and the union brought new activist leadership to Local 814.

The rest of the local business community, including the other non-unionized hotels, might have dissociated themselves from the antics of Miramar management by pledging not to interfere with the rights of their workers to organize. They could have pledged, for instance, not to hire outside union-busters.

Maybe I am a Pollyanna, but what would this have cost the hotels? After all, they would merely be pledging to abide by the law, its spirit as well as its letter, and if, as the hotels claim, their employees do not want to join unions, what did they have to fear? The hotels, SMART, and Local 814 probably all disagree, but I think such a pledge would have obviated the need for, or forestalled politically, the living wage ordinance.

We will never know. The hotels chose to battle Local 814 at every turn. Loews Hotel, the focus of Local 814's organizing efforts, hired the same union-busting firm that worked for the Miramar.

As precedents established at the NLRB during the Reagan and Bush years increased the difficulty of organizing, unions have turned to political action—in this case, the living wage ordinance.

From the start SMART and Local 814 designed their proposed ordinance to put pressure on the non-union hotels, specifically the big profitable hotels along the beach, because these are the businesses the union wants to organize. The original proposal for a living wage excluded small businesses, such as most restaurants, covered only the Coastal Zone, and, most crucially, allowed union contracts to supersede the ordinance.

Businesses complain that Local 814 and its allies are using the living wage ordinance to pressure them to sign union contracts. But for years corporations have used politics to subvert the rights of workers and unions. Turnabout is fair play.

[Note: the council, by a 5-2 vote, asked staff to prepare a living wage ordinance.]

The pending execution of Timothy McVeigh in April 2001 prompted me to write about the death penalty. Later, after the 2004 election, it turned out that I was writing about "values."

"The punishment of death is pernicious to society, from the example of barbarity it affords." —From Cesare Beccaria, *Of Crimes and Punishments* (1764)

Last December a federal judge permitted Timothy McVeigh to waive any further right of appeal. The government has set May 16 as the date for his execution.

At the same time that the federal government is preparing to execute its first criminal since 1963, the death penalty is under the most sustained public attack since the Supreme Court nearly abolished it almost thirty years ago. Questions about verdicts have led even conservatives to wonder whether it is a good idea for the state to kill people. In Texas, the state that most frequently uses the death penalty, a legislative committee recently recommended holding a referendum on whether to have a moratorium on executions.

The history of the death penalty happens to be something I know about because of a paper I wrote in law school on the nineteenth century reform of criminal law in England. At the time, 1978, the topic seemed esoteric, because no one was being executed in the U.S. But what I learned then has unfortunately become more relevant as the years have gone by.

Prior to the nineteenth century, the guiding principle behind the criminal law of England, as well as just about every other place, was terror. In England, death was the punishment for more than one hundred crimes, many of them trivial crimes against property. Crime was rampant.

Although the struggle took decades, reformers ultimately prevailed. They reduced the scope of the death penalty essentially to one crime, murder. They also devised a more humane penal system and caused the government to establish a modern police force. Crime declined.

Looking back, the most surprising aspect of the reform was that evangelical Christians provided the political muscle to push the new laws through Parliament. That's right: the religious beliefs we identify as conservative today were then associated with the radical cause of penal law reform.

Reform, however, did not begin with the evangelicals. It began with Cesare Beccaria, a nobleman from Milan, who wrote a quintessential Enlightenment book, *Of Crimes*

Colonel Robert S. Baker, a wealthy sheep rancher from northern California, visits Santa Monica area and purchases Rancho San Vicente,
Santa Monica (30,260 acres) for $55,000 from the Sepúlveda family
and 2,000 acres of Rancho Boca de Santa Monica for $6,000 from the
Reyes family. Baker later purchases 160 acres of Rancho La Ballona
from the Machado family and marries landed heiress Arcadia Bandini
de Stearns.

and Punishments, which put thinking about crime on a rational basis. The book is just as
trenchant today as it was when it appeared in 1764.

Beccaria's book was a big hit. Sixty editions were published by the end of the century
in all the major European languages, including an English translation in 1767. In the
1770s and 1780s, prospects were good for reform of English criminal law along the lines
of the new thinking.

The English reaction, however, to the excesses of the French Revolution, and the wars
with France, doomed for decades the prospects of enacting any new laws based on ideas
associated with the Enlightenment. Reform finally succeeded in the 1830s. Although the
ideas behind reform came from philosophers, such as Jeremy Bentham, the political will
and the necessary clout came from evangelical Christians, who, emerging from Method-
ism, steadily took over the established Anglican Church in the early 1800s.

The leader of the evangelicals was William Wilberforce, best known for leading the
fight to abolish the slave trade. The evangelicals supported criminal law reform from
humanitarian principles and because they believed the brutality and chaos of the system
based on "the barbarous custom of hanging" (Wilberforce's words) induced the poor
into lives of crime, and therefore jeopardized their ultimate salvation.

Although the evangelicals were conservative when it came to the political and economic rights of the working class, they pioneered the notion that social problems were
political problems, and they changed public opinion in fundamental ways.

So what does this all mean today?

America remains in a prolonged period of political reaction against the social and
political upheavals of the '60s. Nothing better exemplified that reaction than the death
penalty tidal wave that rolled over the country in the '80s and '90s.

Given the country's overall religious bent, secular liberals who want a more humane
society, including the abolition of the death penalty, might consider addressing their arguments to those who are often their opponents, namely the mass of pious Americans. But
how might one do that?

Purely rational arguments do not work against the death penalty. Yes, the only purpose of punishment should be deterrence and rehabilitation, and, yes, the death penalty
does not deter crime, but these arguments will not persuade one who believes in retribution when statistics relating to deterrence are, at the end of the day, just statistics.

Beccaria made all the rational arguments against the death penalty, but ultimately he
devised a subjective argument that was better, an argument that appealed to our better
instincts. Laws, he said, "are intended to moderate the ferocity of mankind," and they
"should not increase it by examples of barbarity."

1874

Baker sells three-quarters of his Santa Monica lands to U.S. Senator
(from Nevada) John Percival Jones for $160,000 and one-quarter to
his wife, Arcadia Bandini de Baker, for $50,000. Jones, a silver baron,
plans to build a railroad from his mines in the eastern Sierra to a
port in Santa Monica.

Most people, myself included, would say that if someone must be the first federal prisoner put to death in thirty-eight years, Timothy McVeigh is a worthy candidate. The enormity of his crime, the innocence of his victims, the desolation of their survivors. The fact that he attacked the very government responsible for a "domestic tranquility" that is the envy of the world, despite its imperfections.

But killing McVeigh increases barbarity.

McVeigh's crime should remind us of who we are, of what we have, and what we aspire to be.

Cesare Beccaria wrote, in what must have been a bitter moment, that "the history of mankind is an immense sea of errors, in which a few obscure truths may here and there be found." If we focus on those truths, perhaps all men and women of goodwill can, together, abolish the death penalty.

One does not have to be devout, nor Christian, to be moved by the words Thomas Fowell Buxton, a disciple of Wilberforce, said on May 23, 1821, in the House of Commons, in support of a bill to reform the criminal law: "I hazard nothing when I say, that a very religious man cannot, in many cases, be a prosecutor. He deeply feels, that his own dearest hopes depend only on the pardon which he shall receive; and he knows, that the condition on which he asks forgiveness to his own trespasses, is the forgiveness he extends to the trespasses of others. He cannot, therefore, for many crimes, call down upon his brother sinner the exterminating vengeance of the law."

I took my first opportunity to write about education and schools when the Santa Monica Malibu Unified School District hired a new superintendent, John Deasy, a progressive-minded educator from Rhode Island.

MAY 11, 2001

Welcome to Santa Monica (and Malibu), John Deasy.

I sat in on the *Lookout's* interview with our new superintendent and I was impressed by his comment that he would involve himself in state government. That's good, because, realistically, whatever people believe the cities of Santa Monica and Malibu should do, Sacramento is where the money for education is.

It was not always this way. My son Henry, who will start middle school at John Adams next year, and his friends refer to the years of their parents' youth as "the olden days." Well, back in the olden days, things were different.

Did you ever wonder why we have a special elected local government for schools, while cities and counties handle everything else? Apparently people once had the quaint idea that schools were so important they needed their own government. Children can't vote, and people knew that to protect the interests of children in their future, and the interests of society in education, they needed to insulate schools from politicians who might prefer to spend money on police, or potholes, or parks, or whatever cause, good or bad, they thought would win them more votes.

Local school boards had the right to levy taxes and the responsibility to do one thing and one thing only: educate future citizens.

Of course, nothing works perfectly. Schools reflected every ill that infected society as a whole. For instance, some localities are richer than others. Some have grown-ups who are more willing or able to pay more taxes for schools. The system was not fair. In the 1970s the California Supreme Court held in the *Serrano* cases that school funding had to be equal around the state. The basic holding of *Serrano* was undoubtedly correct. It is wrong to base educational opportunities on the relative resources of communities.

There have been, however, serious unintended negative consequences from *Serrano*. To balance funding, the state capped spending on education. When people in wealthy districts could not pay for good schools in their communities, many decided to pay for private schools, and the public schools lost important constituents.

(There is no limit to the tax subsidy private schools receive through tax-deductible contributions. For example, Crossroads, a local private school with 1,125 students, recently raised $17 million to build a sports facility. Assuming a combined federal and

1875
February: Construction begins on a 1,740-foot wharf at "Shoo Fly
Landing," at the foot of Railroad (now Colorado) Avenue.

California marginal tax rate of 45 percent, that's a $7.65-million subsidy. By way of comparison, only $6 million of the $42 million the school district raised with Prop. X will be used for improving playgrounds and athletic facilities. That's for a district with more than 12,000 students.)

As it happened, the *Serrano* cases also had a lot to do with the voter anger that led to Prop. 13. Prop. 13 had even a greater impact on school finances than the *Serrano* decisions, because of how it limited not only the property tax, but also the power of governments to enact or raise taxes.

Some analysts say that there is no connection between money and the quality of education, but I take a very basic view. If schools are falling apart, if kids don't have books, if teachers don't have credentials and don't make enough money to stay in the profession, if there is no music or art, then schools need more money. When I was a kid back in the olden days, grown-ups built us schools. Today we don't build schools. We buy portable classrooms, stick them on asphalt, and still expect kids to respect public institutions.

But the worst unintended consequence of *Serrano*, and the worst intended consequence of Prop. 13, was not the direct impact on school budgets. No, the worst was that when school boards lost the power to tax, they became ineffective as advocates for children. This change in the political culture of school governance has been disastrous.

Most people would say that education is the number one priority for local government. But compare the powers of a city to those of a school district. If a city wants to build new offices for its police and fire departments, but its bond issue doesn't pass, it can still issue bonds. If it wants more open space for housing, it might create a redevelopment district and borrow $53 million to buy eleven acres of land. If there is a recession, and tax receipts are down, it can tax utility bills.

I don't begrudge these powers to the cities—this is what government is about. But school boards lack these powers, and their weakness has permeated public education. Look at Santa Monica. As the extraordinary votes in favor of the parcel tax and school bonds show, voters here value education more than anything. Yet our school board—or its citizen surrogates—must beg for support from the City because the state allocation is not enough to educate our kids, many of whom are low income.

The City has its own responsibilities—parks, housing, police, etc. But haven't we turned the world upside down? What once had the highest priority now has the lowest. At the state level, it's the same, although recent propositions have given schools more clout. But schools are still at the mercy of the governor and legislators who may have other fish to fry and constituents and lobbyists to please.

1875
July 10: Jones and Baker record map of "Township of Santa Monica,"
with boundaries from the Pacific to Twenty-Sixth Street, and from
Montana Avenue to Railroad Avenue (now Colorado Avenue).

I respect politicians, but what kind of politicians will be attracted to school boards that have no power? If politics is the art of getting things done, then a political entity that has no power may attract people who want to do good, but not necessarily people who are good at doing. Public schools have a tough job and they do it better than most people think. But clearly there are problems. Especially in school governance. At the root of these problems is a political culture of helplessness.

I see two solutions, neither easy. One would be to amend the state constitution to return to local school boards the power to tax, while requiring the state to equalize funding. The other would be even more radical. If state government is to be the source of funding for education, then we need a state school board with the power to tax and the responsibility to see that our children learn. A separate legislative body to make sure schools have enough money—no matter what.

A fter the Santa Monica City Council had indicated its intention to draft a living wage ordinance, staff came back to the council with a proposal.

MAY 18, 2001

Next Tuesday evening the City Council will adopt a precedent-setting living wage ordinance, unique because of how it will affect workers and businesses that do not have a contractual relationship with the City.

I hope the council takes the time necessary to craft a good law. Not only one that will stand up in court, but also one that does the job without too much collateral damage. A bad law will do more harm than good to the workers who are its intended beneficiaries.

The plight of the low-income worker, the region's biggest social problem, is complex. It involves just about every other big issue—the decline in manufacturing, the rise of the service economy, immigration, sprawl, transportation, education, and the need for investment, both public and private. Commendably, Santa Monica is trying to solve a small part of the problem and, perhaps symbolically, to do more than that.

Devising a good law, however, has not been easy. The difficulties begin with the origin of the living wage movement in Santa Monica as part of a drive to unionize big hotels. Nothing wrong with that: if unions could organize the big employers, then their better wages and labor standards would ultimately become the standard for their smaller, non-unionized competitors in the market for low-skilled labor.

But a local minimum wage is not an obvious tool for union organizing. No matter how the proponents of the ordinance try to juggle district borders, exceptions, hardship-exemptions, and the like, unless the council is careful, the end result will be a complicated law, a cumbersome enforcement apparatus, and potentially more unintended consequences than unionized hotel workers.

The response to the proposal from the business community—both the hotels and local businesses as represented by the Chamber of Commerce—has been hysteria. Ignoring the real efforts of the living wage proponents to exempt smaller businesses and restaurants, the business community declared from the start that a living wage ordinance in any form would spell doom.

The hotels' execrable Measure KK killed any chance of constructive dialogue.

Businesses have the attitude that somehow workers are uniquely unentitled to raise the price of the services they provide. Take restaurants, for example. Several restaurants have recently gone out of business in downtown Santa Monica, not because of high labor costs, but because of high rents. No one jokes about "Soviet Monica" when

1875
July 15: With steamers from San Francisco docked at the wharf,
more than 2,000 attend the first auction of lots in Santa Monica.
Sales total $40,000 the first day and $43,000 the second.

property owners all raise rents. Why is it the end of the world if workers agitate for more money?

If it costs more to do business in Santa Monica, if businesses can't survive here, then rents will decrease. As it is now, restaurateurs who make good in Santa Monica must give their profits to the landlord or move on when it is time to renew the lease.

Yet the proponents of the living wage have been disingenuous, too. One of the rhetorical pillars on which they have justified implementing a living wage ordinance in the "Coastal Zone" is the alleged investment the City has made in the district to benefit the tourism industry. Yet assessments on property owners and businesses paid for the improvements on the Third Street Promenade, and regional, state, and federal monies largely paid for beach and park improvements so that these regional resources could better serve not tourists, but the millions who live in nearby communities.

Not only that, but the City encouraged tourism to pay for social services. The City's budget for 2000-01 counted on receiving more than $20 million from the hotel bed tax, about one-sixth of the City's total revenue from taxes. The data consultant Robert Pollin himself collected in his report to the City on the living wage showed that between 1985 and 1999 the City spent only 4.7 percent of its operating budget and 12.1 percent of its capital budget in the Coastal Zone, a district that represents 18 percent of the city's total area.

The City has not subsidized the tourism business, tourism has subsidized the City.

Yet because of a nearly unlimited supply of workers, hotels and other businesses can externalize their costs by paying a sub-living wage without benefits. Taxpayers bear the additional costs of these workers' lives.

Professor Pollin made a point that is certainly correct: All Santa Monica hotels have benefited greatly from Prop. S, the ban on building new hotels near the beach, and the City's other no-growth policies. If the City would use this fact to focus its ordinance on hotels, I believe the result would be a stronger law with fewer unforeseen consequences.

Workers do not benefit from the City's no-growth policies. Because of Prop. S, hotels have not only fewer hotels to compete with for customers, but also fewer to compete with for workers. No-growth policies have also prevented the building of housing so that housing costs in Santa Monica are among the region's highest, even as our population has decreased.

My suggestion: Proceed with caution. Ultimately the biggest problem with the proposed ordinance is that Santa Monica is so small. Its economy is not independent of the region's, or even the world's. What we do will not be much more than an example, but that means we need to get it right.

1875
Lemuel Fisher begins publishing the Outlook newspaper on a weekly
basis; publication continues until 1878.

Symbolic gestures are all well and good, but if the law does not work, then no one
will try it anywhere else.

Santa Monica has a reputation for beautiful weather, but it's a lie. Especially in the spring, when the dreaded "marine layer" ("late night and early morning cloudiness") covers the coast.

JUNE 1, 2001

I predict that when meteorologists have collected and analyzed all the data, the spring of 2001 will prove to have been, in Santa Monica, the coldest, darkest, and most miserable on record. It has been gray, not just west of Lincoln Boulevard, but all the way up and into the college streets.

Which raises the question, when are we going to do something about the marine layer?

Spring in Santa Monica: Foggy mornings that linger into bone-chilling overcast afternoons. Parents huddled together in parkas and fleeces, on cold metal bleachers, watching 5:00 o'clock little league games. "Alfresco" dining under gas heaters. Lending sweaters to underdressed visitors from Pasadena.

There is no question in my mind that the marine layer problem is getting worse, not better, although I can't tell if the situation has deteriorated ever since SMRR took control in the early '80s.

Consider this: if we had sunshine in March, April, May, and June—even if summer started here on Memorial Day, as in the rest of the country, instead of July 4th—surely hotels and the rest of our tourist-based economy could make enough money to pay their workers a living wage.

Of course, if we had good weather in the spring, all those extra tourists would add to the unhappiness of everyone here who resents or is inconvenienced by tourists. But then again, some people already have such a heavy load of unhappiness that they might not notice.

Is the City doing anything about the marine layer? Not so far as I can tell. This lack of attention might have been understandable twenty-five years ago, when smog was so bad that it often obscured the marine layer, but now that our skies are otherwise much clearer, shouldn't the City Council at least direct staff to study the issue?

Perhaps we can have a moratorium on new overcast days, or at least require clearing between eleven and four. Environmental impact reports could evaluate to what extent development adds to the moisture level. Or, what if development reduces relative humidity in the city to a level that attracts more moisture from the ocean? We can hire a consultant to find out.

1875
Santa Monica Methodists organize the Methodist Episcopal Church
(now the First United Methodist Church of Santa Monica) and build
a chapel at Sixth and Arizona.

The clouds, of course, do not originate in Santa Monica, but drift in every "late night and early morning." It's not clear what we can do. The problem begs a regional solution. Perhaps we can make a deal with the Inland Empire to trade moisture for desert air.

Some people will say that Santa Monica cannot do anything about the weather, or shouldn't try. That attitude hasn't stopped us in the past. At least we can talk about it.

M y son Henry was in the fifth grade about to enter middle school. Once again, I felt that my life was "ripped from the headlines," as everyone was talking about education.

JUNE 15, 2001

"There is not a single district in the United States sunk in complete ignorance."
—Alexis de Tocqueville, *Democracy in America.*

"If you can read this, thank a teacher." —bumper sticker.

My son Henry is in fifth grade. As such he is about to make the transition from elementary to middle school. Recently Henry and his parents attended a transition dinner for fifth-graders who will attend John Adams Middle School (JAMS). Henry and his peers talked to veteran sixth-graders, who tried not to frighten the younger kids too much. We parents talked to veteran middle-school parents, who tried to reassure us that hormones and education do not necessarily conflict in all instances.

I bring this up because I find myself looking at the current hot social and political issue—education—from the inside out. Everything I read in the papers about testing, standards, curriculum, school financing, etc., seems aimed directly at me, parent of a fifth-grader.

As it happens, the math curriculum at JAMS has become a political issue, with all sorts of people, primarily parents, weighing in on the question of what kind of books teachers there should use to teach math.

I am frustrated with the current debate over educational issues like curriculum, pedagogy, and testing. The reality of education is simultaneously more simple and more complex than how axe-grinders of all persuasions present it.

On one hand, the issues are as simple as providing a good teacher—the most important determinant, in my experience, of the quality of education—with a calm, quiet place to teach. On the other hand, what makes up a high quality education is complex, even elusive. Certain skills, reading, for instance, are measurable, at least to a degree. But how does one test the ability to think critically, or enthusiasm to learn?

Much of what comprises a good education is immeasurable, at least by any standard less broad than happiness and success in the world. I have a friend who did not take high school seriously. He surfed and rode motorcycles. After graduating, he managed to enroll in a junior college. Something clicked. He studied and transferred to a University of

Sept. 28, 1875
Led by the Vawter family, Santa Monicans organize the First Pres-
byterian Church; the congregation builds its first church in 1876 at
Third and Arizona.

California campus. He did well, and went to an Ivy League graduate school. He received a Ph.D. and is now a full professor at USC.

The American system has always been an open system. An educational system of second chances. Third chances. Other countries reserved educations high in intellectual content for the elite, an elite they usually selected around the time American kids started to spend more time combing their hair than doing their homework.

What America gained from this was the best-educated adult population in the world. More Americans graduated high school, more went to college, more received advanced degrees, than any people on earth. Only now is the rest of the world catching up: According to a study published this week by the Organization for Economic Cooperation and Development, for the first time two countries, Japan and Canada, have higher rates of college graduation than the U.S.

Now we have an education president who wants to use testing to destroy the public school system. We don't need President Bush to do the job, however. The friends of public education can do it quite well themselves. Meddlers, professional and amateur, have stolen the educational system away from the people who understand it best—the teachers.

Consider it non-controversial that the American educational system excels at the college and university level, which has championed the highest levels of scholarship at the same time that it has educated the largest mass of students. American higher education is the envy of the world.

A salient characteristic of American higher education is the respect the teachers receive. I do not mean the respect of students, which, judging from popular culture, has never been high. I mean the respect teachers receive from their institutions. American colleges and universities let the teachers, as a group and individually, run the show. Professors run not only their classrooms, but also their departments. They determine curriculum and, for the most part, who their employers will hire to be their colleagues.

There are no standardized tests to prove how good a job these professors do, but, based on the success of their graduates and, for that matter, the entire economy, they do a great job. Nor is it any coincidence that there is no shortage of people who want to teach at the college and university level, even though the pay is not particularly good considering the educational level of the work force. Compare the authority of a college professor with that of a teacher in the public schools.

Uhhh ... Well, the fact is, there is no comparison.

This is not a Left-Right issue. Educational "conservatives" are telling teachers at JAMS, at the moment, what materials they should use to teach math, but a few years ago, in the celebrated "whole language" fiasco, educational "radicals" dictated how to teach reading. You don't have to be conservative or liberal to think you can teach better than teachers. You need only to have an opinion. A lot of people have opinions. Unfortunately, they disagree.

Parents disagree about how teachers should teach. Education school academics (and their publishing companies) disagree. Administrators disagree. Newspaper columnists disagree about how teachers should teach. Foundations, politicians …

Teachers know how to teach. Some are better at it than others, but collectively they have the knowledge. Let them work it out.

If it all weren't so tragic, it would be funny.

Take the L.A. Unified School District, which has adopted a reading program, "Open Court," that scripts exactly what teachers are to say and do each day. The irony is rich: The L.A. schools are falling apart, there aren't enough of them in the first place, there aren't enough books, huge numbers of the kids don't speak English, their parents were never schooled, the bureaucracy is bloated.

But when some kids don't learn, the solution is to tell teachers how to teach.

Santa Monica is, of course, part of Greater Los Angeles and therefore is automobile dependent. There are no rail or other mass transit links between Santa Monica and the region, even though the City was founded on the basis of railroads and trolleys. This was my first column on plans to reconnect Santa Monica to the region by rail.

JUNE 22, 2001

The weather cleared. Friends from Silver Lake dropped by Sunday for brunch, and afterwards we all took a walk to the beach, the first expedition there this year that required sun block. After some sand castle digging and wave jumping by the kids, we walked to the Pier.

The day was glorious and perfect for a ride on the Ferris wheel. The air was clear, sails crowded the horizon, and views in all directions were inspiring. I derive much pleasure gazing on the Ferris wheel from afar, especially at night when it explodes with color. I am happy to give Pacific Park a few bucks from time to time to pay for it.

Some months ago, at one of the hearings of the Civic Center Working Group, City Council Member Richard Bloom said something that has stuck with me. He said that if we build a city to serve the needs of local people, it will at the same time serve the needs of visitors—that visitors are attracted to cities that treat their residents well.

Sometimes the equation works the other way. For instance, a Ferris wheel in an amusement park on a "pleasure pier" is a quintessential visitor-oriented use. But isn't it great to have one of our own to ride whenever we want? Isn't it great to drive home at night from a trip up the coast, to see in the distance first the glimmer, then the glow, and finally the whole thing turning like a combination lighthouse and prayer wheel?

* * *

Next Thursday the MTA Board, which now has as a member a real transit user, Santa Monica's own Pam O'Connor, will take the next step in determining the future of transportation on the Westside. The board will vote on how to proceed with plans for improving bus service on Wilshire Boulevard, and whether to build a light rail line or dedicated busway along the Exposition corridor.

If the board follows the staff report, it will take incremental rather than drastic action. However, in this case, discretion may be the better part of valor, because for various reasons the bold steps the MTA needs to take in the long-term are not feasible now.

Under the MTA board's prior direction the building of a dedicated busway down Wilshire was to have priority over an Exposition corridor project.

Public comment, however, favored Exposition light-rail and there was considerable resistance to the Wilshire busway. The Santa Monica City Council, for instance, voted last week to oppose any busway that would displace parking or lanes of traffic on Wilshire, in effect opposing any dedicated bus lane. The City of Los Angeles is concerned that a busway would interfere with cars making left turns.

The board may now be ready to uncouple the Exposition project from the Wilshire project. This will be good for both. The MTA can test the busway—which in this country is a more or less untried technology and something difficult to add to a busy boulevard like Wilshire—in stages, and development of Expo light-rail can proceed on its own terms with separate environmental review.

But don't expect to board a tram in Santa Monica any time soon. The MTA staff is recommending at this time to design the line only as far as the Robertson/Venice intersection. The fact is they don't have the money to build more than that and may not have even that until 2008.

The need for big transit solutions has become ever more apparent because the futility of improving the road system has never been more obvious. CalTrans is now preparing to spend $50 million to add bits of new lanes to the intersection of the Ventura and San Diego freeways. The intersection was built in 1956 to handle 200,000 cars a day; it now handles 551,000. You could double-deck the whole thing and it still wouldn't handle today's load.

CalTrans will spend the money even though it admits that the $50 million will not buy any reduction in travel times.

We need to channel the growth in transportation demand into transit, and the only way to do that is with capital intensive projects that can move a lot of people. The long-term silver lining in the MTA's inability at present to devise workable busway on Wilshire Boulevard is that planners and the public will have to take another look at extending the Red Line subway from Wilshire and Western to points west.

Mass transit is expensive, but so are roads. According to an article this week in the *L.A. Times*, the Southern California Association of Governments has recently completed a proposal for the first phase of a system of truck-only highways: four truck lanes (two in each direction) on a 37-mile stretch of the Pomona Freeway that would cost $4 billion.

The money might be there for transit if we stopped wasting $50 million a pop on highway non-fixes.

1876
First Santa Monica school opens in the First Presbyterian Church.
School trustees build first school building on Sixth Street on land
donated by Jones and Baker.

* * *

Speaking of capital projects, intensive or otherwise, Santa Monica's transit mall is taking shape. The new wider sidewalk is now in place on a few blocks on the south side of Santa Monica Boulevard, and in a few weeks the other side of the street will be completed, along with the intersection of Santa Monica and the Promenade.

Unfortunately, the Architectural Review Board recently voted to recommend privatizing part of the sidewalk. One reason for widening the sidewalks is to allow restaurants to provide outdoor dining as a way of enlivening the street and improving the pedestrian ambiance, but the ARB has voted (contrary to staff's recommendation) to allow restaurants to wall off parts of the sidewalk with permanent structures, weather guards, and umbrellas.

The ARB's recommendation will now be considered by the Planning Commission and ultimately the City Council, but if they follow the ARB, the City will repeat the mistake it made on Ocean Avenue, where "outdoor" dining has become enclosed dining, and the public gets no "ambiance" benefit.

A better model is the Promenade, where outdoor dining is open and there is a connection between the people watchers at the tables and the people watchers passing by. Given that the restaurants will be using a large portion of the new sidewalks, it is important that this space not be privatized.

The more columns I wrote about Santa Monica, the more I learned how much I needed to learn about its history, which was longer and more complicated than I suspected.

JULY 13, 2001

This Sunday, July 15, marks the 126th anniversary of the day Senator Jones auctioned the first lots in a newly subdivided Santa Monica.

Jones, following the precedent of real estate developers since at least the days of ancient Rome, arrayed his streets on a grid. He numbered them eastward from the ocean. He named the east-west streets for western states, except that what is now Colorado Avenue was called "Railroad Avenue" for the railroad that ran by it and connected the new town with Los Angeles. Santa Monica Boulevard was Oregon and Broadway was Utah. The source of Jones's wealth was the Comstock Lode, and he named the widest street, what is now Wilshire, for Nevada. The first lot, at Ocean and Utah, went for $510.

I took these facts from *Santa Monica Bay: Paradise by the Sea* by Fred E. Basten. This is an excellent picture book about the history of Santa Monica, provided one can get past the fact that there is nothing in it about Santa Monica's African-American community, nor anything about Hispanics once the Sepulveda, Marquez, and Reyes families sell the land to Colonel R.S. Baker in 1872.

Colonel Baker thought the bluff overlooking the ocean would make a good sheep ranch. He got wise quick, however, and sold most of his holdings to Jones two years later for about a 300 percent profit. Jones wanted to build a port to serve a railroad he wanted to build from Los Angeles to his silver mines in Inyo County.

Some days I think history is destiny, some days I think it's bunk. No matter what future one wants or predicts for Santa Monica, one can choose a past that suits one's argument: port or resort; high-class or honky-tonk; congenial small town or Raymond Chandler's Bay City; industrial powerhouse or sleepy suburb. Your call.

No one ever built much in Santa Monica to last, and the only constant, aside from change itself, has been the continued need for investment to keep the place from expiring from terminal shabbiness.

The port failed. A great era of resorts, like the Arcadia Hotel that stood near the present site of Rand's headquarters, replaced it. The resorts deteriorated during World War II and the Cold War when Santa Monica became a blue-collar manufacturing town, as a major locus of the aviation industry. The Santa Monica Freeway presaged a boom in

Senator Jones loses fortune in crash of Comstock mining stock; Collis Huntington of Southern Pacific squeezes the Los Angeles & Independence by reducing fares and freight rates between Los Angeles and San Pedro; Jones forced to sell railroad to Huntington at a loss.

---

apartments and Santa Monica became both a bedroom community for commuters and a retirement center for seniors.

No "vision" of Santa Monica ever proved permanent, yet every phase left some imprint, and sometimes seeds for a revival.

Traffic now crawls on the freeway, and Santa Monica looks again to its own resources. Office workers have replaced factory workers, tourism is again a mainstay of the economy, and, irony of ironies, the MTA voted two weeks ago to start a process that may return rails to Colorado Avenue.

Happy birthday, Santa Monica, and many happy returns.

I'm an immigrant to Southern California. I grew up in Philadelphia, and some local customs still charm and/or amaze me.

JULY 19, 2001

Last year the Dodgers built a new section of seats between the dugouts, more or less at dugout level. The purpose was, according to the Dodgers' website, to make Dodger Stadium "more economically competitive with other ballparks across the nation." Meaning, the Dodgers want to soak up more revenue from businesses that would pay large sums to lease "sky boxes" and the like if the Dodgers had not built their ballpark in mid-twentieth-century California, when quaint notions about democracy led to the building of wonderfully open and egalitarian modernist edifices like Dodger Stadium.

Meaning, further, that until the Dodgers build their own "retro" stadium complete with tiers of exclusive boxes for the corporate elite, the Dodgers will have to rely on these open seats virtually on the playing field, along with a few boxes they squeezed into the club level, to justify the price Fox paid for the team and/or to pay the salary of Kevin Brown.

(I know poor Hispanics lost their homes in the building of Dodger Stadium, and that American ideals of democracy have always stood on the backs of the poor, the persecuted, the enslaved and the otherwise discriminated against, but these topics are outside the scope of this column and much better dealt with during football season.)

Last week, I watched a game from the Dugout Club. Please don't be jealous.

How wonderful are the Dugout Club seats? Let me count the ways. Start with parking. Four Dugout Club tickets come with two parking passes—the ultimate L.A. perk.

After they park, Dugout Club ticket holders descend below the grandstand, pass through security, and have their hands stamped with invisible ink. Finally they reach their seats by way of the "Dugout Club" itself, a bar and restaurant for the exclusive use of Dugout Club ticket holders. The food at this restaurant, which will deliver orders to your seat, is "complimentary"—to the extent there could be such thing as a complimentary lunch.

One final touch: The seats have cup holders.

Extra parking, free food, cup holders—and we were so close that a player in the on-deck circle turned around and answered a question someone nearby yelled out. We could hear the umpire call strikes, and people addressed the umpire as "Blue," just like at little league games when the "blue" makes a bad call, as in "Oh, Blue ..."

1878/79
Huntington closes the Santa Monica wharf and has it torn down;
Southern Pacific uses the Los Angeles & Independence tracks only
for passenger excursions between Los Angeles and Santa Monica.

The game up close was vivid, more like the game in baseball literature than the game I was used to seeing either from the stands or on television. The home-plate umpire came over between innings to get a drink of water. You could see him relax for a moment, before putting his game face back on (he resembled a Marine drill sergeant) to return to the ball and strike wars.

So—how did I get these tickets? I got them through normal channels: i.e., someone gave them to me. Ever since moving to Los Angeles a couple of decades ago I have been fascinated with how Dodger tickets work as currency, both social and economic. The distribution of Dodger tickets would make a suitable topic for dissertation—by a student of economics or anthropology.

Back in the old country, that is, Philadelphia, if you want to see the Phillies play, you arrive at the stadium and buy a ticket. If you expect the game will be crowded, you might buy tickets in advance, to guarantee a good seat. But good seats are available to every game, because the Phils don't sell many season tickets.

But season ticket holders have owned half of Dodger Stadium—the better half—forever. Their tickets float around town, making new friends and keeping the old. Dodger tickets and Hollywood Bowl tickets—I am convinced that the same families and businesses bought them all about the time William Mulholland gazed upon the gushing waters and said, "There it is. Take it."

My Dugout Club tickets came from my friend Kevin, who invited my son Henry and me to share the tickets that he received from a school friend whose company has the seats. Kevin is an architect and his friend is a contractor, and Kevin and the friend might do business someday. (I don't suggest that had much to do with the transaction, but I am encouraging Kevin to do some business with this fellow because obviously, any contractor who owns Dugout Club tickets must do very good work.)

The funny thing about the Dugout Club was that aside from the above-described benefits, sitting there wasn't much different from sitting in any other seats I've sat in at Dodger Stadium. It was the same crowd. I did not feel like I was in some place that Henry would call "too fancy."

I didn't recognize anyone famous. Everyone I spoke to was sitting in these seats for the first time. They got their seats the same way I got mine. People wore tank tops, shorts, tees, and polo shirts. Girls wore their softball uniforms. The couple next to us lived in Rowland Heights and knew which ballplayers on the Dodgers and the Mariners came from Rowland Heights. They got their Dugout Club tickets from work.

I dedicate this column to all those friends and business acquaintances who over the years have shared their Dodger tickets with me. For a Phillies fan who moved here

1880
Santa Monica population falls to 417.

---

twenty-three years ago, being one of the millions each year who attend Dodger games was one way I became a Southern Californian. So thanks.

I went on vacation with my family in the summer of 2001 to a family reunion in Washington state. Just as I had with our visit to New York in December, I wrote about the trip, and writing about my travels became a regular part of the column. When I traveled, there always seemed to be something that I could relate to Santa Monica.

JULY 27, 2001

Port Townsend is a small town on the Olympic Peninsula in Washington, at the entrance to Puget Sound. A fine natural harbor, its founders intended it to become the great port for the Pacific Northwest. Merchants built fine brick and stone buildings. The federal government built an impressive granite customs house on the bluff overlooking the harbor. The county built a brick courthouse. Even the German government built a beautiful consulate in high Victorian style.

But the railroad stopped at Seattle, and Port Townsend never grew up. The old buildings remain, however. Hippies and craftspeople discovered them in the '60s, I'm told, and now, filled with boutiques and bookstores, restaurants, and bed and breakfasts, they serve the great trade of our day—tourism.

Santa Monica began with a similar misconception, that the railroad would come and make Santa Monica Bay a great port. Go to Port Townsend if you want to know what Santa Monica might look like today if a large body of water separated Santa Monica from Los Angeles. Or, go to Port Townsend just to have fun. I spent five days there last week when the extended clan of Grubers met there for a reunion. Thank the ambiance, perhaps, but it turned out to be our most complete gathering in thirty-seven years.

About seventy descendants of my grandparents and in-laws attended, from all over. The Grubers have scattered over the country and beyond: My sister lives in Italy and one cousin just took a job in London. We have all manner of jobs and lifestyles. Most no longer have the name Gruber. By communing with so many people who not only look like me, but who also are just as opinionated, I got a reminder of who I am. Perhaps there are shy and retiring families who have quiet reunions, but that's not us.

I was also reminded that "who I am" owes a lot to "who they were." When looking at my family and its history, I don't know if I can separate my predilections from my sociological destiny. My father's parents, Frank and Rebecca Gruber, were immigrants from Romania who settled in Akron, Ohio. Like many immigrants before and since, they opened a little store. Frank had started to sell life insurance, too, when, in 1930, just as the Great Depression was getting serious, a drunk driver killed him as he stepped off a curb, leaving Rebecca to raise their seven children alone. At the time, my father, the third child, was nine.

1884
W.D. Vawter and his son E.J. Vawter purchase 100 acres from the
Lucas family for the purpose of residential development.

Rebecca invested her life insurance proceeds in an apartment building, but she lost it all as the Depression deepened. She lost the store, too. The bank went under and she lost her $80 savings account. She made ends meet, with a lot of help from her neighbors. With that history, how could I not rate the needs of the working poor, of immigrants, higher than those of, say, hotel owners?

My father's older sister and brother took jobs to support the family, instead of going to college, but my father's public school teachers encouraged him to pursue an academic education. He won a college scholarship and his mother made sure he took advantage of it. That changed his life and, since he met my mother at college, enabled mine. With that history, naturally I believe in not only the opportunity for every kid to go to college, but also the expectation that even immigrant and poor children are entitled to and can handle an academic education.

My father and his siblings, male and female, served in World War II. They came back and took advantage of the G.I. Bill. They found good jobs and started businesses. They bought homes the government helped them buy. They prospered, and their many children went to college and they prospered, too, to a level beyond what Frank and Rebecca could have contemplated when they got off the boat.

With that history, I don't believe the role of government at all levels in creating jobs and building housing is some abstract concept that doesn't affect real people. Economic development is not something for people who have all they need to look down their noses at. If traffic congestion is a problem, don't blame development, don't exile young families to the desert sprawl: Build a transit system.

My grandmother ultimately moved to Los Angeles and, notwithstanding that she had lost one nest egg in an apartment building, she and her second husband invested their savings in a six-unit apartment in the Fairfax district. They lived in one unit, and the other five apartments and Social Security provided for their retirement. With that history, perhaps, I learned not to take for granted capitalism and capitalists, and to appreciate specifically the importance of investing in cities, because there are risks involved in doing so, and people can put their money elsewhere.

Sometimes I worry that I have an inconsistent set of beliefs. I like government regulation and investment, and I like unions and minimum wages, but I also like developers and entrepreneurs and I am skeptical about a lot that government does—especially when it is at its most well intentioned, like it was with urban renewal. Perhaps my ideas are consistent only with my own history.

You have your own past, and no doubt your own beliefs based on it. Or perhaps you have managed to transcend your past, like my cousin who lives "off the grid" in Arizona. The past should not be destiny. Even I can't relate every idea I have to some problem that confronted my grandmother. But I can't get too far away from her, either.

O ccasionally I write about a big-picture planning issue. In this case, the topic was balancing growth and quality of life with prosperity, but what surprised most of my readers was the population data I unearthed about Santa Monica. Santa Monica, it turned out, had not been bursting at the seams.

AUGUST 3, 2001

As the *L.A. Times* told the tale in a front-page story last Sunday, during the Reagan years the FBI, ironically under the (ironic?) supervision of traitor agent Robert Philip Hanssen, monitored the activities of liberals and liberal organizations that the government believed might be susceptible to Soviet influence. My home town, Philadelphia, came under particular scrutiny.

According to the *Times*, quoting from FBI memoranda obtained under the Freedom of Information Act (after fifteen years of stalling!): "[FBI] agents in Philadelphia were concerned that it was 'a fertile region' for Soviet influence operations. Among the causes: 'the decaying industrial base, high blue-collar unemployment, homeless[ness], racial tensions, influential religious community, and concentrated liberal academic environment of the region.'"

The *Times* article could explain a lot. Perhaps the destruction of the urban centers of our civilization, through disinvestment, white flight, freeways, drugs, etc., was all part of a Soviet plot to create the appropriate context for revolution, not, as previously thought, the result of politicians catering to the interests of suburban real estate speculators and shopping center magnates.

I only bring this up because once, back in 1994 when Tom Hayden was collecting signatures to put the Civic Center plan on the ballot, he accused me of trying to turn Santa Monica into Philadelphia. I now suspect the FBI duped Hayden to goad me into revealing a Soviet plan to foment revolution on the Westside. In any case I didn't know how to reply to Hayden, which probably proved to him that I was in fact working for the FBI.

Actually, Santa Monica and Philadelphia have at least one thing in common—they have both been losing population. Between 1990 and 2000, Philadelphia's population declined 4.3 percent from 1,585,577 to 1,517,550, while Santa Monica's population declined 3.2 percent from 86,905 to 84,084. Of course, Philadelphia's population reached its peak decades ago, at about two million and has declined almost 25 percent, while Santa Monica is still within 5 percent of its 1980 peak of 88,314.

But Santa Monica's population decline is contrary to popular wisdom, which holds that Santa Monica is more densely developed than its neighbors. In fact, Santa Monica's

population density of 10,100 per square mile is significantly lower than the average density of 13,000 per square mile that exists in the area between downtown L.A. and the ocean that the MTA studied for its Westside transit projects.

The perception persists that Santa Monica is "built-out" or "overdeveloped" even though it consists mostly of one- and two-story buildings even in the districts that are not zoned single family. This perception permeates all discussion about development. I remember shaking my head last year at the Planning Commission hearing on Target when commissioner Jay Johnson complained about Santa Monica's continuing population growth.

Johnson unfortunately was in good company, or company that should know better. In 1996 the City's Master Environmental Assessment predicted that our population would be 90,777 in 2000, and the sign on Lincoln Boulevard at the entrance to the city states our population as 94,000.

In certain respects, the decline in Santa Monica's population is more dramatic than the decline in Philadelphia's. Philly's population decreased in the context of stagnant population growth in its region, as the population of the Philadelphia metropolitan area increased only slightly during the past several decades. But Santa Monica's population decreased while the population of the region boomed. Between 1990 and 2000, as the population of the L.A.-Long Beach metropolitan area increased 11 percent, and the population of outlying districts increased even faster, Santa Monica was the only city of significant size in Los Angeles County to show a decline in population.

Proponents of "smart growth" promote increased density within the urban core of the region as the most promising solution to sprawl. They point out that Southern California is going to add millions of new residents in the next couple of decades no matter what, and if those people don't live inside the core, in places like Santa Monica, they are going to live outside it. More sprawl will perpetuate the social and environmental problems we have today, including in Santa Monica.

Santa Monica is inseparable from the region. Our poverty rate is equal to the national rate, we have gangs, homelessness, substandard housing (but not enough of it!), declining industrial employment, and, of course, bad traffic. Sprawl, not density, has caused the region's traffic congestion, and investment in outlying areas at the expense of the urban core is the root cause of urban decline.

I often get the feeling that the anti-density, anti-development people want to say that they disagree with the "growth will happen no matter what" part of the smart-growth argument. They want to say, "Why do we need to have growth? Why can't we stop growing and reach a happy stasis?"

Good questions. Put another way, do cities—do regions, for that matter—do better growing or not growing?

I can best answer the question with a word: "Philadelphia."

The Philadelphia metropolitan area stopped growing about forty years ago, and guess what—Philly and its suburbs have the same problems Los Angeles has, but worse.

If you don't believe me, ask the FBI.

O ne of the crazy things about local politics is how NIMBYism can go to extremes. In the summer of 2001, what some residents of Santa Monica didn't want in their backyard was a Trader Joe's grocery store and a 500-seat concert hall.

AUGUST 10, 2001

Wow. Tuesday my household was in the eye of the news. The police, searching for an armed robber in flight, blockaded our street. Then, that evening, I made dinner using key ingredients that came from Trader Joe's.

It's one of our favorite quick pasta dinners. Sauté some garlic and anchovies in olive oil, then add a can of chopped tomatoes. Put the water on for the pasta. Thaw and peel a bag of frozen shrimp. When you put the pasta in the pot, sauté the shrimp in some more garlic and oil. Dump the shrimp into the tomatoes, drain the pasta, put everything in a bowl, salt and pepper to taste, and ... *Ecco la pasta*. As my father-in-law used to say, "Imagine how much this would cost in a fine New York restaurant."

Need I mention that we bought the tomatoes, the shrimp, the olive oil, and the garlic at Trader Joe's?

I have the feeling that whether one shops at Trader Joe's will soon be a political issue, pitting neighbor against neighbor.

I read Planning Commission Chair Kelly Olsen's lawyerly memo to the planning department about whether the proposed new Trader Joe's at Twelfth and Wilshire has unanticipated zoning problems. I have no opinion whether he is correct, as there is never anything obvious about zoning. But even if Olsen is incorrect, the new TJ's will become a political issue because it will need a conditional use permit to sell alcoholic beverages, and the store will come under Planning Commission review regardless of the zoning. If Olsen is right, TJ's will need considerably more approvals, including, perhaps, an amendment to the zoning ordinance.

In any case, Trader Joe's proposal may test the commission's avowed "resident friendliness." Few institutions are more popular than Trader Joe's.

It may also soon be controversial in Santa Monica to be a music-lover. Wednesday night I attended the public meeting Santa Monica College hosted to discuss plans for a 500-seat theater at the Madison School site at Eleventh and Santa Monica Boulevard. The closest concert facility to Santa Monica is Royce Hall at UCLA, so a new venue, even a small one, would be a welcome addition to the cultural landscape.

You would have thought the College wanted to build a car dealership.

The reaction was hysterical and I don't mean funny. One neighbor characterized the proposed theater as "Lincoln Center West" and said that she and her neighbors would "pay for the pleasures of others who don't want to drive downtown." Another neighbor said that Eleventh Street would become clogged with rich people driving to concerts from the northern part of the city. Another worried that the traffic would force the City to put traffic humps on nearby streets.

I have to blame the hysteria, at least in part, on members of the City Council who have treated the idea of this small theater, which will not only well serve the college but also the many Santa Monicans who would appreciate a local venue for music and dance, as if it were a paper mill or, heaven forbid, a department store.

Of course the biggest concern of the neighbors was parking, even though the existing lot is beyond adequate and the area around Madison has been designated a preferential parking zone. Why not establish preferential parking on all residential streets in the city, but only on one side of the street? By having preferential parking everywhere, we would get over the neighborhood vs. neighborhood, block vs. block antagonisms we have now, and by leaving one side of each street open for anyone to park, we will get over the business and visitor vs. resident antagonism. We would also more efficiently allocate the resource.

Just an idea.

I hope the neighbors near Madison School conclude that a small concert hall is just what their neighborhood needs. Something they can be proud of, but also something that enlivens their streets, makes them more secure. People who like music also like to eat, and perhaps someone will turn that ugly tire store on the corner into a neighborhood-friendly restaurant or coffee shop. Maybe some nights neighbors will walk there and see their friends.

[Note: the Madison site theater—built mostly with funds raised as part of a Santa Monica College bond issue—opened in the fall of 2008 with a varied program of concerts and theater. The theater was named the "Broad Stage at the Santa Monica College Performing Arts Center" to honor Eli and Edythe Broad, whose foundation donated ten million dollars to endow programming.]

Because Santa Monica has had mostly left-wing government for twenty years, there is a tendency to ignore the reality that the city is highly segregated and that its left-wing leaders have done little to change that fact. I've tried to hold their feet to the fire.

AUGUST 17, 2001

Tuesday night the Santa Monica City Council faced the result of a shameful episode of squeaky-wheel politics, namely, the City's flaunting of the state law requiring the inclusion of second units ("granny flats") in single-family (R-1) zoned districts. Naturally, the council punted, referring the matter back to staff. You see, there wasn't enough "public input," as only five speakers addressed the council, and one of them was the attorney, James Isaacs, who took and won the case challenging the City's ordinance that limited occupancy of second units to relatives and care-givers (i.e., no renters). Unsure of what to do without a horde of homeowners to advise them, the council asked staff to return with more research and, presumably, more "public."

Some history. The City Council, in a series of votes since 1996, with a majority that has included sitting members Ken Genser, Kevin McKeown, and Robert Holbrook, ignored the advice of its own attorneys and planning staff and forced planning staff to develop "findings" to support the result the council wanted to achieve. (To give credit where credit is due, Mayor Michael Feinstein has consistently voted in favor of second units.)

Attorney Isaacs took the City to court and won (and the City had to pay his fees). In finding that the council had violated state law, the court of appeal dismissed the City's claim that it could, under the law, ban second units entirely based on its "findings," which the council based entirely on anecdotal evidence supplied by homeowners.

Squeaky-wheel government at its worst.

Even if the council punted, some of what its members said deserves study. Kevin McKeown said, soulfully and as if on cue, "In Santa Monica we value diversity," and went on to say that the "diversity" Santa Monica values includes single-family neighborhoods.

Let me tell you something: If Santa Monica were in South Africa, Kevin McKeown would be on a hunger strike. That is because, with the exception of a few neighborhoods, Santa Monica is segregated. North of Wilshire, only 1 percent of the population is African-American and only about 5 percent is Hispanic, even though blacks and Hispanics make up 20 percent of Santa Monica's population as a whole. The R-1 areas in Sunset Park are also overwhelmingly white.

An amount equal to 31.43 percent of all of Santa Monica's land, and 47.18 percent of its residentially zoned land, is zoned R-1. Restrictive covenants once segregated these areas by race. Now these areas are out of bounds to anyone unable to make a large down payment.

True, one cannot assume that owners of second units will rent them to poor people or to minorities. This has been one of the arguments Ken Genser has used to rationalize his votes against second units. But this argument ignores one thing: the law. The California legislature has already decided that regardless what Genser thinks, second units are part of R-1 zoning.

Do squeaky wheels grind slow and fine?

For the first year I wrote my column, I tried to avoid criticizing the Planning Commission from which I had been "purged." But then the commission's chair, Kelly Olsen, started to do things that annoyed me.

SEPTEMBER 7, 2001

Over the weekend, wife, child, and I stopped at Cha Cha Chicken for takeout and then drove up Topanga Canyon to see some Shakespeare at the Will Geer Theatricum Botanicum.

Weather balmy, road winding, bees pacifistic, show wonderful. Go.

The play was *Twelfth Night*, in which Sir Toby Belch and his boon companions provide the low humor. At one point, addressing the puritanical scold Malvolio, Sir Toby says, "Dost thou think, because thou art virtuous, there shall be no more cakes and ale?" I know it indicates I spend far too much mental energy on Santa Monica politics, but when I heard that line, even under the stars in Topanga, I could only think of Planning Commission Chair Kelly Olsen doing his best to stop Trader Joe's from opening a store at Twelfth and Wilshire.

"Dost thou think, because thou art virtuous, there shall be no more sesame crackers and Chilean wine?"

Lately, Olsen has provoked me much as Malvolio provoked Sir Toby. It's not so much his attempt to write the staff report on Trader Joe's, but his going on in the press about how wonderful he and the Planning Commission are. In an interview last week in *Santa Monica Bay Week* headlined "Residents Doing Better with Planning Commission Now," Olsen not only took credit for recruiting half the commission, but also, from how he talked, you would have thought Washington, Lincoln, et al., had come down from Mount Rushmore to adjudicate our conditional use permits.

"They are bright, they are dedicated, and if I had not been surrounded by these kinds of people, we couldn't have accomplished all the things we have done," said Olsen, modestly.

"Unlike their predecessors, Olsen suggested that the new commissioners think for themselves, working together fluidly in a collegial environment," inscribed the *Bay Week* interviewer.

This appreciation is reciprocated. Praise of Olsen from Commission member Julie Dad can approach North Korean "Dear Leader" standards. She recently wrote to the *Lookout,* before the commission elected Olsen to another term as chair, "[m]y own hope

J.W. Scott, proprietor of the Santa Monica Hotel, opens the Arcadia Hotel near the present-day Civic Center. The five-story hotel boasts 150 rooms, a bathhouse, ballroom, dining room, flower gardens, and panoramic views.

is that Kelly Olsen will be elected to another term as Chair of the Planning Commission, in order to cement the path which has been carved."

Perhaps self-love and back-scratching harm only the self-deluded, but Olsen does not mince words when it comes to impugning others. In the same *Bay Week* interview, Olsen said that when he joined the Planning Commission, "it was a rubber stamp for projects and ideas of developers" and that the "opinions of people in the community were not being heard."

It wasn't only the commission. In those dark days Before Olsen, before the carving of the path, before anyone hoped to cement the path, planning staff did not seriously scrutinize proposed developments, but instead facilitated them to the point that, in Olsen's words, "the law was bent to fit the project."

According to *Bay Week*, in "Olsen's view, the core problem was that the senior city staff and the planning commission were entirely too cozy with each other, thanks heavily ... to the influence of John Jalili, the former City Manager regarded as pro-development."

Olsen is not the only one singing this tune. In June City Council Member Kevin McKeown spoke at a Wilshire/Montana Neighborhood Coalition meeting about how the council had appointed a "whole new neighborhood-friendly Planning Commission."

My term on the commission ended when Olsen's began, in 1999, so the "old commission" Olsen calls a rubber stamp, and which McKeown presumably believes was less "neighborhood friendly," was the one that included me. I am a bit embarrassed to use this pulpit to defend the old Planning Commission, since I was on it, but I will get over that. None of the other former members of the commission have the time, inclination, or ego to respond to Olsen, and his public bashing of the City's professional staff is particularly low. He knows they will not defend themselves.

There is nothing wrong with pointing out the differences between the old commission and the new, but it is wrong to accuse people falsely of being rubber stamps, of bending the law, of making decisions behind closed doors. I'd like Olsen to give evidence for any of these charges, or even an alleged example. Beyond my personal pique, it is important to set the record straight about what happened before Olsen joined the commission because otherwise people might get the idea that how one properly represents "residents" and "neighborhoods" is to ignore the law and the needs of the community.

A little history.

Michael Feinstein once justified an ordinance restricting development in residential neighborhoods by saying to me that Santa Monica would always be booming. But in the mid '90s, Santa Monica was doing anything but. Remember riot and recession?

1887
"Santa Monica Improvement Club," founded by Senator Jones and
Colonel Baker, hosts regional tennis tournament.

Remember real estate prices declining so much that people—even residents of Santa Monica—complained they couldn't sell their houses or had negative equity? Remember the earthquake? The red tags? Much of Santa Monica was in ruins, and the priority that the City Council established was to rebuild the city.

As for the public mood, in 1994 the voters of Santa Monica—including Kelly Olsen, then a member of the City Council—overwhelmingly approved a development plan for the Civic Center that opponents had described in apocalyptic terms.

Autres temps, autres mores.

Olsen says the commission and staff were in cahoots with developers, but, ironically, until the economy started up again in the late '90s, not much private development came before the commission, and much of that was earthquake-related.

The biggest project was the rebuilding of Saint John's Hospital after the earthquake. Commission and staff conducted extensive hearings and caused the hospital to make substantial changes to its plans. At one point the commission had staff hire an outside architect to evaluate technical issues. Of course, no one could solve every potential problem or allay every fear or anxiety.

The commission was hardly a rubber stamp, but, more to the point, if it was anti-resident and pro-developer to work with Saint John's so that Santa Monica would have a state-of-the-art hospital for the next one hundred years, then I expect everyone on the commission would plead guilty.

Olsen claims to speak for and listen to the "people in the community," but some of our residents need jobs, or hospital care, or housing, or grocery stores. Many go to restaurants, and some even go to bars. Shopping is the third most popular leisure activity, according to a survey the City conducted in connection with developing the open space element of the general plan.

There are young people who like to dance, or do whatever else young people do. Residents like to see plays and movies, and listen to concerts. They and their visitors go to amusement parks and the Pier. Santa Monica even has legal and moral obligations to people who live outside its borders.

"Neighborhood" and "resident" are loaded terms—but no one owns them.

More anon. I'll write more about this next week.

I concluded my September 7, 2001, column expecting to write more the next week about the meaning of "neighborhood," but by the next week the word neighborhood had a different meaning, and writing a local column was not going to be the same job it had been the week before.

SEPTEMBER 14, 2001

This summer I sailed on Puget Sound with my Seattle cousins. Experienced sailors, they said to look at the horizon if I felt seasick.

I am glad I live in Santa Monica, because this week I could look west, to the Pacific, hoping that the unchanging line between sea and sky would calm my emotions, even as the ship I stand on rolls with the storm.

I grasped at other straws, too. Tuesday evening I attended a special service for peace at my synagogue, which was unusual for me. I am not religious.

I went to synagogue to hear something different from what I had heard all day on television. There are certain times when only religious figures speak to the better angels of our nature. Priests and rabbis can speak of compassion and loving thine enemy instead of retaliation, of justice instead of punishment. They also can say nothing, when everyone else is making noise.

I was not disappointed. Our rabbi did not say much at the service. It was not a time for a sermon, and he let the old songs and prayers—and silence—do most of his work. He did, however, include in his prayers a prayer for people who were so "wounded" that they would celebrate at the news of such destruction. He was referring, of course, to those Palestinians who cheered the news of America's loss.

Although I understand the rabbi's point, I disagree with his description of these Palestinians as being "wounded." If you perceive a nation as your mortal enemy, it is not unusual to cheer its loss. I am sure my parents celebrated when Allied bombers turned German cities into rubble, and I would not fault them for it. Hell, I celebrate in retrospect.

The word that best describes the collective psyche of our enemies is angry, not wounded.

Why do Islamic extremists hate the U.S. so much? Understanding that is key, not only to defeating them, but also to ensuring a lasting peace.

The resurgence of Islamic fundamentalism as a political force throughout the Muslim world is a reality that frightens many. But appearances are deceiving. Remember how

1888/89
Santa Monica purchases twenty fire hydrants and volunteers organize the Santa Monica Hose and Ladder Company.

mighty the Iraqi army appeared before the Gulf War. Islam has been on a losing streak for a long time. The word that best describes Islam is besieged, not resurgent.

For Americans analyzing the history of the past four or five centuries, the dominant narrative has been the rise of the West and western ideas. Conscientious chroniclers may identify crimes like extermination of indigenous peoples and the slave trade, or complain about more venal sins like fast food and pop culture. Critics may criticize the bad western ideas, like all-pervasive materialism, rather than extol the good ones, like democracy and human rights, but no matter what, the big story has been the rise of the West, and we have identified this with progress.

Muslims must look at these centuries differently—as a constant battle against the encroaching West. The Arabs reached their high-water mark in the eighth century, and by 1492 were gone from Europe. The Ottomans surged, but peaked in 1683 outside Vienna. In the eighteenth and nineteenth centuries, Islam retreated broadly, in eastern Europe, north of the Black Sea, and in the Caucasus. European imperialism overwhelmed Muslim populations in North Africa, subcontinent Asia, and the East Indies.

In the twentieth century, the West almost consumed itself in wars hot and cold, but in the meantime destroyed the Ottoman Empire and accomplished the economic domination of Islam by co-opting Arab political leadership to control the oil resources of the Middle East.

The second half of the twentieth century was especially galling: the United States, the brash apotheosis of all western values, became the dominant world power (capable of utterly destroying the strongest Muslim army at long distance and without breaking a sweat) and the West, to atone for its own sins against Jews, established the State of Israel right on the fault zone straddling the western and the Islamic tectonic plates.

As a Jew I find it ironic that a Jewish state is the West's spear point into Islam, but I imagine the irony is lost on Muslims. Imagine the shame of a hundred million Arabs stuck somewhere in a mental twelfth century defeated by a few Jews who had experienced the worst of the twentieth.

But also as a Jew, I understand this attitude well. In a former time when a great empire extended into the Middle East, bringing peace and prosperity and liberal thinking to the world, the Jews resisted with the stiffest necks. Think of Afghanistan as Masada and you may better comprehend what motivates Islamic radicals.

We cannot judge Islam on the basis of the extremists and the terrorists, just as we would not have others judge us on the basis of Timothy McVeigh, Buford Furrows, and Mormon polygamists. There are hundreds of millions of Muslims who just want to get along. But those millions are not the ones crashing jets into the World Trade Center, and

the violent rejection of western values by the Islamic extremists is exceptional. Other traditional societies—Hindus in India, Buddhists and Confucians in China, Japan, Vietnam, and Korea—largely accept the materialistic western agenda, although they jealously guard their political independence.

No armed resistance—conventional warfare or terrorism—has ever had or will have any effect on the continued advance of western culture. Bombs cannot stop the spread of ideas and technology, and, even if they could, we Occidentals are warlike and, although democracy and some of our higher behaviors may sometimes temper our bellicosity, we will always respond to violence in kind.

We Americans have, in fact, already started fighting back: The passengers in the fourth jet, when they learned what was at stake, did not hesitate to join the terrorists in battle—and win. (We shake our heads at Islamic "suicide bombers," but at the Battle of Midway, American pilots won because they took off from their carriers not expecting that they had enough fuel to hit their targets and return.)

I hope we are as smart as we are tough. I have a fantasy that the U.S. will obtain and show the Taliban convincing evidence that Osama bin Laden is guilty, and that the Taliban will give him up to our justice system. Think what a triumph it would be to show that we can give our sworn enemy a fair trial.

I know that is a fantasy, and an unlikely one. We rightly characterize these atrocities as acts of war. We will not limit ourselves to judicial process.

I accept that, but as I look out over the Pacific, trying to calm my emotions, I see peace for half the globe, notwithstanding that other "day of infamy" sixty years ago. In a vast sea that recently saw vast strife, ships, and planes carry trade and tourists and the hope of mutual understanding.

But I also think of Vietnam, where we lost a war because we did not understand what the other side was fighting for.

In the day of missiles and nuclear weapons, and, yes, terrorism, peace does not depend on the Seventh Fleet alone. The Pacific is peaceful because our former enemy, Japan, and the nascent powers of Asia realize that their interests are better served by being part of the modern world, not setting themselves against it.

Sooner or later we must reach that understanding with Islam or the twenty-first will not be the peaceful century we want it to be.

[Rereading these words in 2009, particularly those about giving our enemies a fair trial, I cannot help but reflect sadly on what happened with the Bush administration's policies of torture and such.]

The next two weeks I wrote two more columns in response to September 11, but ultimately I had to return to writing about Santa Monica. After all, the president said Americans should go shopping. I picked up where I left off: expressing outrage about Kelly Olsen and the Planning Commission.

OCTOBER 5, 2001

Although on September 11 City Manager Susan McCarthy admirably set the tone for the City by insisting that the public's business should continue as usual, I am only now ready to make my contribution to the national recovery by resuming my fulminations over Kelly Olsen, chair of the Planning Commission.

In my September 7 column I discussed comments Olsen made in an interview in *Santa Monica Bay Week* castigating the "old" Planning Commission, which included me, and planning staff. He accused the old commission of rubber-stamping the plans of developers, and he accused staff of facilitating development to the extent of bending the law. I suggested that Olsen might provide evidence of such conduct, or even allegations of a specific incident, but so far neither Olsen nor anyone else has done so.

Olsen has a history of grandstanding and making overblown comments, beginning with overstatements of his own accomplishments both politically and professionally. So you say, "What's the point?" Olsen is and will remain who he's been for all the years he's been involved in Santa Monica politics. Santa Monica is still a wonderful place.

To some extent, my motivation to continue this discussion arises from personal bewilderment. Perhaps I lack self-awareness, but I am astounded when Olsen says the old commission focused on the "quality [of] life for the developers," or made decisions "behind closed doors," or when Planning Commissioner Julie Lopez Dad says the public didn't "have enough access for input," or when Council Member Ken Genser implies the commission was not "respectful of neighbors and neighborhoods." (These quotes appeared in news reports.)

Of course not everyone was pleased all the time, and sometimes tempers flared, but I cannot remember any time when anyone on the commission was disrespectful of anyone who appeared before us. I know that if I had shown any disrespect, the four people who chaired the Commission during my tenure—Ken Breisch, Eric Parlee, John Zinner, and Kathy Weremiuk—would have let me know it. They are among the more decent people you will find in Santa Monica, even if you disagree with their views.

I enjoyed my years (1995-99) on the Planning Commission immensely. Perhaps because we were in a recession for most of the time I was a member, and there was not much private development to consider, we worked on challenging projects, such as revisions of the housing, circulation, and open-space elements of the general plan, the Recreation and Parks Master Plan, the non-aviation land at the airport, the BIG [beach improvement group] projects on the beach, the downtown plan, 415 Pacific Coast Highway, the north of Montana development standards, etc., etc.

There were issues that were controversial, such as the rebuilding of Saint John's Hospital, extending the hours of Pacific Park, allowing second units in R-1 districts, changing the uses at Edgemar, and reviewing various conditional use permit (CUP) applications for alcohol sales. Although there was not much in the way of new private development, there were affordable housing projects like Menorah Housing, which was controversial because of its impact on a public parking lot.

By 1998 developers started proposing various small condominium projects. Although the applications for CUPs to permit these projects rarely aroused opposition from immediate neighbors, perceptions developed in the community that (i) a lot of affordable rental housing was being lost to make way for the condos and (ii) a lot of development was occurring in residential areas.

Although I would argue that both these perceptions were wrong, it must have been the granting of these CUPs that stoked the ire of the self-nominated guardians of the "residential community." When the City Council appointed Geraldine Moyle and Julie Lopez Dad to the Planning Commission, Moyle said, speaking of the old commission, "CUPs [were] given out like candy on Halloween," and Dad said, speaking of the new, "We're not obligated in any way to say yes by right ... There'll be no rubber stamping."

There's that rubber word again. My recollection is that both staff and the commission were always cautious about approving anything, even applications that appeared on the consent calendar, but perhaps I am wrong. I wonder if Moyle or Dad could cite one instance where the old commission granted a CUP casually, or otherwise without regard to the facts.

But it is true that the Planning Commission then and now has a lot of discretion when it comes to approving or denying CUPs. The law says that although the commission is to use "fixed and established standards," the commission must balance "the public need for and benefit to be derived from the use against any adverse impact it may cause," and, in addition to satisfying a host of specific requirements, any proposed use must "not be detrimental to the public interest, health, safety, convenience, or general welfare."

Over the years and particularly in the past twenty, the City has engaged in extensive public processes to reduce development standards. I happen to believe that the standards the City has adopted are generally good, and that the proof is in the pudding—the

1890
City of Santa Monica takes over operation of the Santa Monica
Library from the Women's Christian Temperance Union.

desire people have to live in Santa Monica, the quality of our life, and the quality of our economy.

What we see now is that some residents and politicians, who purport to speak for everyone, do not accept those standards. They do not believe they are restrictive enough. They want to use the subjective interpretation of words like "general welfare" and "adverse impact" to prevent development that is consistent with the standards the community has established but inconsistent with their own desires.

This is not only a due process problem, but also a democracy problem.

The Saturday night before Thanksgiving 2001, Deanna Maran, a student at Santa Monica High School, was murdered at an unsupervised party in Westwood, the upscale neighborhood where UCLA is that is a few miles east of Santa Monica. Deanna had an altercation with another fifteen-year-old, Sabrina Sarkissian, because Sabrina was breaking flowerpots in the backyard and Deanna thought Sabrina should be better behaved. Sabrina called her older half-sister, Katrina Sarkissian, on her cell phone, for help. An hour or so later, when Deanna and other friends from Santa Monica were on the front lawn of the house, waiting to go home, Katrina arrived. She attacked Deanna with a knife and stabbed her in the chest. Deanna died in a friend's car on the way to a hospital in Santa Monica; the friend didn't know that UCLA Hospital was much closer. The next day, Katrina killed herself with an overdose of sleeping pills—she collapsed during a police interrogation and died. I attended Deanna's memorial service at the high school.

NOVEMBER 30, 2001

By the time the memorial for Deanna Maran ended Monday afternoon, it was dark enough. Dark enough so that the snapshots projected on the back wall of the Greek Theater at Santa Monica High School were clear, and it was plain that all the talk about Deanna's smile had not been just talk. Dark enough so that candles kindled when it was still light, now lit the faces of the rememberers. Dark enough to shadow the tears, but not so dark as to obscure the gleam of a smile recollecting a happier day.

People use words like "senseless" and "tragic" to describe the deaths of children—also known as "teenagers"—that we read about in the back pages of the California section of the *L.A. Times*: the killings and car-crashes that result from adolescent bravado, behind a weapon or behind the wheel, sometimes fueled by drink or drugs or inexplicable desperation, or unfathomable anger. Sometimes, as with Columbine or Santee, these deaths make the front page.

But these words do not tell us much—how could the violent death of a fifteen-year-old ever make sense, or be anything but tragic?

Deanna Maran was fifteen. I did not know her, although she lived down the street from the house I moved into last year. I have watched the accumulation of candles and flowers and photographs in front of her house grow steadily.

Deanna made straight As at school. She played three sports and sang in the chorus. She came from a loving family—her parents had already raised three accomplished sisters, and she had a younger brother.

1891
Huntington and the Southern Pacific revive plans for turning Santa
Monica into a deep water port to prevent the federal government
from digging a port in San Pedro that would be open to competitors,
such as the Santa Fe Railroad.

She was adored.

At the moment, despite various reports in the press, much is unclear or at least unconfirmed about what happened at the party in Westwood where Deanna was fatally attacked. The death of her alleged assailant is still a mystery along with any information about her, or about how the party came to be, and how an argument escalated into murderous violence.

Without more authoritative information, it would be wrong to speculate about responsibility. But we know, using what words we have, that Deanna Maran's death will never make sense and will forever be a tragedy.

A fter the demise of Target's plan to build a store in downtown Santa Monica, the next controversial development in the city was a mixed-use apartment/retail project on the former site of the Boulangerie, a once-popular bakery and restaurant on Main Street in (my) Ocean Park neighborhood. The project was largish by Santa Monica standards—more than one hundred units—and pushed the usual buttons. Traffic, of course, and because its three stories qualified to some as "massive overdevelopment." That the proposal was consistent with a comprehensive plan the neighborhood had developed for Main Street only a few years before was irrelevant to the critics.

NOVEMBER 30, 2001

Before La Brea Bakery and their crusty wonders, before Il Fornaio brought us the ciabatta, there was the Pioneer Boulangerie on Main Street. My wife lives for good bread, and she lived on the transcendent sourdough Pioneer baked only in the brick oven on Main Street. Then some fool replaced the real brick oven with a fake one, the bread became insipid, and the Boulangerie, which had been the most popular destination in Ocean Park, closed. (Maybe it wasn't only the bread, but the moral is clear.)

For seven years the site has been a huge litter-strewn eyesore. For a time there was talk of locating a Trader Joe's there, but that didn't work out. For three years developer Howard Jacobs has been preparing a proposal to build a mixed-use complex of apartments and retail on the Boulangerie site and the parking lot across the street. Next week the Planning Commission will review the project.

I have no idea if the plan will be controversial. Jacobs presented the project to two annual congresses of the Ocean Park Community Organization (OPCO) that I attended, and at both meetings he received constructive suggestions rather than impassioned opposition. But OPCO is hosting a workshop on the project tomorrow, and perhaps its board of directors will take a different view.

In the meantime I have reviewed the 411-page Environmental Impact Report the City prepared, at Jacobs's (considerable) expense. If you read the EIR, you will learn, among other things, the following:

If the Stone Canyon Reservoir fails, within 24 minutes several inches of water will flood portions of Santa Monica near the I-10 freeway, but the Boulangerie site will not be affected.

The 250 people this project would add to Santa Monica's population of 84,000 will not have a significant environmental impact nor require changes to the public transit system.

On the winter solstice, a thirty-five-foot tall building will cast a shadow on the sidewalk that will last more than two hours and thus adversely impact the pedestrian experience.

In other words, preparing a 411-page EIR for an urban, mixed-use, in-fill project, on a busy street is a complete waste of time and a perversion of every purpose the California Environmental Quality Act was enacted to serve. But EIRs in Santa Monica exist for one purpose—to provide pseudo-scientific and pseudo-environmental grounds to attack projects based on their supposed impact on traffic.

Sure enough, based on the unique Santa Monica standard that adding any traffic to a dysfunctional intersection (levels of service D, E, or F) is a significant environmental impact, the EIR finds that this project will have a significant impact on four intersections, one of which is an intersection with stop signs that the City installed for the purpose of slowing traffic. But the EIR also says that even without the North Main project those intersections would be at dysfunctional levels by 2009. So where is the impact?

What this EIR fails to do that might have been logical or even helpful is to compare the impact of this project consisting of needed housing and neighborhood-serving retail with the traffic generated by the old Boulangerie, which was a regional draw and whose parking lot was constantly full.

In fairness, whoever is responsible for this EIR does make the important point that trying to mitigate these alleged impacts on traffic—by creating turn lanes and narrowing sidewalks—would make things worse because of the adverse impact on the pedestrian environment. I understand, however, that Jacobs, the developer, in his eagerness to secure approval, has offered to pay for these "mitigations." Let's hope the Planning Commission resists this offer. But let's also hope that they approve what is an excellent re-use of the old Boulangerie site, notwithstanding the imaginary impacts on traffic.

In the meantime, there was more news about the Trader Joe's. The Planning Commission's Kelly Olsen questioned the code, and the chance of buying the store's cannellini beans without having to traipse across town seemed to go down the drain.

DECEMBER 7, 2001

When I was on the board of the Ocean Park Community Organization (OPCO), a rumor reached us that Trader Joe's was looking at the old Boulangerie site for what would have been its first Santa Monica store. The OPCO Board then included such no-growth stalwarts as Laurel Roennau, John Bodin, and Mike Feinstein, but they knew enough to button up when everyone else on the board gushed at the prospect of Ocean Park having its own Trader Joe's.

(By the way, taking advantage of a good deal Trader Joe's has on cannellini beans, I recently devised a recipe that has rapidly become a family favorite. Chop two purple onions and sauté them in about four tablespoons of olive oil. Meanwhile, empty two cans of cannellini beans into a smallish baking dish. When the onions are soft but not mushy, add them with all the oil to the beans. Add a few chopped tomatoes, fresh or canned. Season with salt and pepper. Sprinkle bread crumbs over the top and bake at 350 for an hour.)

Of course, where NIMBY angels like Roennau, Bodin, and Feinstein once feared to tread, Kelly Olsen, chair of the Planning Commission, rushes in. Back in July Olsen emailed Planning Director Suzanne Frick to argue that the zoning code precluded converting a tire store at Twelfth and Wilshire into a new Trader Joe's. Olsen's point was that Trader Joe's could not continue using a rear parking lot that sits on residentially zoned land because the parking standard for a grocery store was more intensive than that for the existing tire store. The tire store was classified as an auto repair shop for zoning purposes, and Olsen explained to Frick that the requirement for auto repair shops was one space for every 500 square feet, as opposed to one space for every 250 square feet of grocery store.

Depending on whom one talks to, Olsen's *ex parte* meddling either (i) resulted in, or (ii) merely coincided with, three months of delay in planning staff's review of Trader Joe's application for administrative approval.

The bad news, as reported last week in the *Lookout*, is that on November 15 staff finally replied to Trader Joe's and told them that their plans were not in compliance with the zoning code.

1891/93
Huntington extends the Southern Pacific tracks along the beach to a
point north of Santa Monica Canyon, where he constructs "Port Los
Angeles," also known as the "Long Wharf."

The good news is that staff rejected Olsen's parking intensification argument. Olsen, sadly, did not notice that parking requirements for auto repair shops are based primarily on the number of service bays, not square footage. It turns out that the parking requirements for the old tire store and the new Trader Joe's would be the same.

What might be even better news is that both staff and Trader Joe's believe they can resolve their differences over the code and the plans. Unless Trader Joe's becomes so frustrated that they just give up, there remains hope that someday residents of the western half of Santa Monica will not have to drive across town for good deals on cannellini beans.

* * *

Trader Joe's never was much interested in the Boulangerie site. The old restaurant and retail complex has been unused for years, except as a staging area for Pioneer trucks and the City's sewer repair equipment. Wednesday night developer Howard Jacobs presented to the Planning Commission his proposal for a mixed-use, but mostly housing, project on the site. The Commission, predictably and unanimously, voted the project down.

Even the commissioners had to acknowledge, however, that Jacobs had diligently tried to work within the Santa Monica rules, whatever they might be at any given time. Commissioner Barbara Brown said Jacobs "had done a great job so far." Commissioner Jay Johnson said that with a little more work the project could be "world-class," and the commission agreed with Johnson's suggestion to deny the project "without prejudice," so that Jacobs could quickly return to the commission with an improved—presumably world-class—project.

As if any developer in his right mind would voluntarily appear before the Planning Commission.

Consider that last month the commission rejected a two-story, four-unit condominium project on Twenty-Second Street near Santa Monica Boulevard as being "not compatible with the neighborhood" even though the adjacent lots had two- and three-story structures.

Jacobs and his 133 units never had a chance.

Nonetheless, Jacobs's project, though comparable in size to the Target once planned for downtown, engendered minimal controversy. Jacobs has presented his plans at numerous public meetings, and most people agree that Main Street is a perfect place to build apartments.

1892
Abbot Kinney, who later developed Venice, California, and his partner
Francis Ryan purchase an oceanfront strip of land from the Vawter
family and form the Ocean Park Development Company.

A mere eight members of the public appeared before the commission with opinions about the project, and five of them spoke in favor. Of the three who opposed, one was Laurel Roennau, who opposes everything, and another was a neighbor who wanted to postpone construction of the project for "five or ten years" so that he could get over the trauma of the City's sewer reconstruction project.

This lack of NIMBY fervor caused consternation on the dais. Commissioners badgered the pro-project speakers with leading and rhetorical questions. Wait a minute: Wasn't this the commission that promised to treat members of the public, and their opinions, with respect?

Planning staff opposed the project, notwithstanding that the project actualizes major City planning objectives, is less dense than what the zoning permits, and has "significant" environmental impacts that are in fact either trivial or temporary. The alleged traffic impacts, for instance, are Kafkaesque. Can we believe that the traffic from 250 residents and a little bit of retail will significantly affect traffic flow at the Fourth Street on-ramp? It's not development, but the on-ramp itself that draws traffic to both Fourth and Main.

Traffic analysts can spin numbers and predict that the project will generate cars that will slow traffic down at intersections on Main and Fourth, but the import of this analysis conflicts with the fact that on both streets the City has reduced the number of lanes and incorporated various traffic-calming features, precisely for the purpose of slowing traffic.

Staff hung its opposition to the project on tenuous interpretations of vague and general policies of the general plan, ignoring the multiple incentives the City's laws and policies give to building housing in commercial zones like Main Street. For instance, staff cited a provision in the land use element of the general plan that calls for good transitions between commercial and residential areas, ignoring the plain meaning of the provision, namely that mixed-use projects, like Jacobs' project, are to be encouraged precisely because they make good transitions.

I can't figure staff out.

Perhaps staff opposes a project like this one because staff doesn't want to be chastised by the Planning Commission as soft on developers. After all, staff recommended approval of the four condos on Twenty-Second Street and got burned. Or, perhaps staff opposed the project because it views the Planning Commission, because of its psychological incapacity to deal with developers, as irrelevant to the essential role of planning in our society: the process of molding developer desires to public needs and wants. If this was the case, then staff's motive would have been to create negotiating room with the developer for the inevitable appeal to the City Council.

But under either scenario, all our significant planning decisions are being made on an *ad hoc* basis, our zoning standards are hopelessly vague, and we are stuck with an eyesore blighting one of our most important streets.

Two of the ongoing issues in Santa Monica are whether to elect city council members on a district basis (we now elect them all at-large) and whether to have an elected mayor with administrative power (the mayor now is chosen by the City Council and has no more power than the other members of the council). In 2001 an initiative, the "Voter Election Reform Initiative for a True Accountability System" (VERITAS), was floated to change the City Charter. The formal controversy masked real political frustrations. What will be familiar to those who follow local politics in other places is the obsession of politicians with pleasing the voters least likely to be made happy by whatever the politicians do.

DECEMBER 14, 2001

Watching war and politics in Afghanistan, one must be thankful that we live in a society where it is war that is politics by other means and not the other way around. But watching politics in Santa Monica, people are not thankful. They are grumpy. People are so grumpy about local politics that the City Council Tuesday evening instructed staff to return with proposals to amend our election laws, and members of the public have placed an initiative on the ballot that would dramatically change our political system.

I get a little grumpy, too, but it is good to have a little perspective. There is nothing terribly wrong with politics in Santa Monica, certainly when compared to local politics elsewhere. For instance, elections are contested in Santa Monica. This is no small good: Consider that the most powerful politicians in the region, the Los Angeles County Board of Supervisors, rarely face meaningful opposition. Our politics and our politicians are clean. The biggest hint of a scandal involved the unauthorized use of a photocopier. Our bureaucrats are clean, too. No credible person has ever charged our staff with improprieties.

Furthermore, and this is where some readers will start feeling grumpy, the most powerful political force in the community is just what reformers say should be the most powerful political force in a community: a local organization that relies on a broad base of residents. Love it or hate it, but Santa Monicans for Renters Rights (SMRR) has mobilized ordinary citizens into effective collective action, precisely what everyone says political organizations should do.

Although everyone—certainly myself included—has something to complain about from time to time, Santa Monica is a well-governed city. We are just a small part of a megalopolis, but our city operates its own police and fire departments, its own bus line, and takes care of one of the region's great resources, the beach, as well as the urban center for a subregion with several times its own population.

Naturally, those who have been losing elections to SMRR are not in the best frame of mind. Although they would do better to look inward, at why their message has proven unpopular, or outward, at why SMRR has such credibility among the voters, the losers in recent elections prefer to blame "slate politics," as if SMRR invented the campaign contribution.

I, as one who has often opposed SMRR candidates but who was, until I started writing for the *Lookout*, a SMRR member, can understand this frustration. SMRR has especially dominated elections since 1998, and the opposition has not done well since the early '90s. I miss the creative tension that existed for most of the past twenty years between SMRR and its opponents—tension that kept both sides on their toes.

What I see now is an organization, SMRR, that is dangerously complacent yet infuriatingly anxious—smug, yet so cautious that it won't take a stand that might alienate even one noisy voter. I also see a group that has not replaced its activists from within, but rather has shown itself susceptible to manipulation by outsiders with energy and their own agendas.

Yet, when I look at the opposition, I see politicians who doom themselves because they won't let go of right-wing positions that the majority of Santa Monicans just don't like, such as union-bashing by the hotels, or homeless-trashing by the terminally irate. The local business interests that traditionally fund the opposition proclaim their right to pay workers whatever they want to pay them, thus alienating most voters. At the same time they are so "protectionist" that they do nothing to support, and in fact oppose, smart development that the majority of Santa Monicans want—such as the Target store.

At the same time, one wishes that the most important vote was not the one that 120 or so members of SMRR take to determine SMRR's endorsements. That doesn't feel democratic. Nor does it feel democratic that a candidate needs $100,000 to mount a serious campaign.

One proposed solution, or, rather, several proposed solutions, are contained in the VERITAS initiative, which has recently submitted what sponsors believe are enough signatures to qualify it for the ballot. Its most significant changes would be to have our seven council members elected by district, to impose term limits, to have the mayor elected directly by the people, and to give the mayor the power to veto ordinances.

Much of the money behind the signature campaign for VERITAS came from businesses opposed to SMRR, and people have tended to view VERITAS from a pro-SMRR or anti-SMRR perspective. The proponents of VERITAS, however, Irene Zivi and Paul

1893
The Southern Pacific opens the Long Wharf, which extends 4,720
feet into the sea. The S.P. has exclusive access.

DeSantis, have been pushing proposals like it for a while, and originally they had support from SMRR city council members.

I take Zivi and DeSantis at face value, that they genuinely expect that their proposals will improve politics in Santa Monica, by giving representation to minority interests (with districts), by making it easier (i.e., cheaper) for independent candidates to run, by reducing the power of incumbency (with term limits), and by using an elected mayor to galvanize political interest among a sometimes apathetic electorate. But I predict the VERITAS proposals would make things worse, from the perspective of both government and politics, and not because SMRR would probably have a lock on four or five districts.

While once reformers promoted electoral districts to give voice to minority interests, current thinking is that minority voices are best heard when many people are listening. For instance, the Hispanic interests behind the living wage movement might not have had as much influence on the five SMRR council members if only one ran in the Pico Neighborhood. At the same time, we need only look at Los Angeles to see how district elections have increased the power of incumbency, as it is easier for a council member to dominate the politics of a single district than a whole city.

In principle, there is nothing wrong with an elected mayor, but the mayor under VERITAS would only have the power to break ties in the City Council and the power to veto, as the executive power of the City would still be in the hands of the city manager. The VERITAS supporters talk about "separation of powers," but this mayor would awkwardly sit half in and half out of our "legislature"—bargaining a threatened veto, on the dais, against whether there were five votes to override.

Perhaps we should adopt a true mayoral system, as in bigger cities, but in that case the voters should consider that separately. This points to the biggest problem with VERITAS—it jumbles too many proposals together. Zivi and DeSantis may have the best of motives, but dramatic proposals like these should emerge from a more measured public process.

Two thousand one was coming to an end, and I wrote more about the national situation, looking for silver linings. As it turned out, during those days after the deposing of the Taliban in Afghanistan I was entirely too optimistic about both the nation's post-9/11 unity and the nature of the Bush administration. This column is painful for me to read seven years after I wrote it.

DECEMBER 28, 2001

> *"[We] have made a donation in your name to*
> *The Armed Forces Foundation*
> *and*
> *The American Civil Liberties Union"*

—Sentiment inside a Christmas card I received from a business acquaintance.

This time of year it is traditional to be optimistic, and I expected to focus this week on various good things that happened to me in 2001. Good things that interjected themselves in between the hyper-politics of the Bush ascendancy and the political trench warfare that followed, the unutterable sorrow of September 11, and the anxieties a suddenly more dangerous world unleashed, the war that ensued and its surprising course, and, not to trivialize the foregoing, the highs and lows of Santa Monica politics.

I thought I might write about the joys of the John Adams Middle School music program, or the fantastic smoked fish, sausages, rye bread, and poppy-seed cakes I discovered at the Ukraina Deli on Wilshire near Twelfth, or the serendipity of someone getting around to making *The Lord of the Rings* movie just when my son turns twelve.

But it is hard to write with a light touch after September 11. I admire those, like the writers at the *Onion*, the satirical website, who can. (See their article, "Entrepreneur Stuck with 40,000 Unsold Bin Laden Urinal Cakes," if you want to know what I mean.) Still trying to be optimistic, however, I have found something to be happy about. Something ponderous. A bipartisan foreign policy.

It took the worst disaster in our history, a terrible, murderous attack, but for the first time in three decades Americans now have a politically unified foreign policy. Not to discount the skill and professionalism of the Powell-Rumsfeld-Cheney-Rice team, but this Republican administration has adopted Al Gore's foreign policy. Before September 11, the Bush administration was turning toward neo-isolationism, but now, by necessity if not with ardor, they have embraced the nation-building, the multilateralism, and the engagement in the hard problems of the world that they previously scorned.

Democrats have supported the administration with near unanimity. What's more, a major cultural shift has occurred in the left wing of the party. The left wing has literally rallied around the flag. I knew a change was in the air on Rosh Hashanah, the Jewish New Year, which occurred just days after September 11. I attend a synagogue with a politically active, left-wing rabbi, and it came as something of a surprise when, at the close of the first service, the rabbi led the congregation in "God Bless America." A surprise, but quite moving.

It is possible to support both the ACLU and the Armed Forces Foundation.

This cultural shift, not only to accept patriotic symbols without embarrassment, but also, and more importantly, to acknowledge that not everything the U.S. does in the world is suspect, is just as important to the nation as the Bush administration's acknowledgment that neo-isolationism cannot work in today's world, that we will not find security behind a strong military and nothing else.

Although September 11 kicked it into gear, the Left's cultural shift did not come from nowhere, but developed gradually with the end of the Cold War, as the Left began to reacquire internationalist ideas and urged, in particular, a stronger American role in the Balkans and elsewhere in the world to protect human rights. The great divide in American foreign policy was always between internationalism and isolationism, but, historically, foreign policy was not predominantly partisan. Both parties had their internationalists (Teddy Roosevelt, Woodrow Wilson) and their isolationists (William Jennings Bryan, Henry Cabot Lodge).

America's true bipartisan foreign policy was born at Pearl Harbor and continued until the day in 1968 when Lyndon Johnson told his fellow Americans that he would neither seek nor accept the Democratic nomination to run for reelection. While the parties had stuck together to fight fascism and contain communism, they came apart over Vietnam. Aside from the unique tragedies of that unfortunate war, the issue that drove Democrats and Republicans apart was that Democrats no longer agreed that all issues of foreign policy were subservient to the conflict between the "free world" and the "evil empire," or that Cold War considerations justified any action on the part of the U.S.

Fortunately, the Soviet Union obliged the foreign policy establishments of both parties by imploding. Unfortunately, when that happened, the parties were still stuck by habit and culture in their adversarial postures. The votes in Congress on intervention in the Gulf and in Kosovo were embarrassingly partisan. Democrats, leery of another Vietnam, could not support the first Bush's righteous war against Iraq, and Republicans,

1895
In a deal with resort developer Abbot Kinney the Santa Fe Railroad
builds the first pier in Ocean Park.

unwilling to concede any authority to that Vietnam-era draft-dodger, Bill Clinton, could not support his righteous war against Milosevic.

A bipartisan foreign policy will be a good thing. But beyond an America forced to involve itself in a world it can never turn its back on in any case, what will having a bipartisan foreign policy mean? It should mean, in the long-term and notwithstanding the current popularity of President Bush, good news for Democrats. The less foreign policy is a political issue and, crucially, the less Republicans can tar left-wing Democrats as unpatriotic, the more elections will turn on domestic issues where the Democrats have a proven advantage.

I am something of a left-wing Democrat, albeit one who considers himself a super-patriot. But my belief that a bipartisan foreign policy will make it easier to elect the liberals I vote for is not the reason I believe it will be a good thing. These past three decades of the culture wars have been nasty. It is not good that Americans make assumptions about each other's love of country based on their politics.

These negative assumptions go both ways. It is wrong for people on the right to characterize anyone who questions the value of a missile defense system as unpatriotic just as it is wrong for people on the left to characterize anyone who joins the military as a jingo. If we can get beyond these assumptions, i.e., if we can put Vietnam behind us, that would be a silver lining. Not one that by itself lifts the cloud of September 11, but something shiny to be hopeful about.

Happy New Year.

2002

A few weeks later, President Bush informed us of the "Axis of Evil" and a bipartisan foreign policy went out the window. So much for my pretensions at punditry. But I still had Trader Joe's and Kelly Olsen to write about.

JANUARY 11, 2002

If you made my cannellini bean recipe, you might want a good vegetable to go with it. Nothing goes quite so well with white beans as greens (nothing so well as a leg of lamb, that is), and I like to cook them with anchovies.

Use spinach, kale, collards, or Swiss chard for this recipe. Unless you are cooking spinach, you need to steam the greens first. I use an old James Beard technique: Remove the toughest parts of the stems, wash the greens, and stuff the still-dripping leaves into a big pot. Add salt, cover and cook over medium high heat. Stir several times over the course of about fifteen minutes, until the greens have cooked down and the stems are *al dente*. Drain the greens. Rinse with cold water or let them cool, and then squeeze out as much liquid as possible. Chop.

Heat two or three or four tablespoons of extra virgin olive oil (nothing fancy: the kind you can buy at Trader Joe's for five or six dollars a liter) in a skillet and add several cloves of chopped garlic and half a dozen chopped anchovy filets. Cook for a moment or two until the anchovies dissolve, then add the cooked greens or uncooked spinach. Sauté for a few minutes, remove from the pan, and serve hot or cold with lemon.

Anchovies are my secret ingredient. Most times when I sauté a little garlic in oil, I add a few anchovies. Just about any dish that is good with garlic is better with anchovies, too. Home cooks don't cook much with anchovies because the little cans are a mess. Forget them. The filets inside resemble bits of leather shoelaces, and since you typically only need a few, you are stuck with a half can that spills or gets lost in the refrigerator.

Better you should buy anchovies in jars at Bay Cities Imports on Lincoln (thirteen varieties at last count). Guidi Marcello on Tenth Street also carries anchovies in jars, including fat whole anchovies in oil and parsley. Sometimes Trader Joe's, which apparently will not be building a new store in Santa Monica, carries anchovies in thirteen-ounce cans. That's more than even I will use in months and months, but they are good quality and you can drain the oil they come packed in, dump the anchovies into a plastic container, replace the oil with extra virgin, and keep them in the refrigerator. They will last forever, and you can take two or three filets out whenever you need them.

The best anchovies come salted in one-kilo cans at Bay Cities, but you have to rinse off the salt, soak them in water, and filet them yourself. Standing around filleting anchovies is not everyone's pleasure, but it's something to do while listening to city council meetings. A good anchovy in good olive oil is one of life's small sublimities. Toast a little piece of stale bread, top it with an anchovy privileged to have bathed in extra virgin olive oil, and pop it in your mouth. That's quality of life.

"Quality of Life." The be-all and end-all of local politics.

Tuesday night at the City Council's hearing on budget priorities, City staff presented a summary of the City's 2001 Resident Survey. The City uses the survey to identify its priorities. Staff reported that the three issues people in Santa Monica most often identified as the most important facing the City were "too many homeless," "traffic," and "too much growth." But staff did not mention out loud the actual percentages of Santa Monicans who are concerned about those issues, although if you looked closely enough, the percentages were included in the overhead projections.

According to the survey, in fact only 22 percent of Santa Monicans said they were concerned about too many homeless, only 21 percent were concerned about traffic (and this after years of having our streets torn up for sewer repairs and other projects), and only 14 percent were concerned about too much growth. For that matter, among other issues, only 11 percent were concerned about parking and only 8 percent about crime.

Not only that, but survey respondents could mention up to *three* "important issues facing Santa Monica." Meaning that even given three chances to complain about something, only small fractions of Santa Monicans mentioned what staff called "the three most important issues facing Santa Monica." Call me speculative, but I'm guessing that the failure of staff and the survey's executive summary to highlight these actual statistics means that someone is kind enough not to embarrass those politicians who have staked their political careers on the dubious premises that Santa Monicans are in an uproar

---

about any of (i) traffic, (ii) parking, (iii) growth and development, (iv) the homeless, or (v) crime. Obviously, more than 75 percent of Santa Monicans wouldn't waste their breath on any of the above.

So what should Santa Monica do with its money?

Let's start with the premise that a kid involved in a gang has different quality of life issues than either me, the resident who likes anchovies and olive oil, or Kelly Olsen, the resident who worries about traffic and development and who didn't want a Trader Joe's at Twelfth and Wilshire. When it comes to the City's priorities, it's the kid in the gang, or the kid who's at risk of joining a gang, and probably his mother and father and his girl-friend, who need the most attention. Beyond basic services, the City's resources should go to education, jobs, affordable housing, and recreation before they go anywhere else.

But when it comes to choosing between the ready availability of olive oil and ancho-vies, or restaurants and shopping, or a theater or movie, or whatever else makes urban life enjoyable, and traffic, don't tell me that the people of Santa Monica value their abil-ity to make a left turn more than they value their ability to taste life in its fullest flavors.

Columnists like to write about bad news. Bad is more interesting than good, and sells more papers, just as murders sell more commercials for TV news. But one of my arguments has always been that Santa Monicans were generally happy about their city and their government, and that NIM-BYs and other residents with their own agendas used a sense of crisis to set the governmental agenda. I often write about "good news" to counteract this tendency, and one reason my column has had an impact on Santa Monica politics as opposed to other local commentators is that I occasionally say nice things about our politicians. Psychologists call this "intermittent reinforcement." I had an occasion to be nice after the City Council approved the Boulangerie mixed-use project.

FEBRUARY 15, 2002

I did not attend the City Council meeting Tuesday night even though the main item on the agenda was Howard Jacobs' Boulangerie housing development, an issue I have closely followed. My parents are in town, and I chose to have dinner with them and watch the proceedings on television. My parents are, it should be no surprise to other parents, my most loyal readers. While Santa Monicans write letters to the *Lookout* taking pains to make it known that they do not read me, my far-off parents read their middle-aged son's weekly mutterings as loyally as they read his grade school book reports.

My father was eager to watch the City Council in action after so often having read my musings over this august body of legislators, spiritual heirs of the first democratic councils of ancient times, guardians of liberties hard fought and hard defended, neighbors elected by neighbors to pursue the public good. So we watched together while the others finished their dinners. Naturally, I expected the council members to live up to their billing and say the most ridiculous things imaginable, argue childishly and at length over the most petty political points, pander to the most strident elements of the public, and thus validate my new life's work in the eyes of my father.

Why did the City Council choose this week to be reasonable? What am I supposed to say when my dad says things like "they don't seem so bad?"

The City Council's approval of the Boulangerie project leaves me with little to complain about. The council members understood the project and the issues, both local and global. Most of them took pains to say that the current iteration of the development was better than what the Planning Commission rejected. This is a subjective judgment, but,

1897

U.S. Government chooses San Pedro as site for a "free harbor," open
to all railroads.

at the risk of being churlish, it seemed to me they were trying not to hurt the Planning Commission's feelings.

Certainly from a development standards perspective, the project is much the same as the one the commission rejected—the same number of units, with only a reduction of 1,750 square feet in size. True, the architect extensively modified the exterior, by breaking the façade into sixty-foot pieces, adding setbacks and stepbacks, and mixing up architectural styles, and both he and the City Council may consider that new design makes the project both different and better.

I can't argue with that, but is our process working if the City Council is deciding how many doors a corner shop should have and staff dings a building for not looking like it's as wide as other buildings? What happened to the Architectural Review Board? There is nothing wrong with the Planning Commission or the City Council on appeal giving the ARB direction and advice, but whether a project is consistent with the general plan and the zoning ordinance should not depend on what it looks like. Not, at least, if we have a separate design review process.

But the process failed in other ways, too. This project was consistent with zoning standards the City Council had previously enacted. Jacobs indicated all along—including in front of the Planning Commission—that he was willing to modify his plans if the City would tell him what it wanted. Planning staff, however, is not willing to do any planning. Perhaps they just don't want to be yelled at, but instead of engaging a developer in dialogue to improve a project, they say merely yes or no, after the developer has spent huge sums in design and financing. They justify their timidity by the most mechanistic use of environmental analysis.

Environmental Impact Reports are meant to be tools for decision-makers, not straitjackets.

If, for instance, architectural "permeability" is a goal of planning, why not empower our planners to work at the inception of a project with developers of big projects, before they have spent a fortune in plans, to break them up with new streets or walkways? Unfortunately the idea that our planners would work with developers during design is anathema here because so many people view developers as an enemy to be defeated.

It's not taking anything away from the City Council to say that the public testimony preceding their deliberations Tuesday night set the table nicely. Just as at the Planning Commission, few speakers opposed the project, which will be the largest development on Main Street. Perhaps the usual naysayers saw writing on the wall. Many supporters of the project, such as Ralph Mechur, Suzanne Kaplan, and Mario Fonda-Bonardi, have

1897
Senator Jones and others form the Santa Monica Land and Water
Company, which buys water rights to thousands of acres in the
Santa Monica Mountains, thus providing the city with a private but
independent water supply.

---

been active in Ocean Park for years, and they described how the project was consistent with the Main Street plan.

Other supporters, including nearby neighbors, spoke about how the development would bring life to a dead section of town. How unusual: People testified to the positives of development. They expressed what everyone knows, that we like living in Santa Monica precisely because there are other people here, and shops we can walk to, coffee shops we can meet our neighbors in.

In our system, government plans, developers build. We need them both. And they need to talk.

The same conflict between positive and negative visions of urban life plays itself out in Santa Monica with respect to Santa Monica College. Santa Monica has something of a town vs. gown conflict. While SMC, a two-year community college, is wildly popular with most residents, some of its immediate neighbors in the Sunset Park neighborhood resent it, and historically they have had a lot of clout within the anti-growth wing of SMRR.

FEBRUARY 22, 2002

Santa Monicans and Malibuans have a chance to shore up Social Security on March 5, when we can vote for Proposition U, Santa Monica College's $160-million bond issue.

Huh? What does Social Security have to do with SMC's need to upgrade its physical plant? Social Security, contrary to general belief, is not an investment program, but instead a pay-as-we go mutual support system. Workers today pay for the retirements of pensioners, and in turn, when they retire, future workers will pay their benefits. The whole system depends on the increasing productivity and earning power of successive generations of workers. The more productive they are, the more money they earn, and there is more money to pay benefits.

This is important to remember when considering all expenditures for education, but especially long-term investments in educational institutions, like Santa Monica College, that provide continuing education to both young people entering the work force and current workers. Aside from the intrinsic benefits of education, education increases earning power.

People who are no longer in school or who no longer have children in school sometimes believe that they are being altruistic when they pay taxes for education, but this is not true. As they approach retirement, they have a direct interest in what money younger workers make. The more money flowing into the Social Security system, the more benefits the system can pay. There is a lot of talk in Washington about what will happen to Social Security as the baby-boom generation retires. This is not the place to analyze this complex policy question, but it is safe to say that the best security for Social Security is continued investment in people.

Although no one submitted official opposition to Prop. U—the shame would probably be too great even for the city officials who like to mutter darkly about SMC—there is opposition on the Web. While the underlying theme of the opposition is yet more yammering about traffic (always the lowest common denominator of local political discourse), the opponents make the particularly noisome argument that Santa Monica

College does not deserve our support because only a fraction of its students live in Santa Monica and Malibu.

Are we supposed to believe that Santa Monica and Malibu somehow stand alone, independent and self-sufficient when it comes to education? While many Santa Monica students take courses at SMC, many more go outside the district for their higher educations, and many who start at SMC move on to other institutions to complete their educations. Our children benefit from investments made in other jurisdictions just as out-of-district students at SMC benefit from our investments in SMC.

And we all benefit from being a better-educated people.

Vote Yes on Prop. U.

It turned out I was wrong about there not being public opposition to Prop. U. Council Members Ken Genser and Richard Bloom both opposed it, and their colleagues Michael Feinstein and Kevin McKeown declined to express support or opposition, which was tantamount to opposition. The proposition won handily without their support.

MARCH 8, 2002

Discretion might have been the better part of valor for the anti-growth opponents of Prop. U. Richard Bloom and Ken Genser turned a fiscal issue, raising taxes to support Santa Monica College, something the Howard Jarvis Taxpayer Foundation might (and did) oppose, into a vote on growth. Now that the anti-growthers lost in a landslide, and would have lost in an even bigger landslide if turnout had been greater, can we get beyond the idea that there is a consensus against growth in Santa Monica?

I know the NIMBYs will now say that they didn't lose anything, that "everyone is for education" and that's why they lost, but that's not true. Not everyone is for education. I remember when Santa Monica NIMBYs opposed building the new elementary school in Ocean Park. And, excuse me, but you are not for education if you are against it when you think it adds to traffic.

The no-growth element in Santa Monica politics has not won an election since the defeat of Michael McCarty's beach hotel proposal for 415 PCH. The most clear-cut vote was the one in 1994 for the Civic Center Plan. Tom Hayden, Mike Feinstein, and others mounted a well-publicized anti-growth campaign against it, but it passed with 60 percent of the vote. Then in 1998, Santa Monicans voted to authorize the City to build more affordable housing, one of the most difficult votes ever to win.

But it is also worth looking at the votes on bond issues. No bond issue in Santa Monica has received less than 64 percent of the vote in recent memory. I do not mean to equate the popularity of schools and libraries and public safety buildings, and, in some quarters, affordable housing, with the popularity of growth. But given that anti-growthers are willing to fight bond issues, and equate building schools with development, it is fair to argue that the popularity of bond issues indicates that the public has a more nuanced attitude toward growth than that of the neighborhood organizations who purport to speak—or harangue—on their behalf, and from which Santa Monica's anti-growth, "neighborhood-protectionist" politicians have emerged.

It should not have been a surprise, but it was to many, that the City's 2001 Residents' Survey found that only 14 percent of Santa Monicans consider too much growth, and

only 21 percent consider traffic, to be important problems facing the city. These figures are consistent with past surveys. These votes and survey results do not mean that Santa Monicans want to give developers carte blanche. Certainly the initial round of downzoning in the '80s made sense.

But there is no evidence that there is a consensus either against growth or in favor of the way the City conducts its business. While part of the attack on Prop. U was based on plain NIMBYism, another part was based on the college's presumed "arrogance." Anti-SMC city officials say that the college does not listen to the people the same way that the City does. The college, however, did two percentage points better on Prop. U than it did in 1992 on a much smaller bond issue in a presidential election year, when presumably more Democrats, who tend to support bond issues, were voting. Notwithstanding all the college-bashing, the college is more popular with voters than ever.

Perhaps our anti-Madison Site Theater council members should think twice the next time they want to criticize that modest effort at civic improvement. Just as a swallow does not a summer make, a few neighbors who have irrational fears about traffic doesn't mean the electorate as a whole doesn't think a little culture would be a good thing.

Santa Monicans by and large are progressives; i.e., they believe in progress, and they do not believe that the best—or only—measure of a society is how smoothly flows the traffic. It is true, of course, that anti-growth candidates have won elections to the City Council, but could any of them have won without the endorsement of Santa Monicans for Renters Rights? None of the four council members who did not support Prop. U, for instance, have ever raised much money for their own campaigns.

The anti-growthers have been quite effective at running and winning at the SMRR nominating convention or in the SMRR Steering Committee, but that doesn't mean they speak for SMRR on growth. The disconnect between the four and the rest of SMRR on Prop. U was dramatic. SMRR-endorsed officials or appointees dominate various entities, beginning with the college's board of trustees, that endorsed Prop. U, including the school board, the Rent Control Board, and the Commission on Older Americans.

So what does this mean, politically? Word is that the SMRR leadership is unhappy that Bloom and Genser went public with opposition to the bond, after the leadership had agreed, in deference to the sensibilities of its anti-growth council members, not to have SMRR take an official position. But I'm not sure what this unhappiness means. I told a friend—a liberal, former SMRR stalwart—that I heard the SMRR leadership was unhappy at the antics of the SMRR council members. His jaded response was, "AGAIN!"

1899
Hatsuji Sano leases land from the Southern Pacific and establishes
Japanese fishing village near the Long Wharf.

At the same time, all signs point to SMRR's opposition taking its usual suicidal route far to the right of the Santa Monica electorate. Meaning that as long as SMRR wrongly believes it needs NIMBY votes, as long as NIMBYs can mask their conservative agenda by giving lip service to liberal ideals, and as long as the SMRR opposition doesn't even pay lip service to those ideals, the anti-growthers, who represent the mainstream of neither SMRR nor its opposition, will set the agenda in Santa Monica.

S anta Monica has tony residential districts, especially "North of Montana (Avenue)," and many people lump Santa Monica in with the adjacent upscale Los Angeles neighborhoods of Brentwood and Pacific Palisades, and with Beverly Hills, and consider Santa Monica to be an enclave for the wealthy, but this badly misstates the case. About 70 percent of Santa Monicans rent their homes or apartments, and, as I wrote previously, Santa Monica has a significant population of poor and working class people. It also has a serious and long-running gang problem in the Pico Neighborhood.

MARCH 22, 2002

I have a stack—more than an inch thick—of mailers I received in the 1998 and 2000 Santa Monica elections. It's interesting—I just leafed through the whole pile and I found only two references to gang violence, one in each year. In 1998, two weeks after gang violence erupted in a series of deadly shootings, Richard Bloom released an attack piece on Bob Holbrook based on Holbrook's leaving the city for a vacation after the shootings. Although the piece did not offer much in the way of constructive suggestions, at least Bloom mentioned the violence—something all the other candidates apparently thought would be in bad taste. In 2000, Herb Katz published a thirty-page booklet, a serious attempt to get beyond postcard politics, that included this one statement about youth violence: "[W]e need to adopt a zero tolerance policy for gangs and gang violence in Santa Monica." Good idea!

But that's it. Oh sure, there are many references in my pile to "public safety." Usually the incumbents (usually from Santa Monicans for Renters Rights) tout the decrease in crime in recent years, while the challengers try to use "public safety" as code words for attacking the City's homeless policies. No one, however, tries to win votes by suggesting constructive measures the City might take to keep kids out of gangs.

The lack of political focus replicates itself in policy. The City each year gives money to various well-meaning social service organizations. I don't mean to dismiss the efforts these people make, but judging by what is going on in the streets, the results have been meager. I wonder what would happen if the City Council and city staff (at the council's direction) put into finding ways to intervene in the lives of at-risk youth half the intellectual energy, let alone the time and money, they now put into counting cars at intersections, or enacting building moratoriums, or theorizing about sustainable cities and building codes, or prohibiting monster mansions or second units, or second-guessing

1899
Marion Jones, daughter of Senator Jones, becomes national tennis
champion; repeats in 1902.

architects, or agonizing over parking in all forms, or thinking about whatever else the council members and their squeakiest wheel constituents want to obsess on.

These issues can be important, but has "how to create more real jobs for youth" ever appeared on a City Council agenda? And what's the good of being for the living wage if you are against jobs?

The lack of political and policy focus on youth violence is not surprising given the priorities of Santa Monicans themselves. Most Santa Monicans are happy. According to the 2001 Santa Monica Resident Survey, the highest percentage of residents who identified an issue as one of the "most important" facing the City was the 22 percent who said there were too many homeless. Undifferentiated "crime" was cited by only 8 percent. There was not even a category for gang or youth violence.

Yet the bullets are flying in what the *Santa Monica Daily Press* likes to call, strangely and without historical precedent, the "east side," or "East Santa Monica." (Is Seventeenth and Delaware east?) But labels are important. Describing part of the city as geographically apart, or even identifying one part of it as a separate neighborhood, serves to isolate that area from the consciousness of those who don't live there. Can a town of only 85,000 people in only eight square miles afford to have the "other"?

Slicing the Santa Monica Freeway through Santa Monica created dead ends on a lot of north-south streets in Pico. Did the freeway builders know they were creating metaphors as well?

The incomprehensible atavism of gang violence—deadly violence over what?—is a challenge to us all, to the moral content of our lives and our society. Sometimes I hope, perversely, that these shooters are fighting over who can sell drugs on a particular street corner. At least that would show some purpose. But marginalized kids, brown and black, fighting over "turf"?

We have this image that Santa Monica is a place where we have the luxury to think only of ourselves, but we don't. We may not be able to make all children happy and well-educated, and turn them all into happy and productive adults, but we have a moral duty to focus our community efforts on helping those who need the most help, instead of those who don't need much help at all.

People who build upscale neighborhoods call dead ends "cul-de-sacs," but there is still no way out.

As if to exemplify the importance of every issue other than poverty and gang violence in Santa Monica politics, a particularly nasty controversy erupted during 2002 over the possible creation of "historic districts" in Santa Monica's single-family home zones and the landmarking of houses as "historic" to prevent demolition. Homeowners opposed to landmarking gathered signatures to put the "Homeowner's Freedom of Choice Initiative" on the ballot. This law would have required the City to obtain the consent of homeowners before declaring their homes landmarks or placing them in historic districts. The initiative pitted homeowners against homeowners—the preservationists versus those who wanted the right to remodel or tear down their properties as they saw fit. This was mostly a civil war within the wealthy North of Montana district, and there is nothing quite so uncivil as rich people having at it.

APRIL 5, 2002

"'But we shall live to see the day, I trust' went on the artist, 'when no man shall build his house for posterity. ... If each generation were allowed and expected to build its own houses, that single change, comparatively unimportant in itself, would imply almost every reform which society is now suffering for.' ...
"'How you hate everything old!' said Phoebe, in dismay. 'It makes me dizzy to think of such a shifting world!'"
From Nathaniel Hawthorne's, *The House of the Seven Gables.*

In case it has been a few years since you read Hawthorne's "romance," the artist and Phoebe fall in love and—no surprise—he has the "presentiment" that he will in the future plant trees, make fences, and even build a house for another generation. Word is that notwithstanding the fine Victorian the artist and Phoebe built in Iowa for their posterity (after selling the creepy seven-gabled seventeenth century edifice Phoebe inherited back in Salem), all their grandchildren moved to California. One bought a lot in King C. Gillette's "Regent Square" subdivision on Eighteenth Street in Santa Monica, and built a 1,300 square foot imitation Spanish adobe that her granddaughter now wants to sell to a family of Iranian immigrants who want to tear it down and build a 4,000-square-foot imitation Cape Cod.

Phoebe's great-great-great-great granddaughter was at the Landmarks Commission meeting Tuesday night where the City's historical consultants presented their report on updating the City's Historic Resources Inventory for the North of Montana area. There

she hooted and hollered and expressed great indignation because the consultants identified the Regent Square tract as a potential historic district.

I was there too, and it was the nastiest meeting I have ever attended in Santa Monica.
I have been to lots of meetings with all sorts of people in attendance, but this was the first
where the public couldn't control itself and follow instructions—and common courtesy—
not to applaud some speakers while jeering others. It wasn't only the overt rudeness, but
also the fact that nearly all the outraged residents walked out before hearing what the
commission had to say.

Yet this might have been, on an average basis, the wealthiest and best-educated collection of members of the public ever assembled for one meeting in Santa Monica. Maybe
the school district can make Roosevelt School available so that immigrant workers who
grew up in Central American dictatorships and who politely appear at city council meetings to advocate for the living wage can give democracy lessons to the North of Montana
mob. (Applause, however, for Greg Poirier, a property owner on Eighteenth Street and
a leader of the anti-historic district group who used a portion of his three minutes to
admonish his neighbors to have better manners.)

But there is nothing obvious about historic preservation. Even in Hawthorne's time
Americans had conflicted attitudes about the past. Our history is not so long, and that
means whatever exists, whatever has survived even fifty years, feels important. Yet our
culture is built on ideas like what's new is best. In cities, the desire to preserve, particularly the idea of preserving whole districts, conflicts with the organic process of incremental growth, through countless independent decisions, that makes cities fascinating
places to live and gives them a texture that is worthy of having a history.

Historic districts presume a value in homogeneity, which makes sense only if the
homogeneous quality is remarkable.

As a taxpaying member of the public, I want to know where the benefits go. Owners
of historically protected properties can get a 50 percent reduction in their property taxes.
If the very wealthy people living on, say, Adelaide Drive, are going to pay less taxes, then
I want to be sure there is a public benefit. So judgment is in order. What I did not see
in the consultant's report were convincing arguments for the historicity of the houses in
the districts they propose creating, beyond that the houses are now more than fifty years
old.

Perhaps these arguments will emerge later when the commission looks at specific
districts, but just because King Gillette invented the razor blade, is that a reason to preserve the (undistinguished) houses that people built on the cookie-cutter lots he drew on
a map? Eli Broad has a famous art collection—should his sprawling developments be

1900
Santa Monica Christian Scientists build the first Christian Scientist
church on the West Coast, at Seventh and Oregon (now Santa
Monica Boulevard).

---

immutable history, too? Rich people ninety years ago may have hired the top local society architects to build their houses in the Palisades Tract, but was their work any good? At Tuesday night's meeting, one opponent of historic districts expressed the fear that historic districts would attract busloads of tourists. My fear is a little different—that no tourist would care about what we are preserving.

The current battle, while ostensibly about historical districts, is in fact political. One side wants to use historic districts as the equivalent of sumptuary laws to prevent the building of big houses: "Monster Mansions, Part Two." Recently a member of the Landmarks Commission resigned, making this very charge, that the commission was more interested in controlling growth than preserving history.

But the other side is no less political. Not only do they see historic preservation as another infringement by government on sacred property rights, but they also want an issue to galvanize homeowners against the SMRR incumbents on the City Council who appointed the Landmarks Commission and hired the consultants to update the Historic Resources Inventory.

As is often the case, the question is not what is history, but who would own it.

One characteristic of local news is that tragedies that would be statistics to a national writer were personal to me. I had known David Attias since he was a baby, and Deanna Maran had lived down the street. My own son was about to become a teenager, and he attended the same middle school that served the Pico Neighborhood, locus of Santa Monica's gang problem. I thought a lot about kids.

APRIL 12, 2002

Two weeks ago, my twelve-year old son Henry and I were skiing with our friend Dana and her two kids. To be more precise, Dana and I skied, and the three kids snowboarded. Dana is an expert skier, while I am permanently intermediate. The kids are not virtuoso snowboarders, but because of a snowboarding technique aptly named "falling leaf," they can slide down nearly any run a mountain can offer, no matter how steep or bumpy. We usually skied together, on the intermediate, "blue" runs, but a few times Dana took the eager kids down double black diamond runs that were so ridiculously steep and covered with moguls that at best I could give them a sideways glance.

The next day Dana's husband, Kevin, joined us. Kevin, because he is a cool guy, has switched to snowboarding, and he and the three kids decided to take a snowboarding lesson together. During the first run of the lesson, on not difficult terrain, the instructor demonstrated a new way of making turns. Henry tried it, fell, and broke his arm. Dana told me, later, that, sorry as she was that Henry broke his arm, she was sure glad it didn't happen when she took him down the double black diamonds.

My wife, who teaches philosophy, tells me there is a concept called "moral luck." Sometimes people do dangerous, negligent, or even illegal things, but nothing bad happens. Other times, people do merely careless or even well intentioned things, and terrible things happen. Should we take consequences into account—the implication of Dana's remark—when we ascribe blame or praise for what people do?

But in fact an expert skier who takes kids who know falling leaf down a double black diamond is not negligent or less than conscientious. Nor, speaking for myself, is a parent who says "okay." One needs to weigh the chance of a bad result—injury—against the likelihood of a good result—not only the fun the kids will have, but also the boost it will give their confidence and their skill. Growing up.

On a ski slope they mark the trails—green circles, blue squares, black diamonds, double black diamonds. Information to make conscientious choices by. Yet there are always patches of ice, and, especially in the spring, thin cover, and one can always find a way to break a leg, or worse. They don't print all that stuff on the lift ticket for nothing.

1900
Santa Monica voters vote 305 to 218 to prohibit saloons in the city;
alcohol may still be served in restaurants and hotels with meals cost-
ing more than 25 cents.

Speaking as a parent, I'm starting to get the feeling that, as my child gets older, the ice-encrusted bumps and the tufts of grass sticking through the snow are starting to overwhelm the helpfulness of the trail markings. Not only that, but I've never skied some of those gnarly runs myself. But without sending Henry down some black diamonds, how do I teach him how to ski—or board—the moguls?

I know—get him a lesson. But that's how he broke his arm.

O f course, there are many more serious dangers to a kid than icy slopes. There's no question that modern life puts a lot of pressure on innocent children—both on them and on their innocence.

APRIL 19, 2002

"The whole reason for parties is that parents aren't there." —A friend of Deanna Maran, as quoted in the *Los Angeles Times* a few days after her murder at a party in Westwood where there were no parents.

As I reported last week, my twelve-year-old Henry broke his arm snowboarding. The Saturday after we returned to Santa Monica, Henry's soccer team had a tournament in Torrance. This soccer team is the first tournament team Henry has been on in any sport, and, even though he couldn't play because of his injury, he wanted to travel with the team. The coach kept him busy with a clipboard, keeping track of who took shots on goal.

Players and parents all went to lunch at a nearby Coco's. We took over a long table, parents at one end, boys at the other. As happens when ten parents find themselves together, a big discussion ensued along the lines of how can we protect our kids from the violence, sexual imagery, and general chaos purveyed by TV, movies, music, electronic games, and all the rest. The discussion went back and forth. At a certain point, after I recalled the limited universe of popular culture choices we parents grew up with— for example, television that consisted of just three heavily censored networks—I found myself sputtering, "I hate the good old days."

Thinking back, though, afterwards, I wondered if I had been rash. My gut tells me that more freedom is good, but do I have evidence? What is better (or worse)—the vulgarity of MTV, or censoring Elvis Presley's hips? Does having more choices make a better society, when so many of those choices are dehumanizing?

One's answer depends, no doubt, on one's view about whether society is better. I believe that today's culture that celebrates freedom to live as one likes, regardless of race, gender, sexual orientation, politics, religion, etc., is both improved over the tightly wound and hierarchical social compact of fifty years ago, and inseparable from the explosion in media and expression.

One can disagree.

And you may ask: Am I, being the father of only a twelve-year-old, qualified to answer the question? Perhaps you want me to ask the question again in three years. That's when Henry will be fifteen, just the age of the boy who last week took his mother's Jeep Cherokee out for a spin on Arizona Avenue, with four friends as passengers, and

1900
Residents of the area of south Santa Monica now known as Ocean
Park vote 341 to 59 not to secede from Santa Monica.

crashed into eight parked vehicles. Fortunately, no one was hurt. (A great example of the "moral luck" that I wrote about last week.)

Fifteen was also the age of both Deanna Maran and the girl she argued with about flower pots at the party in Westwood. Fifteen was also the age of the boy I quoted above, on the reason for parties. When I read what he said, I found it unbelievable, but my wife suggested that I probably had the same views when I was fifteen. Although at the time I was confident of my invincibility, the '60s were not a particularly safe time to be an adolescent, either.

When a terrible and unexpected crime occurs, people want to understand it, and the tendency is to make generalizations. Partly this is constructive—Deanna Maran's parents, for instance, believe her death reflects disturbing social trends, and they have tried to use her death to attack violence as a social phenomenon. But if we go too far, and see every pathological act as the result of social forces, then we tend to erode the sense of individual responsibility everyone—at least every sane person—has for his or her own actions. In the process we probably make misjudgments about society, too.

Usually, when it comes to crimes, we can rely on the justice system to pursue the issue of individual responsibility. Deanna's killer, however, killed herself the next day. While her suicide is itself evidence of mental imbalance, Katrina Sarkissian's death means there will be no trial and no public examination of the events, and the life, that culminated in her being at an unsupervised party with a knife.

The District Attorney has determined that the state has only enough credible evidence to charge Sarkissian's half-sister, a juvenile, with crimes that are not serious enough to cause the proceedings to be open to the public. It appears that unless there are civil suits, there will be no public proceedings to determine what happened.

"The people have a right to know." A crime is a public event. Had Katrina lived, and even if she had been tried as a juvenile, her trial would have been public, because of the magnitude of the crime. Although we need to respect the privacy rights of juveniles, the DA should find a way to release the results of the police investigation to provide the public with a credible account of what happened. Perhaps the DA could blot out the names of all juveniles. Now that Katrina Sarkissian is dead, and her privacy is no longer an issue, the DA should disclose any information the police obtained that could illuminate her actions that night.

Evidence can still be relevant even if it is not sufficient to justify prosecution.

Otherwise, we are awash in rumors, which do no one any good, least of all the families of all the young people involved. The Marans live down the block from me, and since Deanna's death we have become friendly. I don't mean to plead their case, but one can imagine what it is like not knowing what happened, hearing one thing, hearing another.

The others involved, not only the families of Katrina Sarkissian and her half-sister, and the girl herself, but also the family at whose house the killing occurred, have been largely silent. No doubt they have their own grief to deal with, and probably frustration with, if not anger at, their bad moral luck. No doubt they are concerned about their own responsibility. But it is hard for me to understand how not knowing what happened will help them in any way to "deal with it," whatever it was or whatever it in the future may be.

As for us, the public? We need to know, because we need to deal with it, too.

It was coincidence, but my son's broken arm and my musings about child raising happened to coincide with the start of Daniel Attias's trial and the arraignment of the surviving sister of the girl who murdered Deanna Maran in Westwood.

APRIL 26, 2002

I am borrowing the title for this column ["Grief Enough to Go Around"] from a caption that appeared in a Santa Barbara newspaper over a photograph of the parents of David Attias. In the photo they stood outside the Santa Barbara courthouse, immediately after their son's first court appearance, expressing their sorrow that David had killed four young people in Isla Vista a few nights before and their compassion for the families of the victims and the community as a whole.

"Grief enough to go around."

David Attias's trial began in Santa Barbara this week. David, who was eighteen in February 2001 when he crashed his car down a crowded Isla Vista street, is charged with murder and has pleaded not guilty by reason of insanity. The trial is expected to last eight weeks. The Attiases are friends of mine. In fact, I have known them since David was two, and in my other life as an entertainment lawyer, I represent David's father, although I have nothing to do with David's defense or any other aspect of the case.

Daniel Attias, David's father, is a successful television director. After David was arrested, the press tried to tie the case to "Hollywood" excess and other stereotypes. As someone who knew the Attiases, and something of the truth, I resented this. I am not going to pretend that my emotional attachments don't color my perspective on the case. Fortunately, the press backed off when it learned of David Attias' life-long difficulties with mental illness, and his family's attempts to deal with them.

Coincidentally, this is also the week that the fifteen-year-old half-sister of Katrina Sarkissian, the seventeen-year-old who stabbed fifteen-year-old Deanna Maran to death last November, is scheduled to be arraigned on a battery charge related to the attack, as well as a felony charge of making criminal threats arising from a separate incident. I say "coincidentally," although it doesn't seem like coincidence to me. The Marans live down the street from me, and we have become friends since Deanna's death.

The fact is, my friends the Marans are the parents of the victim of a tragedy, and my friends the Attiases are the parents of the perpetrator of a tragedy. I have tried with difficulty to imagine what it would be like for my wife and me to be either couple, and what we would do and how we would handle our grief, our fear, and our anger.

When I first heard of Deanna Maran and learned that she died at an unchaperoned party, I wondered how it could be that dozens of affluent teenagers from good schools and presumably good families were at a party without adults, drinking, and fighting. Weren't these the same kids who knew never to ride in a car without buckling up? As a parent, I wondered about the parents of Katrina Sarkissian, the girl who stabbed Deanna, and the parents of the half-sister who had called on Katrina to retaliate against Deanna after Deanna and she had had their own scuffle. I wondered about the parents of the boy who threw the party.

I wondered and wondered and I was starting to speculate, when I remembered the Attiases and how the press had treated them. And I thought about how parents don't choose their children, and who was I to throw the first stone, especially since I didn't know much about what happened. So I stopped speculating. But still, months later, almost no reliable information, such as a chronology of what happened that night, has been made public.

The Sarkissian family and the family of the half-sister have been silent, except for two statements by Matthew Bernstein, the half-sister's father. He made a statement after the release of the coroner's report on Katrina's death, that all he was concerned with at that time was his daughter's sanity, and he was recently quoted in the *L.A. Times* to the effect that the tragedy was Deanna's fault.

The press, uncharacteristically respectful of the privacy of the Sarkissians and the Bernsteins, has not reported on anything about their girls that might shed light on why one sister would use her cell phone to call the other to come to a party to back her up in a fight that was over, and why the sister would arrive for that purpose an hour later with a knife and ready to fight.

My emotional attachments are showing. I agree that like the Attiases, the Sarkissians and the Bernsteins have privacy rights. They have much to grieve over themselves, and it is not helpful to make generalizations about people because of where they live, how much money they make, or where they send their children to school. Nonetheless, at a certain point, with or without objective information, people will ask their own questions and draw their own conclusions.

Why? Because violence among the young—incidents of madness like the Isla Vista and Westwood tragedies, as well as the persistence of gang-related madness here in Santa Monica—in the midst of what to the rest of the world appears to be a well-ordered and prosperous society, is appalling. We grown-ups must consider what we can do to stop it.

1903
Santa Monica voters vote down a total ban on alcohol in the city, 544
to 287.

Last week I expressed the hope that the District Attorney's office would release evidence they and the police gathered in the case to provide an authoritative account of what happened at the party. I don't know if they will, and the decision will likely rest with Juvenile Court. I don't know enough to venture an opinion about what happened the night Deanna Maran died, or an opinion about who is responsible, but I am in no way embarrassed to say that I want to know the facts.

S anta Monica is part of "L.A." and occasionally I had occasion to take
note of that. One such occasion was the tenth anniversary of the riots—
or insurrection—that ripped L.A. after police officers who beat Rodney King
were acquitted.

MAY 3, 2002

I have a few personal memories of the 1992 riots, some good, some bad, probably not
that different from anyone else's. Especially the bad memories. The abiding image I have
in my mind—from television, of course—was rage—misguided but at least predictable—
quickly transmuting into consumerism, as opportunists seized the day to load what they
wanted into the back seats of their cars and thus prove their oneness with the culture.

We here in Santa Monica were a part of what was going on, but also, to a degree,
detached, in both dictionary definitions of the word: unconnected and aloof. Santa Mon-
ica is no Garden of Eden when it comes to race and ethnic relations, but my friend Abby
Arnold, who at the time was rehabbing a house next to the Korean-owned mini-mart at
Seventh and Marine, remembers how on the first afternoon after the verdict the African-
American and Hispanic neighborhood kids surrounded the store to protect it.

On the second night, the Thursday, neighbors came over to our house for dinner. We
lived on Marine Street then, near Fourth, a stone's throw (no pun intended) from Venice.
Our son was two, and our guests had toddlers, too, and we all ate spaghetti and watched
the riots on television. That's how one knew the disturbances would be riots, not a revolution, because everyone knows the revolution will not be televised.

Just six blocks away, across Rose Avenue, in Oakwood, some of the worst violence
was taking place, as the mob chased people from their homes. This was some of the small
fraction of the overall violence of the riots that was directed at people, not property.

My personal bad memory is the panic that overtook our housekeeper, an immigrant
from Guatemala. Just before the riots she and her husband had purchased an appliance
of some sort. She could not find the receipt, and she was sure that people would think
she had looted it. The shame would have killed her.

My good memory, my best memory, is of actor Edward James Olmos showing up
with a broom that Friday morning to start the cleaning up. Woody Allen famously said
that 80 percent of life is just showing up, but Olmos showed that you have to pick the
right time and place to do so. The rioting stopped then, in what would have been only the
second full day of it. That was no coincidence. Olmos's Gandhian act did more to quell
the madness than the National Guard or the police. It might not have been on his mind,

---

but Olmos also allowed me to be the best person I could be and ever have been, for a day at least, because the next day my friend Kevin and I took our shovels and brooms and dust masks and joined the clean-up.

I once met Olmos at a film festival and had the opportunity to thank him personally, but now that I have this public forum, let me do it again. So, thanks, Eddie, but one question: Could you send some push brooms and shovels to Jerusalem and Jenin?

In fact, if anyone reading this column is interested in showing up to stop the violence between Israelis and Palestinians, local rabbi Neil Comess-Daniels, of Temple Beth Shir Sholom, conducts a vigil every Friday, from noon to one, at the northwest corner of Twentieth and Wilshire. The only condition for joining the vigil is that one must be willing to stand next to two signs: "No Suicide Bombings" and "End the Occupation."

So far the weekly vigils have been effective, as the Israelis have withdrawn most of their troops from West Bank towns and there have been many fewer acts of terrorism.

I am Jewish and one of the most unfortunate columns I ever found myself writing was this one, where the subject is the manipulation of procedures by (mostly) Jews to gain access to affordable housing.

MAY 17, 2002

When I was on the Planning Commission I voted yes on the Menorah Housing Foundation's senior affordable-housing project on Fourth, just north of Wilshire. It's a great project. In land-starved Santa Monica, the developer and the City utilized the air rights over a parking garage to create sixty-five units for low-income seniors, conveniently located near downtown.

Great project, but now I am feeling a little bit had. Menorah assured the Planning Commission that the project would be open to all, without regard to race, ethnicity, or religion, notwithstanding that the developer is an offshoot of the Jewish Federation Council of Greater Los Angeles, a private, religious-based organization.

Legally, of course, the apartments had to be open to all, because the funding for the $9.5 million project came mostly from public sources: $7 million from federal Housing and Urban Development funds and $2.37 million from the City of Santa Monica. As recounted in the *Lookout's* recent two-article series, however, not one of the Fourth Street tenants is Hispanic or African-American. Nearly all of the tenants are white. Specifically, Russian immigrants.

According to the 2000 census, more than half the population of Los Angeles County is Hispanic or African-American. According to a recent Rand survey, the population of Santa Monica is 20 percent Hispanic and African-American. But the population north of Wilshire, where the Menorah development is located, is less than 7 percent Hispanic and African-American.

We need housing. We do not need housing that perpetuates racial and ethnic segregation.

Although much has been made of the City's inability to require affordable-housing developers who receive federal funds to give preference to Santa Monica residents, because of federal regulations that proscribe local preferences, giving local preferences is not the answer. The federal regulations make sense, not only because the lack of housing is typically a regional problem, but also because if localities could give preference to locals, given that most localities in America are segregated, federal housing money would end up reinforcing segregation.

However, in the case of the Fourth Street project, manipulation of the federal rules resulted in the very outcome the rules are supposed to prevent: more segregation. It would be easy to point fingers, but I am willing to accept at face value Menorah's claim that it aims for its application process to be non-sectarian, and it does appear that Steve Wagner, Menorah's director of operations, did try to encourage non-whites to participate in the lottery for apartments in the project.

I also have nothing against Russian immigrants, and I don't blame them for trying to improve their living conditions. My great-grandparents were immigrants from what was then Russia, or at least ruled by Russia, and as a regular customer of the Ukraina Deli at Twelfth and Wilshire, I consider myself a direct beneficiary of the cultural diversity more recent Russian immigrants have added to Santa Monica.

Nor can I blame whatever group it was that organized the mini-vans of white applicants who swamped Menorah's lottery with 2,854 applications, more than 80 percent of the total. Presumably, based on the results, these were nearly all Russian immigrants, but no one says that everyone has to be responsible for everyone else.

So who is to blame?

When public money is involved, both public authorities and private developers need to take a proactive stance to insure that each housing development responds to the needs of the entire community. Certainly the federal rules should have an "emergency brake" procedure available, so that special outreach can take place when it appears that normal operation of the rules will result in an outcome that contradicts the purpose of the regulations.

But perhaps the question should not be "who" is to blame, but "what," and that what refers to ingrained attitudes we have. My guess is that no matter how much outreach Steve Wagner would do, many non-Jews are not going to apply to live in a development built by an organization called "Menorah." At the same time, Joan Ling, of Community Corporation of Santa Monica, which has an admirable record in fostering diversity in its developments, told the *Lookout* that CCSM has a hard time getting whites to live in the Pico Neighborhood—a neighborhood, by the way, that has a substantial white population.

Attitudes. Perceptions. Tribalism. Fear.

I n 2002 a new planning issue arose in Santa Monica, when the anti-growth majority on the City Council voted to lower the threshold for discretionary development review in downtown Santa Monica to a level that would mean every apartment building would require specific council approval, even if the development satisfied all of the conditions of the downtown zoning the council had enacted a few years before with the specific intention of encouraging denser, mixed-use development.

MAY 31, 2002

Last Sunday my wife and I drove to Ojai to have lunch with our friend Lia. Unhappy with the bleak prospect of the Ventura Freeway, we took the back route, by way of Route 118, through hill and dale and Moorpark and Fillmore and Santa Paula. While a meal cooked by Lia, eaten with good talk in the shade on her back porch, is a destination worth nearly any trip, the drive through agricultural Southern California was a trip worth nearly any destination. If you have a hankering for Tuscany, but don't have the money or the time, go get yourself lost between Fillmore and Santa Paula.

What a place like Fillmore needs is some refugee from a cold climate to buy a house there, fix it up, and write charmingly about the locals and their foibles: "Under the Ventura Sun." Fillmore, to complete the illusion, also could use farmers making fresh cheese and roadside restaurants featuring local wines and homemade pasta, and centuries of history and art, but let's not quibble when on a glorious day you can still outrun the encroaching housing developments whose colorful flags line the off-ramps in perverse tribute to medieval pageantry.

While mostly I stick around Santa Monica, on several recent weekends I've driven hundreds of miles in and around the "Southland." I've been quite the tourist, and not only to the Italianate portions of the local landscape. My son's soccer games took me to the 1950s sprawl cities of Lakewood and Downey, located on the flats of the coastal plain. My Baedeker was D.J. Waldie's *Holy Land: A Suburban Memoir*, a meditation on the life and times of a suburb, Lakewood.

For those of us who are as quick to dismiss suburban life as suburbanites are to damn the city, Waldie's book is worth reading as a reminder that when people have a choice in where they live, they tend to like what they choose. For instance, my neighborhood in Ocean Park has several corner grocery stores. From time to time they need to renew their permits, but if the City ever tried to close one of them down, my gentle neighbors might riot.

Yet if the City tried to permit a corner store in a residential neighborhood that doesn't have one, the gentle neighbors there might riot.

The point being that there is no moral content to whether a neighborhood has a corner store, or, perhaps hitting the bigger point, the moral content of someone's life is a function neither of being able to walk to a store to buy a carton of milk nor having a little bit of backyard.

But what would be the moral content of covering Southern California completely with subdivisions with names like "The Highlands" or "The Village at the Brook?"

Forget morality, what about mobility, with all those new residents unable to go anywhere without driving? According to a story in the L.A. *Times* last week, planners expect, over the next twenty years, that 71,000 homes will take the place of dairy farms in a fifty square-mile area near Chino. Two hundred thousand people will replace 350,000 cows. According to another story, in an obscure corner of wild country near Brea in Orange County, oil companies want to build 3,500 houses.

I don't doubt that people like to live in Lakewood, or will enjoy the "Village at the Brook" lifestyle, but it doesn't work anymore and we have to make with the alternatives.

Last week I muttered about how four members of the City Council had voted to make it harder to build apartments in downtown Santa Monica. I'm still muttering. It's not that I have any illusions, or delusions, that building more apartments in our downtown will solve the regional sprawl problem. For instance, in the past few years "massive overdevelopment" downtown has resulted in about 500 apartments. "Building booms" of this scale are drops in the bucket when it comes to accommodating Southern California's continued growth.

Yet one can oppose both increasing density and developing Ahmanson Ranch [a proposed development in the western San Fernando Valley] only if one can see only sand from the vantage point of an upside-down head.

B y June, the trial of Daniel Attias was coming to an end. Originally I had not intended to write about the trial, but it was hard not to.

JUNE 7, 2002

"I am but mad north-north-west; when the wind is southerly I know a hawk from a handsaw."—Hamlet

As you read this, the jury in the trial of David Attias is deliberating, or may have returned a verdict, in the initial "guilt" phase of the case. Attias is on trial for having killed four pedestrians and injuring another when he ran his car down a crowded Isla Vista street in February 2001. At the time Attias, from Santa Monica, was eighteen and a UC Santa Barbara freshman.

The charges consist of four counts of second-degree murder, which is homicide without "special circumstances" but with "malice aforethought," four counts of manslaughter by reason of driving while under the influence of marijuana, and one count of driving under the influence and causing great bodily injury. Attias faces life in prison if the jury convicts him of the most serious charges.

Attias has pleaded not guilty by reason of insanity. What this means under California law is that if in the first phase of the trial the jury finds that the prosecution has proved that Attias' actions included all the elements necessary to constitute any of the alleged crimes (or reduced versions), and is thus guilty, then the trial will move into a second phase, during which his sanity at the time of incident will be the sole issue. If acquitted, Attias will be committed to psychiatric care.

As readers of this column know, I am close with the Attias family, having known them, and having represented David's father, Daniel Attias, as an entertainment lawyer, since David was two. I attended several days of the trial as their friend.

I had not intended to write about the trial. My sympathies in favor of the defense would be obvious. The issues the case raises, however, are of considerable interest, especially to Santa Monicans, given that the Attiases live here. None of the local media has the resources to cover a two-month trial in Santa Barbara, and the *L.A. Times* has only run one substantive article about it. (The headline, "TV Director Testifies in Son's Murder Trial," fairly indicates what the *Times* identified as the "local angle.")

I attended only three days of the trial—once during the prosecution's case, then the last day of the defense's case, and then the first day of closing arguments. I followed the case as best I could by reading the Internet editions of the *Santa Barbara News Press* and

UCSB's *Daily Nexus*. Although I witnessed only a little of the trial, driving up and back to Santa Barbara three times allows one time to ruminate on the issues presented by an insanity defense, and I hope that some of those ruminations, keeping in mind my sympathies, will be helpful to those readers who want to know what the case is about.

Notwithstanding the bifurcation of the trial into "guilt" and "insanity" phases, Attias's mental state was the key issue for both the prosecution and defense throughout the trial. To prove "malice aforethought" in the absence of and express intention to kill, the prosecution must show that Attias acted with a conscious disregard for, or reckless indifference to, human life. "Conscious disregard" and "reckless indifference" are, of course, mental states. The District Attorney wanted to persuade the jury that Attias acted out of anger, while the defense sought to show that his actions were the result of his mental illness and that, in effect, he did not have the capacity either to have a conscious disregard, or to be recklessly indifferent.

To a great extent, both sides relied on the same evidence. The DA called more than one hundred witnesses, most to testify about Attias's behavior before and after the collision. The defense augmented these accounts with additional testimony about Attias, particularly to illuminate a childhood of well-documented mental illness, and called to the stand psychiatric experts, both hired by the defense and court-appointed, who tried to explain what Attias' mental illness was all about.

To summarize the psychiatric testimony, throughout his life Attias has suffered from various developmental and psychiatric disorders, some of which would make him unable to control his actions or his temper. At times he was hospitalized, and for many years he attended special schools. Ultimately a diagnosis of bipolar disorder was reached, and under medication, Attias was able to graduate from high school.

In October 2000, however, shortly after arriving at UCSB, he stopped taking his medication. His behavior became more psychotic, with elements of schizophrenia, as he started to have delusions. After the collision, when he was in jail, he had full blown psychotic episode, which was ultimately treated with large dosages of several anti-psychotic medicines.

The prosecution emphasized two issues: that much of Attias's day-to-day behavior was normal, but that at the same time he was prone to anger and rage. To the DA, Attias's refusal to take his medications, against the advice of his family and friends, was itself a manifestation of his malice. In his closing argument, the DA described Attias's actions that night as "Columbine with a car."

Analogizing insanity to a riptide that roils below the surface, not apparent to untrained observers, the defense pointed out that Attias's "normal" day-to-day behaviors were also normal to madness, and that as for Attias's failure to take his medications, the very

nature of insanity is not to be aware of it. The defense used testimony of prosecution witnesses to buttress the case that Attias was delusional. As for the reference to Columbine, the defense reminded the jury that the killers there had planned their attack in advance and knew whom they wanted to kill.

In the courtroom, family and friends of the victim sat on one side and family and friends of David Attias sat on the other. The groups avoided eye contact. What struck me was how alike the families were. Loving parents who tried to raise their children with values and high expectations. Under different circumstances, they would be friends, but the aisle down the middle of the courtroom divided people into "us" and "them." I hesitate to speak for the families of the victims, but I doubt anyone on either side felt like that.

Most of the victims were Jewish, and so is David Attias. At one point I had a fantasy that cases like this should be submitted to rabbinical courts, a fantasy no doubt predicated on some latent cultural image of wise rabbis carefully meting judgment while knitting up the torn fabric of the community. In all honesty, however, I don't know if rabbis would be more holistic or the proceedings less adversarial.

The adversarial system is unmatched for illuminating the truth, and given that evidence can be contradictory, we trust juries to decide, for instance, whether a David Attias is evil or ill. But the purpose of these proceedings should, more than anything it seems to me, be to comfort those who have lost their loved ones, and at that level, I wonder how proceedings like these help. I agree that without reference at all to vengeance, it would be a comfort to see an evil person punished for his crimes. But in a case like this, would it provide more solace for the living for the jury to determine that the victims died at the hands of a cold-blooded murderer or as the random victims of unfathomable madness?

I don't know. Thankful not to be in those shoes, I won't insult those who are by guessing.

[Note: in the initial phase the jury convicted David Attias of four counts of second-degree murder, but then, on June 20, after more testimony and deliberations, the jury found him to have been legally insane. The court committed David to a state mental hospital. I didn't write about the verdict, which was reported in the local press.]

There are reasons that Santa Monica is ordinary, but there are also reasons it is special. I am lucky to have both to write about. The outlaw beach culture that had such an impact on popular culture through "Xtreme" sports and other means, the history of which was celebrated in the documentary "Dogtown and Z Boys," arose in our backyard, forged by kids isolated at the edge of the continent.

JUNE 24, 2002

One advantage of writing a column is that, having had my say about the City's budget, I could skip the City Council meeting Tuesday night. My son Henry had just finished his last substantive day of sixth grade, and the family decided to celebrate by seeing *Dogtown and Z Boys*, the documentary about the 1970s' renaissance of skateboarding in Ocean Park and Venice (a geographical state of mind the skateboarders called "Dogtown").

It was one of those long warm nights that make one forget the marine layer, and we walked up Main Street, through the Civic Center, to the Laemmle theaters, to see the five o'clock show. The movie is terrific. It evokes a different Santa Monica, certainly a different Ocean Park, a rougher and poorer version than the one we have today.

It is more than interesting that two of the crucial "street" styles of the '70s that have since had such an impact on pop (and other) culture—the outlaw beach culture celebrated in the movie and "hip-hop"—both arose in isolated populations of kids living, as the country sprawled into suburbia, in the backwash of urban disinvestment, i.e., in Dogtown and the South Bronx. It reminds me of how some anthropologists describe evolution as occurring in isolated populations that adapt to new challenges in changing environments.

The movie also has intriguing messages about art. While rap artists from the Bronx worked with words and music, and put their work on records, and thus identified themselves and were identified as artists, the Dogtown skateboarders described their dances on wheels as "almost like art." They were not willing—not then, at least—to take the leap into self-conscious reflection, and the wider culture didn't encourage them to do so. Yet the compulsion of the top skateboarders to push themselves further—for their own satisfaction—reminds one more than anything of the artistic impulse.

After the movie we walked to the Pier. Like I said, the evening was warm, glorious. The crowd was numerous, but soft. We ate dinner outside, then walked home along the beach.

At home, I turned on the TV. I had missed the council's vote to do the right thing and give the school district $1.5 million, but I tuned-in in time to see the council give extra funds to the Convention and Visitors Bureau and the Historical Society. Maybe the two groups can get together and send tourists on historical tours of Dogtown.

I am sure glad I turned on the TV because what I wouldn't have missed for in the world came soon after: Mayor Michael Feinstein expounding on the importance of resolving zoning standards for Santa Monica's car dealerships so that they don't lose their franchises, leave Santa Monica, and take their sales taxes with them. The rest of the City Council agreed, and the council pushed the planning department's consideration of the issue up ten months, from July 2003 to September 2002, in the schedule of the department's priorities.

Irony is a columnist's daily bread and it's much easier for someone to give it to you for free than to have to stare into a computer screen trying to make it up. The Santa Monica City Council, led by its Green Party mayor, worried about the business climate? Lord have mercy, nothing like a blip in the increase of sales tax revenues to make Green Party politicos think about that other kind of green.

For discontented locals, Santa Monica has become a congested hell ruled by scheming developers. But outsiders—such as travel writers for the *New York Times*—see a town that is cutting edge, hip, and sustainable. It's hard to reconcile such unhappiness with such desirability.

JULY 1, 2002

"Though only five miles or so from the heart of Los Angeles, Santa Monica feels a world away from the urban sprawl, the clogged freeways and the downtown traffic jams that make a visit to this part of Southern California often seem so maddening."—From "36 Hours in Santa Monica, Calif.," the *New York Times*, June 14, 2002

I'm going out on a limb here, but I suspect the *Times* reporter forgot to interview Planning Commission Chair Kelly Olsen for the recent travel piece on Santa Monica. The article said nothing about the horrific traffic, the sea of alcohol we swim in, or our living hell of code and CUP [conditional use permit] violations.

Of course, the *New York Times'* thirty-six-hour version of Santa Monica, which consisted, in part, of drinks at Casa del Mar and dinner at Michael's, an early morning walk on the Pier, the Farmer's Market downtown on a Saturday morning, shopping, more good meals at Ocean Avenue Seafood and Rockenwagners, the Novel Cafe, skating lessons (in Venice), and the California Heritage Museum, is not anyone's everyday version of our town.

But then, what is the true Santa Monica?

The mansions on Mesa or Georgina, or the myriad dingbat apartments lining the cross streets of the city's mid-section?

The city of convenience, where nearly anything one might want is within a ten-minute drive or a fifteen-minute bus ride, or the city of morning commuters clogging Twenty-Sixth Street, or the line of cars heading south on Twenty-Third Street at five p.m.?

The city of "massive overdevelopment," or the city of sagging bungalows and crumbling stucco?

The cutting edge, hip, sustainable, progressive city of the arts, or the epitome of Southern California provincialism?

Rich city, or poor city?

I n July 2002 I went on vacation to Italy. By then, writing the column was something of an addiction, and I couldn't stop while I was away.

JULY 8, 2002

A while back I wrote about "moral luck," the concept about whether the goodness or badness of one's actions depends on their result, rather than the intention behind them. There's a related concept, perhaps not so philosophical, along the lines of "some people get all the luck," regardless of their qualities, moral or otherwise.

With reference to this latter idea, which you may know of as the "lucky stiff" paradigm, I'm writing this column from my parents' house deep in the Italian countryside. You see, regardless whether I have lived a good life or bad, twenty years ago my parents and my sister bought two farmhouses in a little village in Umbria, midway between Rome and Florence, and so gave the rest of the family a perfect place to go for vacation.

Of course, context is everything. For example, years ago, not long after my parents started spending six months of the year at their Italian farmhouse, my wife and I took our honeymoon in Italy—as she likes to say, "one week in romantic Amalfi and one week with Frank's parents in Umbria."

Umbria is a small, landlocked place that reached its historical peak many centuries ago. Popes lived down the road, in Orvieto, during one exile or another. Orvieto and another town, Todi, which is up the road, used to battle each other back and forth for the fate of the medieval world. Umbria is a good place to be from if you are a saint who wants to establish monastic orders. Everyone knows that the ascetic and spiritual Saint Francis was from Assisi. Fewer know that the worldly Saint Benedict (and his sister Saint Scholastica) were from Norcia, a town in the wilds of eastern Umbria now famous for making the best salami in Italy.

Once my wife and I drove to Norcia to buy some sausages. In Norcia we asked one of the butchers why the best sausage came from Norcia and he shrugged: *È l'aria, o l'acqua*—"It's the air, or the water."

My parents' house is down a bumpy gravel road from a little village. The village has little in common with Santa Monica. In fact, it's hard to imagine two places that are more different, but I told Jorge Casuso, my editor, that I would try to make these columns relevant to readers in Santa Monica.

To begin with, our village has no beach. It does have a fine view from its little piazza of the valley of the Tiber. The view is so good that during the Orvieto/Todi wars, Todi built watchtowers nearby, overlooking the valley, to make sure Orvieto didn't launch a surprise attack up the river. A few years ago a wealthy Italian family got permission to convert one of the old watchtowers into a house. The windows are small, but it stays cool in summer.

Our village is also different from Santa Monica because there is no place to get an espresso. In fact, there are no businesses at all, except that a couple of years ago a local family converted an old stone tower (the signs say twelfth century, but that seems optimistic) on the piazza into a six-room pensione. Although just a little village, there are a number of fine old buildings here. The village was the seat of three local landowning families in the days before land reform and ruling class dissipation, and they built impressive houses. People here build with stone and bricks rather than plaster and sticks, and the buildings tend to resist termites better than in Santa Monica. Even bricks here come from a 500-year-old brick factory.

The village is a lot quieter than Santa Monica. No sirens or stereos wail in the middle of the night. That doesn't mean that everything is tranquility. Farmers or woodcutters driving tractors like to rumble by at six a.m. They aren't on vacation. This year it took a couple of nights to get used to a strange noise. All night, every ten seconds or so, you can hear the muffled thuds of explosions, much like the sound of distant fireworks. These are part of an operation a local farmer devised to scare wild boars away from his fields.

To answer the question that every Santa Monican is probably asking by now, no, there is no traffic congestion. I'm guessing, based on the figures I learned last week in reading the EIR for that condo project on Sixteenth Street, that Idaho Avenue has about as much traffic in a day as crosses the piazza in two weeks. But then, except for a grocery in the slightly bigger village two kilometers away, a store that is considerably smaller than the typical corner store in Santa Monica, the nearest place to shop is Todi, about a twenty-five-minute drive.

I.e., there is less traffic here, but life is more convenient in Santa Monica.

Todi has been the market town for its little hinterland since Etruscan times, so it's fitting that on its outskirts, down where various roads cross the Tiber, there are now four supermarkets. Notice I said "supermarkets." Forget romantic notions of string shopping bags and a daily gossip-heavy meander among the local shopkeepers. Most people around here drive to and shop in supermarkets much like those in Santa Monica, except here the supermarkets have deli counters with fresh ricotta and multiple kinds of prosciutto, and produce from Sicily instead of the Central Valley.

Italy has sprawl, too. The incredible prosperity of the past fifty years is evident all around: in the new houses sprouting seemingly everywhere, built both by locals whose grandparents were subsistence tenant farmers but who now have cars and satellite TV,

1907
Gilbert McCarroll opens a shoeshine parlor, Santa Monica's first
black-owned business.

and by us tourists and summer people who have supplanted sheep as a mainstay of the economy. Even twenty years ago there was so much traffic in Todi that the whole of its beautiful medieval piazza, the town's principal tourist attraction, had become a parking lot. The local administration responded by severely limiting parking in the center of town (including banning parking from the piazza) and by improving public transportation, first in the form of buses and now a funicular from parking lots on the outskirts.

In general, one can't build new houses here in the open countryside. Todi has sprawled outside its old walls, down the hill toward the river, but by and large farmland has been preserved because the new housing is dense. For instance, Sidis, an Italian version of Wal-Mart, recently built a store near a major crossroads outside of Todi, but four stories of apartments sit above it.

Maybe Santa Monica and our Umbrian village have more in common than I thought. But wait a minute—I'm on vacation.

One of the fixtures of Santa Monica and the Third Street Promenade was the Midnight Special bookstore, which specialized in left-wing politics and culture. For a long time the store had a sweetheart lease in a prime building, but finally the family that owned the building decided they needed to make some much bigger money.

JULY 15, 2002

"Il Progresso Tecnologico fa 'Boink'"—the Italian translation of the Calvin and Hobbes book title, *Scientific Progress Goes "Boink."*

Twenty years ago, when my parents and sister bought a farmhouse down an unpaved bumpy road from an Umbrian village, most farmhouses here, including theirs, didn't have telephones. In those days I worked for a high-powered law firm, and when I visited, I spent much of the time between six and ten in the evening (nine a.m. 'til one p.m. in L.A.) in a house in the village making business calls on a public phone that was in the living room. The family that lived there was more than patient.

The road is still unpaved and bumpy, but we not only have telephone service, we can dial up the Internet with a local phone call. That's how I can file this column. But connectivity is a mixed blessing. For instance, now I know, 8,000 miles away, that Midnight Special is losing its store on the Promenade.

(Memo to downtown developer Craig Jones: Here's your chance to get a good tenant for some of the under-utilized first floor retail in one of your mixed-use buildings.) (Memo to the City Council: How about making it easier to build retail downtown, for instance by scaling back the ridiculous parking requirements, so that stores like Midnight Special and Hennessey & Ingalls, and restaurants can relocate downtown and draw people off the Promenade?) (Memo to everyone else: Why is the City Council so concerned about providing downtown with more parking when business is so good property owners keep jacking up the rents?)

Not far from the house that used to have the public phone, which is owned by Aldo and Pierina, two of the locals who were most helpful to my sister and parents in the years after they arrived here, is a three-basin fountain where the local women, including Pierina, used to do their wash. The water entered at one end and would overflow from one basin to the next. The women washed their laundry in sudsy water the third basin, farthest from the water's source. They would do a first rinse in the second basin, which was a little sudsy, and a final rinse in the first basin, which remained clear.

1908
African-Americans build Phillips Chapel, the first Colored Methodist
Episcopal Church (now the Christian Methodist Episcopal Church)
on the West Coast, at Fourth and Bay Streets in Ocean Park.

I thought the system was ingenious. My sister, who then as now lived in the village year-round, thought the whole idea was ridiculous. She told me that the women all had washing machines and only used the fountain in the summer. They said they used the fountain "by habit," but when it was cold, they used the machines. Whether the women did their summer wash outside at the fountain to save on electricity or to socialize, I don't know, but in any case, water no longer runs through the three basins, and the village women use their washing machines in the summer, too.

Romantics might bewail this as a loss of community, or tradition, or just want the country to remain quaint for goodness sake, but washing clothes by hand in cold water is hard work and now Pierina has more time to spend with her grandchildren.

Not everything around the village has changed. There is still a shepherd who mows my parents' fields and bales the hay. The big round bales add a Van Gogh touch to the landscape. We always buy a wheel of the shepherd's cheese to take back to Santa Monica, but the shepherd doesn't give us a discount even though his sheep eat hay from my parents' fields. Perhaps that is why he drives a Mercedes.

People these days are familiar with the Italian phrase *dolce far niente*—the "sweetness of doing nothing." We *far niente* a lot around here. I'm not complaining—as I wrote last week, I know that I'm a lucky stiff to have family with a couple of farmhouses in Italy, but in the summer it's hot, and, let's face it, in the village there is *niente* to do. For every "culture" day that we manage to defeat the inertia and accomplish—this year we took day trips to Rome and Florence—we need three days to recover.

It's not that difficult to convince oneself that under the right conditions—a hot afternoon, crickets sawing rhythmically, wine at lunch—even a nap can be a touristic experience. After all, it's what the Italians do—or used to do. We walk a lot, and cook, and joke that whatever we do here is touristic. Walking along dirt roads, past ancient scenery, and cooking with great ingredients in brick ovens and in kitchen fireplaces—well, for sure that's why we come to Italy.

Of course, the biggest difference between any vacation and real life is work, and when you don't work, you have more time. Time to take walks, or time to make a fire and wait to cook until there's a good bed of coals. But still I wonder, when I get back home to Santa Monica maybe I can spend more time taking walks. There is the beach, after all, and Palisades Park, and my neighborhood. Maybe I should fire up the barbecue more often, even if it's just to roast a chicken. I could spend less time reading the paper, or watching television, or doing whatever.

Maybe what's so good about doing nothing on vacation is that you realize that you don't have to do everything back home.

B ack home, it was politics as usual. But politics about the little decisions that are important because they make cities work or not.

JULY 29, 2002

The City Council held a hearing Tuesday night on reducing the design review threshold for downtown, but few downtown residents cared enough to testify. By my count, only seven people showed up to support reducing the threshold, and four of them were Kelly Olsen, Ellen Brennan, Arthur Harris, and Joy Fulmer, all City Council regulars of one sort or another. Only two residents of the streets most affected—Fifth, Sixth, and Seventh—showed up.

This low level of public outrage is particularly surprising because, unusual in the context of Santa Monica residential development, there has in fact been a lot of construction. In response to changes the City made in downtown zoning, developers have built hundreds of apartments, so many that supply is having an effect on prices. Perhaps you have seen the billboard on Lincoln advertising new apartments at Seventh and Santa Monica, offering a month's free rent. When was the last time landlords were competing for tenants in Santa Monica?

What a concept—after all the hand-wringing about Santa Monica losing its middle class, something can in fact be done to address our shortage of middle-income housing. Build apartments!

As reported in the *Lookout*, the council voted four to three to subject nearly all development downtown to discretionary review, notwithstanding not only the collective yawn from the public, but also the fact that most council members expressed their commitment to the development standards the City enacted in the 1990s for downtown, and their desire that developers continue to build there.

There is ample evidence that few if any developers will risk running the gauntlet of review, because outcomes have been so uncertain even when proposed developments are well within the standards established by zoning. But what bothers the proponents of the reduced threshold is that some developers have avoided discretionary review by building separate, smaller projects on contiguous parcels—"slicing and dicing," in the words of Ken Genser. They say that quality has suffered.

Both Genser and Planning Commission Chair Kelly Olsen, speaking from the floor, showed slides of the buildings they believe have skirted the City's rules. Olsen's view is that these developments are just too big, and he expressed his frustration that the Planning Commission couldn't stop them from being built. Genser, however, supports the

City's current downtown zoning plan. He believes, however, that if developers had built these "sliced and diced" projects as larger, unified projects, they would have had more design flexibility to make better projects, and that there would have been no need for multiple pedestrian and vehicle entrances that reduce the amount of pedestrian-friendly retail that the City wants on the first floors of these buildings.

Genser's most egregious examples, however, were out of date. His biggest complaint was that each individual project required multiple parking entrances on the street, thus hurting the pedestrian ambiance. Since passage of the downtown design guidelines in 1997, however, all parking entrances have been located in the rear, in the alleys. As for multiple pedestrian entrances to the apartments, they increase pedestrian friendliness. While Genser objects to multi-lot projects that skirt development review, reducing the review threshold means that even bona fide single-lot projects will have to undergo review. He's operating with a hatchet, when a scalpel would be more appropriate.

All the pedestrian ambiance issues Genser raised could be dealt with at the ARB [Architectural Review Board]. For instance, if the council wants more "transparency" for the ground floor retail, then it should give the ARB guidelines to that effect. As it is now, much of the pedestrian-unfriendliness on Fifth, Sixth and Seventh Streets results from the ARB itself, which typically requires excessive landscaping in front of store windows. Genser has a point that a developer and an architect working with a bigger project would have more flexibility, but that point is moot. Developers who have tried to work with the City to develop bigger projects, such as Target, can't get their projects approved.

Which brings me to the good news. For once, there was little demonizing of developers. Perhaps aware that later in the meeting they would be dealing with a ten-unit condominium project on two lots that has kicked around the review process for four years, the council listened to developers like Craig Jones and architects like David Hibbert tell them that if they want housing to be built downtown, they had to make their rules clear.

The council not only listened, but also heard. Three of the four council members who voted to reduce the threshold, Genser, Richard Bloom, and Mayor Mike Feinstein, along with the three council members who voted against lowering the threshold, said that they wanted a faster and more certain review process. In Bloom's words, the council needed to "bring certainty to the planning process," and at Bloom's suggestion the council requested that planning staff return to the council with ideas about how to do so.

Genser and Feinstein, for their part, both suggested, among other ideas, that the council should take another look at the City's unique environmental standards that result in in-fill projects that otherwise would be exempt from environmental review having to undergo it. Feinstein went so far as to say that he might not vote to extend the reduced-

---

threshold ordinance beyond its initial forty-five days unless improvements would be made to the process.

I believe that these three council members are genuine in their desire to let downtown continue to develop as a real urban center. I am not sure, however, what can be done about the review process, which is inherently ad hoc. By reducing the review threshold, the council threw the zoning law out the window. The City already exercises architectural review, through the ARB, over all downtown projects. Like all questions of aesthetics, architecture is subjective. What the council has done now is to make development standards subjective, too.

Target, the Boulangerie projects, even the ten-unit condominium the council approved after midnight Tuesday, in fact nearly every development that has been subject to development review, provide myriad examples of how project opponents can subvert the planning process with specious environmental arguments and subjective views about what a neighborhood is (as opposed to what the City Council has zoned it to be).

Tuesday night, Kelly "Neighborhood Compatibility" Olsen and Kevin "It's the Traffic, Stupid," McKeown made it clear that they consider the review process an appropriate tool for undercutting zoning standards the council enacted as law after considerable public process. If Genser, Feinstein, and Bloom truly want "to bring certainty to the planning process," they will need to think hard how to manage discretionary review.

Good luck.

With the 2002 elections approaching, politics began to heat up in Santa Monica in August, when SMRR and other organizations endorsed candidates for the City Council. The big news items were a split between the Green Party and SMRR, and the failure of "Santa Monicans Allied for Responsible Tourism" (SMART) to endorse incumbent SMRR Council Member Pam O'Connor.

AUGUST 12, 2002

Let me get something off my chest: Mayor Michael Feinstein runs a good meeting. I was reminded of that a few weeks ago when I watched the City Council debate whether to lower the development review threshold for downtown. He's also good at public events. I saw that when Feinstein spoke at the ribbon cutting for the transit mall. Feinstein can be fair with the gavel, gracious to his colleagues and the public, and charming to all.

Too bad that when it comes to politics, he's a hypocrite, an ingrate, and a sore loser.

If you heard some screaming last week, it was the leadership of Santa Monicans for Renters' Rights. Their hands—the ones with which they have been feeding Feinstein and fellow Green Party council member Kevin McKeown for years—were bloody from Feinstein's bites. For six years, Feinstein and the Green Party have played SMRR like a violin, but last week a string broke. The SMRR convention did not endorse the Green Party candidate Feinstein wanted SMRR to endorse, and he went ballistic.

In case you haven't been following the story, Feinstein has for months promoted the candidacy of Josefina Aranda, a twenty-nine-year old Green Party member who recently moved back to Santa Monica after completing graduate school in New York. Aranda, a Latina, grew up in Santa Monica in a working-class family, and both she and Feinstein, and Feinstein's Green Party cohort, Kevin McKeown, have argued that not only SMRR, but also the local living wage movement, should endorse Aranda because of who she is.

Or, rather, because of whom her parents are. As McKeown expressed it, he couldn't fail to understand how the labor movement could fail to endorse the "daughter of a bus driver and a janitor." As it happened, instead of Aranda, both the living wagers and SMRR endorsed Abby Arnold, who has been an active participant in the living wage movement since its inception, and involved in SMRR and local politics for nearly twenty years.

The wailing, the gnashing of teeth, the howls of outrage. "A shameful act," said Feinstein of the living wage vote. "It was not a democratic process," said Aranda. Of the living wage contingent who voted en bloc for Arnold at the SMRR convention: "a divisive,

hostile takeover," said Feinstein, who neglected to mention that he packed the 1996 SMRR convention with bullet-voting Green Party members to make sure he received the endorsement SMRR had refused him in 1994. [Note: "Bullet voting" in Santa Monica refers to the practice of not using all of one's possible votes in an at-large election, so as to magnify the votes for a preferred candidate.]

While many expected Aranda to withdraw from the race when she failed to receive the SMRR endorsement, she defiantly placed herself on the ballot. This no doubt ensures the reelection of SMRR-nemesis Robert Holbrook and could, if there turns out to be a second attractive non-SMRR candidate, and if Aranda siphons off enough votes, result in the election of another non-SMRR council member.

"This is their nightmare," said Feinstein, speaking of SMRR, the organization to which Feinstein owes his political career, to which he owes those junkets to the National Conference of Mayors, etc., to which he owes his appearances in the *New York Times* and other media (all listed on his website), "because now they have to defend their flank."

Ralph Nader couldn't have said it better.

Perhaps the Greens don't comprehend the loathing they inspire in many Democrats, but then the only thing that exceeds that loathing is the contempt the Greens have for anyone in the mainstream Left. Like it or not, SMRR and its leadership have for more than twenty years run one of the most effective grassroots political organizations in American history. The living wage coalition managed to get a law passed that is unprecedented for the rights it gives workers.

Feinstein would be selling rollerblades at Green Party conventions if it weren't for SMRR and the living wage supporters who got the vote out for him in 1996 and 2000, but I have little sympathy for the SMRR leadership. They knew Feinstein. They knew he was in politics for himself and for the Green Party. They should have known he saw Santa Monica and SMRR as ripe for the plucking.

It's not only Feinstein. Unbelievably, SMRR has elected four council members who haven't the social conscience or consciousness to support a bond issue for Santa Monica College.

I don't have much sympathy, but I do have some hope. This year the old liberal guard of SMRR, aided by a lot of energy from a social movement analogous to the original renters' rights movement, rose up and took the organization back. I hope they keep it. These forward-thinking, pragmatic progressives are much better for all of Santa Monica than narrow-minded Green Party ideologues and their allies.

* * *

One has to wonder, however, about the living wage people not endorsing Pam O'Connor. Abby Arnold tried to put a good spin on it by saying that by only endorsing two candidates (herself and McKeown) the living wagers had left open a spot for O'Connor, but it was hardly becoming for them not to endorse a candidate who supported a good 98 percent of their agenda, and whose other votes consistently reflect the interests of low-income people.

Clearly, communications between SMART and O'Connor broke down, but it's not good politics for an interest group to appear to require absolute fealty. It makes it easier for politicians to find reasons not to vote your way. Certainly there are people in SMRR who were offended. It's not my business whether SMRR and labor need each other, but they make a good fit, and they will certainly be stronger if they work together.

A rchitecture is a friction point in the politics of urbanism. I headlined the next column, "World Class City of the Self-Deluded," and it began a series on design review.

"That the plan for the proposed project ... contributes to the image of Santa Monica as a place of beauty, creativity and individuality."—The key finding the Architectural Review Board must make to approve a project.

"What a dump."—Bette Davis's character Rosa Moline, in *Beyond the Forest* (1949)

The key word in the above quotation from the Santa Monica Municipal Code is not beauty, creativity, or individuality, but *image*. The key word in the quotation from *Beyond the Forest*, as one might apply it to Santa Monica's built environment, is *dump*.

The Planning Commission is heading toward approval of Howard Jacobs' north Main Street (Boulangerie) apartment projects. A five-vote majority of the commission, which was sitting as the Architectural Review Board on appeal of an ARB denial, did a credible job in the context of an awkward situation—the fact that the City Council, when it approved the project a few months ago, decided the crucial design issues. The commission gave Jacobs and his architect, Howard Laks, reason to believe their three-year journey through the Santa Monica planning process might soon be over. I can't argue with the justice of that, nor would I.

Instead, at the moment I am fascinated by the commissioners' rhetoric. Whether they grudgingly supported the project or railed against it, the commissioners love to talk about how "special" Santa Monica is and about how any architecture that is less than "world class" is unworthy of our little town.

One hears this line at all levels of development and design review in Santa Monica, from the ARB, the Planning Commission, the City Council, and the public, expressed with typical Santa Monica condescension as "this is good enough for Glendale, or Newport Beach, or the Marina, but not for Santa Monica."

Why it is that the Santa Monicans who go on about how "world class" our architecture needs to be are the same Santa Monicans who go on and on and on about how horrible it is that Santa Monica is no longer a (i) beach town, (ii) suburb, (iii) crumbly slum where the "debris meets the sea," (iv) blue collar arsenal of democracy, (v) patrician redoubt, (vi) glamorous hideaway for Hollywood, or (vii) fill in the blank with your own simplistic fantasy of the golden age, but try to employ the adjective "sleepy" wherever possible.

The French have a word for this: *nostalgie de boue*, literally, "nostalgia for mud," figuratively, what a bourgeois does when romanticizing the poverty of earlier days. *Nostalgie de boue* is the defining characteristic of Santa Monicans Fearful of Change (SMFCs). There was a good example of this at the meeting Wednesday night, when Planning Commissioner and SMFC supreme Geraldine Moyle, a UCLA professor, in despair that someone might actually build a new apartment house, exclaimed (in plummy English tones), "Dogtown dies."

Okay, I like the past, too. In fact, let's rebuild Pacific Ocean Park, or reopen the Boulangerie. But can you imagine what the EIR would say about the traffic?

Santa Monica has its charms, but they aren't architectural. Look around. What do you see?

(i) Awful public architecture. A civic auditorium that on at least three sides is the worst of mid-century junk architecture. A courthouse of Soviet drabness. A main library so undistinguished that, thankfully, no one is trying to save it. A city hall that is—may I say it—charming, quaint, interesting even as an example of a minor period and style, but hardly great architecture.

(ii) Bad private homes that range from the routine work of hack society architects, to form-book genre architecture, to the recent truly monstrous hybrids.

(iii) Horrendous apartments, the worst in stucco boxes on stilts or other slapdash construction, half of which look ready to fall down. Mansard roofs garnished with shake shingles, decorative brick garnished with Mexican tile. Cars behind bars. Accidental post-modernism.

(iv) Depressing commercial buildings that, with a few exceptions, reflect the worst of every cheap business park style of the past four decades.

(v) Lincoln Boulevard.

Each week our colleagues over at the *Mirror* try to find a good building to feature above the fold of their second section. I admire the effort, but the minor delights they manage to drag up are exceptions that merely remind one of the rule. Take this week's choice, the Central Tower on Fourth Street. Aside from the fact that, as is typical in Santa Monica, some benighted owner ruined the ground floor facade, for every Central Tower here, you can find ten buildings just as good in the same style in Hollywood. The same goes for our few good apartments—for every Sovereign or Charmont, there must be two dozen better examples in Hollywood, mid-Wilshire, or Pasadena.

Take a look in some guidebooks if you still believe our architecture makes us "special." In *Los Angeles: The City Observed,* published by our own Hennessey + Ingalls, noted architect Charles Moore devoted only six of 396 pages to Santa Monica, and one of those was about the Pier. Pasadena has a whole chapter—forty-two pages.

All right, forget architecture. What about beauty, creativity, and individuality? In the Getty Trust's *Discover Los Angeles: An Informed Guide to L.A.'s Rich and Varied Cultural Life,* out of 283 pages, only five concern Santa Monica, and one of them is about our just departed Museum of Flying. When it comes to art and culture, besides a cluster of private art galleries, Santa Monica contributes about nothing to the region. No important museums or public art, no concert halls, few venues for live music, no significant stage theaters, not much beyond a decent library and a two-year college.

So where do we get off with looking down our noses at the poor slobs elsewhere who would tolerate anything less than world-class apartment buildings?

Of course, even if the town is a dump, that's no reason not to want the best. I happen to like the best myself. I also like the good. If you want the best, or even the good, and you don't have much of either, the question is how to get it.

So what's my point? SMFCs have their *nostalgie de boue* and their delusions of grandeur for a reason. There is, to continue the French theme, a *politique* of self-delusion, a politics of negation that enables people who fear change to romanticize the past to damn the present as well as the future. It's all in the image.

In my second column on design review, I looked into the inherent contradictions in Santa Monica's architectural standards, which demand both compatibility with a built environment that generally lacks distinction and innovative beauty. What's an architect to do?

SEPTEMBER 3, 2002

"ARCHITECTS. All idiots: they always forget to put in the stairs." —Gustave Flaubert, *The Dictionary of Accepted Ideas.*

For a confirmed Italophile, I sure have been putting on the French dog. De Tocqueville two weeks ago, some French phrases last week, now Flaubert. Oy, such pretension. (Or should I say *"Sacré bleu!"*)

The Dictionary of Accepted Ideas is one of those books just perfect for columnists, like *Bartlett's Quotations.* Flaubert satirized the conventional wisdom of his time and place, which turns out to be similar to the conventional wisdom of every other time and place, assuming we are talking about times and places like nineteenth-century France, where people thought theirs was the best civilization yet.

This is a great convenience for a columnist. For instance, since Santa Monicans know we live at the apex of civilization, I can substitute "articulation" for "stairs" in the quotation above and summarize most of the deliberations that occur at the Architectural Review Board.

Architects don't get much respect in Santa Monica, which is strange in a city whose officials routinely say they want "world-class" architecture and where every building subject to design review is expected to contribute "to the image of Santa Monica as a place of beauty, creativity and individuality."

Usually when an architect appears before the ARB, or before the Planning Commission if someone has appealed an ARB approval, he or she is met with suspicion, along the lines of "What are you trying to get away with," rather than with helpful interest, along the lines of, perhaps, "Let's see what you've got here, oh, yes, that looks interesting, now how can we help you achieve our goals of beauty, creativity and individuality?"

In fairness to our design arbiters, some of the criteria the ARB is supposed to follow contradict themselves. For instance, the City has charged the ARB not only to find that a project is beautiful, creative, and individualistic, but also that it is "compatible with the development on and in the general area." Since most of the built environment in Santa

Monica is at best undistinguished, it's hard to say how a new building could be beautiful, creative, and individualistic, and also neighborhood compatible.

Architecture is important. It's one of those elitist art forms, like orchestral music, that notwithstanding their rarefied natures, tend to tell the future what people were thinking. For us stuck in the present, architecture can be elevating. For instance, the twentieth century was a nightmare when civilization almost destroyed itself several times, but I'll never forget my thinking, when I first had the privilege of seeing Louis Kahn's Kimbell Museum in Fort Worth, Texas, that maybe we were living in a great age nonetheless.

I doubt that anyone can point to great architecture that is a tribute to Santa Monica's design review process. A building more than 10,000 square feet, for instance, that not only looks good today but, assuming it was built to last, will be worth looking at in the future. Perhaps great architecture is not the point. Perhaps the overall quality of buildings has improved since the implementation of design review. This does seem to happen in specific contexts. For instance, the ongoing dialogue over several years between the ARB and downtown apartment developers has led to a general increase in quality.

Yet, even though when they finally approve buildings the ARB and the Planning Commission like to say that they have improved them, most of the time this improvement is merely substitution of one subjective aesthetic ("more articulation") for another.

It's ridiculous to expect that everything built in Santa Monica can be world class, or even should be. In ten years no one will say that the apartments in downtown Santa Monica constitute world-class architecture, but the neighborhood will be a world-class neighborhood. The beauty of Santa Monica—aside from the physical setting—is the casual and cacophonous residue of thirteen decades of varied development. What's lovable about Santa Monica's built environment, what's delightful, what's ineffable even, is the handiwork of many. Santa Monica is not a static thing, not a city stuck in its first generation of development, nor a city like Santa Barbara that cloaks its history in conformity.

Perhaps it is a positive indication of the urban jumble that defines Santa Monica's look, but the worst aspect of design review here is that no one can agree on what to tell the architects. As a result, developers opt for the safest designs to try to please everyone, leaving the architects to make the best of bad situations. In the end, no one is happy.

What's an architect to do?

What's a city to do?

A city that sits in an especially beautiful spot that cries out for good architecture.

I'll be making some specific suggestions in future columns, but as a first step, I recommend that the City start treating architects with respect. Not reverence, just respect.

1911
Million Dollar Pier opens in Ocean Park; it was destroyed by fire two
years later, but three new piers replaced it.

As in not nit-picking. As in saying something more useful than, "it needs more articulation." As in not suggesting, as one ARB member did a few weeks ago, that an architect give a building a "marine theme." (This in a city where "Disneyesque" is a vile epithet.)

Most important, as in showing respect by being willing to take risks. By saying, "why not?" instead of "go away."

The end of summer and the beginning of autumn is one of those times of the year when people like to celebrate communally. Maybe it goes back to the harvest. One way people do that in Santa Monica is to have block parties.

SEPTEMBER 10, 2002

Last Sunday evening, the night before Labor Day, the coolest place in Santa Monica was the alley that runs behind the bungalows and apartment buildings on Marine Street from Seventh to Goldsmith, the little dead-end street that bisects the block. This alley is not normally notable. It has the same cracked concrete, garage doors, back fences, and trash bins of other alleys.

That Sunday evening was this alley's Cinderella night.

Decked out with Chinese lanterns and Christmas lights, with gates open to back-yards, with the entire grilling and barbecuing might of a neighborhood massed in one backyard, and with a bar in another, with lawn furniture escaped, or rather, released, from lawns, to join other lawn furniture to flank an asphalt dance floor in front of the alley's version of a band shell: an open garage, in which a neighborhood band playing for a band of neighbors boogeyed and bluesed. With a moon bounce at the Longfellow end and an arching paper sign at the Seventh Street end announcing "2nd Annual Marine Street Block Party," this alley achieved destination status.

We—wife, child, and I—used to live on Marine, a few blocks away, up the hill near Fourth Street. Now we live elsewhere in Ocean Park, and we eagerly accepted an invitation to return for the block party. There is something about the little neighborhood wedged between the Fourth Street hill and Lincoln Boulevard. A palpable sense of community. Maybe it's the topography. Maybe it's the Mini-Mart at Seventh and Marine. Maybe it's the fact that there is a neighbor there, John Grant, who bothers to organize something as ephemeral as a block party.

* * *

"Community" is one of those words that we all use, but we don't know always know what we mean, or we mean different things, or maybe, even most of the time, we disagree on how to get it, and in this case the "how to" can be more important than the "what is."

This past weekend was the Jewish New Year, the time of year when I participate most fully, and with pleasure and edification, in my synagogue community. But that's not my sole community. Like most people, I don't have one community. In days gone by community came as a package, a function of your locality: the parish church or the synagogue in the shtetl, the local school, the family trade, or the local job. Your choices were made.

Today we choose communities. I chose to live in Santa Monica, I chose my synagogue. I happen to work in Santa Monica, but I didn't use to. My wife works fifteen miles away, across a landscape of many other communities, yet only one-fourth the way across the metropolis.

We even have electronic communities.

Then along comes an event like September 11, and you realize that, even as it's important to know your neighbors, and to dance with them on the asphalt, or to participate in the other communities you choose, the community that no one chooses—the community of people of goodwill that unites the nation, that unites even the world—is the most important community.

* * *

The argument against the living wage that I don't understand is that the law is bad because it's promoted by the union that wants to organize the hotel and restaurant workers. Is this supposed to surprise me?

Three weeks ago the L.A. *Times* ran a story about how organized labor had twenty-seven bills they wanted Gov. Gray Davis to sign.

It's no secret that for several decades unions have had a hard time organizing, especially since Ronald Reagan was president. There are a lot of reasons, but one is that Republican presidents since 1969 have made consistently anti-union appointments to the National Labor Relations Board, which has permitted employers to get away with more and more aggressive tactics to interfere with employees' rights to unionize.

Twenty-seven bills on Davis's desk and the Santa Monica living wage law are evidence that if workers cannot negotiate effectively with business through collective bargaining, workers are going to look to government to solve problems of the workplace that historically have in America been left to negotiation.

They will succeed. Americans do not want workers here to live like workers in the Third World.

About the same time as the twenty-seven bills article, the *Times* ran an obituary for the former head of the United Auto Workers. This is what the chairman of General Motors had to say about his former adversary, who had led the union in strikes against

1912
First Jewish religious services in Santa Monica take place at the
Masonic Hall on Marine Street in Ocean Park.

the auto industry: "We have lost a respected business partner, a passionate leader in community and union relations, and most importantly, a good and honorable man."

There are many successful businesses with adversarial but nonetheless productive management/union relations. The UAW, for instance, worked with the automakers to improve quality and productivity, to revitalize what had been an industry in decline. The hotels and the hotel-workers union should be allies, not antagonists, most of the time.

If businesses make it hard for workers to organize, workers will turn to government for relief. And why not? Don't businesses look to government to solve their problems? Business has to ask itself—would it rather negotiate with unions, or deal with government bureaucracies? If you think unions are tough, try to fire a worker in Europe.

I consider myself pro-business as well as pro-labor. And pro-environment, and pro-housing, and pro-education, and pro-parks. Sometimes my own desires conflict. But I know enough that in this country, if you want to achieve anything, you have to leave something on the table for the other guy.

For my third column on design review, I tried to apply some lessons I learned from the movie business, movies being another art that, like architecture, relies on collaboration and must please an audience.

SEPTEMBER 23, 2002

"The physician can bury his mistakes, but the architect can only advise his client to plant vines." —Frank Lloyd Wright (1953).

When I'm not writing columns, I practice entertainment law, and years ago I produced an art film that was shown in about twelve of the country's smallest, oops, I mean most exclusive, theaters. As the family's "expert" on the movie business, I am often asked by relatives to explain why Hollywood makes so many turkeys. I usually shrug and if pressed further, say, "You know it's hard to make a good movie." If I am pressed even further, I become indignant on behalf of filmmakers everywhere, and I make an analogy that my relatives all get.

The analogy I make is that the percentage of movies that are good is about the same as the percentage of buildings that are good—somewhere between one out of ten and one out of one hundred, depending on whom you are talking to.

It's hard to make a good movie, and it's hard to build a good building.

Another thing my relatives outside the studio zone want to know is what a movie producer does. To answer this question I often compare producers with real estate developers, as real estate development is a business that is well understood in other parts of the country. Producers and developers do similar things. They find properties (real properties, or books or screenplays), hire creative people (architects, or writers and directors) to develop the property, arrange financing, and then hire more people (contractors, technicians, actors) to produce things (buildings, movies, TV shows) that sometimes rise to the level of art but which exist to make money.

In the past few decades it's become the norm for municipalities to require that developers preview building designs before design review boards at public hearings. The idea is that buildings will be better architecturally if the public and the municipality's experts have a chance to give input. Interestingly, movie producers have been previewing rough cuts of films before "locking picture" since nearly the dawn of the industry—to wonderful effect.

Like I said, it's hard to make a good movie or to build a good building.

Recently, the City Council, on the occasion of filling two vacancies on the Architectural Review Board, had a spirited discussion about the board's role and who should be on it. The council ultimately elected another architect to the board, which gives the professionals a majority. The argument against electing a fourth professional was that the ARB should reflect residents' concerns about their neighborhoods, and that was a job best left to residents.

This argument about the purpose of design review is fundamental. The City's design guidelines reflect this dichotomy by trying to promote, all at once, creativity, beauty, and neighborhood compatibility. Generally, wherever public design review takes place, and design reviewers try to reconcile these inherent conflicts, the result is that the worst projects are usually prevented. But the need to satisfy a multitude of "clients" with differing ideas about "what they want the community to be" (to quote from Council Member Ken Genser's argument against adding another professional architect to the board), generally results in, at best, a homogenized aesthetic and, at worst, a degraded one.

While I expect that the council's choice of well-respected architect Bill Adams was a good one, just because an ARB member is an architect does not mean that he or she will do a good job. A few years ago, I attended, as the Planning Commission's liaison to the ARB, a lot of ARB meetings, and the absolute worst member of the board was an architect named Janet Spinks. My favorite Janet Spinks story involves, coincidentally, developer Howard Jacobs. It was Jacobs's Boulangerie site apartments, which received their final approvals last week after years of development, environmental, and design review, that got me writing these columns about design review in the first place.

Four or five years ago, when Jacobs was planning to renovate the apartment building across from Casa del Mar and turn it into the Citrus Suites, he took a trip to Italy. According to testimony he later gave the ARB, he was impressed by the painted wooden shutters with open slats that Italians use to keep heat out and breezes flowing. These shutters not only look great, but also they help keep Italian buildings cool without air conditioning.

Inspired by *bella Italia*, Jacobs had his architect specify operable shutters in his design for Citrus Suites. But at the ARB, these real shutters created a crisis for then board member Spinks. She said that if the shutters could open and close, then sometimes some would be open while others would be closed—and wouldn't that be terrible!

One of the worst things about design review is that it usually operates by consensus. No one wants to disagree with anyone else and all criticisms are considered equally valid, no matter how ignorant. Even though some other ARB members could see the inherent beauty of shutters that opened and closed and fulfilled the purpose shutters have existed for since the beginning of shutters, no one would stand up to Spinks and her remarkable fear of the irregularity of authenticity.

To gain the consensus he needed for approval, Jacobs agreed to make the shutters inoperable—to make them fake—and on your next trip to the beach, you can swing by Citrus Suites and see the fake shutters stuck on the walls. Not only are they fake, but the widths of the fake shutters don't match the widths of the windows they are theoretically protecting from the elements. The effect is ridiculous.

But perhaps Spinks, even with her technical training, truly understood "the feeling of the soul, the gestalt ... of what Santa Monica should be," to quote Genser further, because let's face it, Santa Monica loves fake—or faux, as it's called. Judging from what gets built here, the easiest way to get a building through the ARB or the Planning Commission is make it either faux Pasadena bungalow or faux Paris bordello.

Fee fi faux fum. The new firehouse on Hollister has fake brick siding. Imagine that— a red brick fire house made of fake bricks.

We don't just have faux. We have world-class faux.

S anta Monica has a large population of homeless people who are a continuing source of political controversy, especially at election time. Two
thousand two was no exception.

SEPTEMBER 30, 2002 (This was my one hundredth column.)

Early Friday morning, I cycled up Main Street, past City Hall, on my way to the
Westside Shelter and Hunger Coalition's breakfast and awards ceremony at the Miramar
Hotel. At this annual event, the coalition celebrates formerly homeless people who have
changed their lives, and honors those who helped make those success stories possible. As
I approached the bridge over the freeway, a man in a sleeping bag, lying on the sidewalk,
was just waking up. Propped on his elbows, he gave me a bleary smile.

Top of the morning to you, too.

The coalition's breakfast was a welcome respite from the "debate" on the homeless
that has recently been roiling the city. It was good to hear not only the inspiring success
stories, but also to hear from and speak with people who work hard to save lives, doing
the work that must be done, on behalf of all of us and our supposed civilization.

If you have ever had a friend or relative descend into alcoholism, drug addiction, or
mental illness, and if you could, ultimately, do nothing, just imagine how hard it is for
strangers to help a drunk, or an addict, or a mentally ill person come in from the cold.
Each success story at the breakfast had a list of people and organizations to thank long
enough to choke an Academy Award recipient. These thank-you's reminded me how
much money, time, training, facilities, expertise, and compassion, not to mention an
individual's own determination, is required to turn around the life of anyone who didn't
reach his or her "bottom" until he or she hit the streets.

It was great to spend time with people like John Maceri from Ocean Park Community
Center who walk the walk every day. It was great to be in a room with business people,
such as the members of the Chamber of Commerce's Homeless Task Force and representatives from the Bayside District and other businesses, who have worked closely over the
years with social service providers to respond to the problems of the homeless, and the
problems created by the homeless, with compassion and realism.

But after the testimony at Tuesday evening's City Council meeting on the proposed
ordinances to regulate meals programs in the parks and prohibit sleeping in downtown
doorways, the breakfast could only partially counteract a rapidly intensifying attack of
cynicism.

I'm cynical about the tough attitude emanating from the new leadership at the Chamber of Commerce and other business leaders who want a "zero tolerance" crackdown against the homeless, and who have formed a new "Public Safety Committee" at the chamber. They want the chamber to take on the homeless directly, with tough means hinted at darkly, and they've turned their back on the good work of the chamber's Homeless Task Force. From what they would tell you, the homeless are destroying business downtown. Yet business is good. In the first quarter of 2002, when you would have thought Santa Monica businesses would have been dying from the post-9/11 drop in tourism, a declining economy, and the construction of the transit mall, retail sales on the Promenade were up 6.1 percent from the year before.

The only place in the city where retail sales decreased significantly was Santa Monica Place, a private mall that is the only retail space in Santa Monica the homeless can't get into.

Yet I am just as cynical about the groups from outside Santa Monica who provide meals in the parks for homeless people without any regard to the City's programs for helping people get off the streets. I have doubts that the City can end these meals programs in a manner consistent with the Constitution, but why do I get the feeling that these Good Samaritans are more interested in their own salvation than the needs of their "clients"?

Take Russell Calleros, the Director of Community Service & Justice from Loyola Marymount who has his students picnic for half an hour or so each Tuesday with the homeless in Reed Park. Here's a quote from the LMU website describing the program: "Students travel to this park with the idea of nourishing those in need, but they are the ones who actually leave feeling nourished!" LMU brings these kids and their sandwiches to Santa Monica, instead of nearby Westchester, because, Calleros says, there are more homeless here.

Some "fisher of men," this Calleros. If the LMU students distributed sandwiches in a Westchester park every Tuesday, my guess is they'd soon have a flock, to mix biblical metaphors. But I suppose that would upset LMU's neighbors and whom would that nourish? By lacking the courage to deal with the problems of the homeless in their own communities, these self-righteous do-gooders do them a double disservice. Not only do they fail the stranger in their midst, but by ignoring them they perpetuate the politics of denial—the notion that homeless people are some other community's problem. At the same time, ever more homeless people attracted to Santa Monica anger voters here who naturally believe that no one is doing anything about the problem, notwithstanding the City's considerable efforts.

1914
Santa Monica changes the name of Nevada Avenue to Wilshire
Boulevard to commemorate completion of the boulevard to Los
Angeles.

I'm cynical, too, about the political rant from the Left. This is not about capitalism. As mean spirited as some business people are, they are not upset about poor people, they are upset about people who have diseases—alcoholism, addiction, mental illness. Perhaps this is just as bad, or even worse, depending if you think there is a moral difference between poverty and illness, but class struggle has as much to do with it as it would with an outbreak of leprosy.

I'm cynical about no-growthers and NIMBYs who whine about the crisis in affordable housing when over the years they have done their best to stop the building of apartments all over the Westside, including in Santa Monica.

I'm even cynical about the homeless themselves and their apologists, or at least some of them who testified Tuesday night, who seem to think that being drunk excuses being disorderly.

Mostly I'm cynical about all of us who don't like looking at the homeless but who won't face up to the price of making a dent in the problem. No one wants to pay the taxes necessary for a mental health system that might be able to deal with people deranged or sick enough to spend their lives dying in our streets. Instead we want to make sleeping on the street criminal without even providing enough beds for these potential criminals to "flop" in.

If people were slowly dying in our streets of cancer, wouldn't we do something about it? Problems seem intractable because people try to solve them using means that conform to their own preconceptions, as grist for their conceptual mills. If everyone tried to look at intractable problems from different perspectives, perhaps these problems would not be intractable.

I concluded my series on design review with the following column, which called for placing more confidence in architects, giving them more elbow-room, and taking the risk of letting them be creative.

OCTOBER 7, 2002

I began this intermittent series on design review in August by looking at how "Santa Monicans Fearful of Change" (SMFCs) have turned their delusion that our burg on the bay is so special that all architecture must be "world class" into a political argument against new development. For another example of how SMFCs distort reality to prevent change, consider the ordinance that the City Council recently passed to make permanent the City's "Construction Rate Program." This program prevents, with certain exceptions, the building or even remodeling of an apartment building closer than 500 feet to another multi-family construction project within fifteen months of the first project's having received a building permit.

The City Council enacted this program in March 2000 on a temporary, "emergency" basis. Why? There was a crisis of over development. Between 1996 and 1999 there was a 533 percent increase in development activity in multi-family residential districts. A 533 percent increase sure sounds like a crisis. But not if you look at the actual numbers. In 1996 there were three projects. In 1999 there were sixteen.

Sixteen projects. According to the housing element of the City's general plan, in 2000 there were about 38,300 apartments in the city. That's 38,300 apartments and sixteen new projects in a year, 1999, that was the very height of an economic boom, after most of a decade during which almost no apartments were built. An overdevelopment emergency?

It's Orwellian. The City Council declares an emergency and so there is an emergency. Peace is war.

Most of those 38,300 apartments are built of sticks and stucco. More than 75 percent of the city's housing is more than thirty years old. Much is sagging and decrepit, food for termites. These buildings will be replaced or "substantially remodeled" several times before Santa Monica even approaches the end of its urban evolution—a few centuries hence.

Leaving aside the SMFC critique that no development could ever be good enough for Santa Monica, what if we wanted to improve the design review process so that Santa Monica might evolve with good design? I have a few suggestions. The first is procedural. When a project requires Planning Commission development review, the City should

c. 1914
Japanese film companies film movies in Santa Monica Canyon for
distribution in Japan.

---

eliminate separate Architectural Review Board review and combine aesthetic and development decisions at the Planning Commission level. Separating architectural from development review has not worked.

Why? Because the Planning Commission is hobbled when it cannot consider design issues; developers are unable to use design to deal with potential development problems; the process is extended and made much more costly; and the ARB, when it finally reviews a project, is often stuck with de facto design decisions made by the Planning Commission (or by the City Council). Both the Planning Commission and the ARB—and developers and architects—are justifiably confused when they have to apply concepts, such as "neighborhood compatibility" or "massing," that mean one thing in the zoning/development context and something else in the architectural context.

When a project is big enough to require development review, the City should follow the practice it used for expedited earthquake replacement projects. When the Planning Commission considers the project, have one or two ARB members sit with the commission to consult on architecture and landscaping.

Regardless where and when design review takes place, the subjective nature of aesthetics and the conflict between encouraging both individuality and neighborhood compatibility, which are both stated goals of design review, make the process problematic. Perhaps design reviewers should think more about good buildings and less about good architecture. "Architecture" is a loaded term, overburdened with ideas about art and beauty. Yet few buildings, even in the world's most beautiful built environments, are the product of the self-conscious intellectual discipline and high art that is architecture.

Certain elements are common in good buildings. Good buildings are built to last. How many buildings in Santa Monica do you expect to be around in one hundred years? How many would you want to be around? Beauty is subjective, but people can agree on objective standards for quality materials. If we require developers to build to last, with high-quality materials, then we will have won half the battle.

Good buildings also suit their environments. The Taos pueblo is beautiful sitting there in the desert. It wouldn't look so good in a rain forest, and faux French chateau don't look so good in Santa Monica.

Speaking of context, why does the ARB consistently require landscaping in between store windows and the sidewalk on streets where the City wants to encourage shopping and pedestrian ambiance?

Sooner or later, we have to deal with the beauty issue. When we do, let's show some respect for architects and architecture. I was appalled during the approval process for Howard Jacobs's Boulangerie site apartment projects that both the Planning Commission and the City Council doubted that anyone could design a block-long building that would not be "monolithic." They required that the architect break the building up to look like little buildings, each in a different style.

What does it say about our being a "city of the arts" that we don't believe an architect can or should make a unified statement over one block? The architect in this case did his best, but if we want good architecture, we have to give architects some elbow room. There's no reward without risk.

Then there is the whole question of "styles." Styles are the crutch used by the design handicapped to try to understand architecture. They can't be used willy-nilly. You can't just throw "Spanish" or "Craftsman" onto the façade of a multi-story apartment block and expect Santa Barbara or Pasadena. There is nothing criminal about genre architecture, but unintentional post-modernism—of which Santa Monica has so much—is a disaster.

Notwithstanding how easy it is to complain about design review, it's worth considering those instances where the process has worked well or, at least, where good and innovative design has survived the process. With the exception of single-family houses in multi-family zones, which traditionally receive more leeway from the ARB, most of these success stories are City projects, such as the beach improvement projects, the re-do of Palisades Park, and the Pico streetscape.

The City is a special client. It has the money and the design confidence to weather the process by accepting good suggestions and avoiding compromise with bad ones. Few private developers have either the City's money or confidence.

The City wants developers to make better architecture, yet it has created a design review process that more than anything makes developers waste money and lose confidence in their architects.

Under California school funding law, including under Prop. 13, one way (one of the few ways) that a community may contribute local money to local schools is to enact a parcel tax—a flat fee per real estate parcel, regardless of the parcel's value. Santa Monica had previously enacted a parcel tax, and a renewal with a substantial increase was on the 2002 ballot.

OCTOBER 28, 2002

Only a fraction of Santa Monica voters have children who attend our public schools. Yet Santa Monicans, going back to Prop. ES [a school bond] and the original parcel tax, have given overwhelming support, in the 70 and 80 percent range, to school bonds and parcel taxes. As a parent of a seventh grader, I want to say thank you.

I hardly need to flatter all you good voters out there who support the schools, since you're not the kind of citizens who need flattery. You are the kind who understand how public education serves everyone, and you are all set to vote Yes on Measure EE, the new parcel tax.

But perhaps you want to know something about the education your taxes pay for. Since my son attends John Adams Middle School, known as "JAMS," I can tell you about it from at least one parent's perspective. You are probably aware of how well Santa Monica/Malibu schools do when it comes to standardized tests. If not, read the *Lookout* article from October 17. [Note: the article reported that local schools had done well in state testing, with significant gains at schools in disadvantaged neighborhoods.]

Our schools achieve these results even though they serve a population that is not homogeneously middle or upper class. Santa Monica is not San Marino. A recent survey found that 26 percent of all Santa Monica public school students qualify for reduced-price lunches. At schools like JAMS that are south of Wilshire many students' families do not speak English at home. Many students, when they graduate from high school, will be the first in their family to do so. There is a gap between the academic performance of our students whose parents are wealthier and better-educated and those whose parents have less money and who had less education. John Deasy, the superintendent of schools, has dedicated himself to closing that gap by improving the performance of the latter.

Less-advantaged students here are not consigned to substandard schools as they are in so many other places. Schools here are highways, not dead ends.

What kind of highways? My wife and I both have advanced degrees and we are well-off. The expectations we have for our son, and for his education, are high. We are not

1916
Santa Monica voters approve a water bond of $712,500 to purchase
private water companies and create a municipal water system, and
vote down annexation to Los Angeles. A subsequent bond issue for
one million dollars in the 1920s allows Santa Monica to purchase
wells in west Los Angeles.

so much concerned about test scores, and we have numerous doubts about standardized tests in any case. What we are interested in is critical thinking.

In Social Studies our son's class is studying ancient Rome. The other day he came home talking about whether the Emperor Constantine should have defended the Western Roman Empire instead of fortifying Byzantium. I don't know about you, but when I was in seventh grade, I didn't know who Constantine was, let alone whether he abandoned the Romans.

JAMS also has a special science program, the "Science Magnet." Earlier this month we, along with many other parents, accompanied our son and about fifty classmates on a weekend field trip to Morro Bay. The dedication of the teachers who shepherded this flock of adolescents was impressive, along with the rigorous attitude they made the kids apply to scientific observation. Taxpayers should know that the Science Magnet is not limited to kids who test well—any student can be a part of it if he or she keeps up a C grade in science and participates in extracurricular science seminars the science teachers run throughout the year.

The music programs at Santa Monica schools are fabled. About half the children at JAMS participate in band, orchestra, or chorus. These music classes are academic subjects. Two things, above all, stand out. First, music is intellectually demanding at JAMS. I remember when music class meant fifty kids singing "Jingle Bells" discordantly, but these kids learn music theory and take their playing seriously. Second, participation in the musical ensembles and choral groups creates a culture of achievement that extends beyond the auditorium.

In short, kids here seem smarter than they did when I was a kid. But then I've never bought the argument that schools were better back in the old days. Certainly our son has received a better education so far than either of his parents did, and we attended schools with largely homogeneous middle-class populations.

Like I said, thanks Santa Monica (and Malibu), and, by the way, this is no time to rest on laurels. Measure EE needs two-thirds approval, and every Yes is precious.

As in the nation as a whole, in Santa Monica the 2002 election was a debacle for liberal causes. The parcel tax for the schools failed to achieve the necessary two-thirds vote; given the bad economic climate, asking for an increase was asking too much. The City's groundbreaking living wage ordinance, against which the hotels collected enough signatures to put it on the ballot, lost narrowly, amid charges of misleading campaign tactics on the part of the anti forces. Meanwhile, par for the Santa Monica course, all the incumbent city council members up for reelection won, which meant that Michael Feinstein's Green Party protégée, Josefina Aranda, lost.

NOVEMBER 11, 2002

There are two ways to get elected to the City Council in Santa Monica.

The most popular route, taken by two-thirds of the winning candidates this year, and three-quarters in 2000, is to gain the endorsement of both Santa Monicans for Renters Rights (SMRR) and the Police Officers Association (POA). The other way is not to be endorsed by either SMRR or the POA. That is the Robert Holbrook strategy.

Clearly, a candidate is in trouble if he or she obtains the endorsement of only one of the two organizations. Viz., Abby Arnold and Matt Dinolfo.

Another thing we learned in this election is that the endorsement of the Westside Greens is quite effective, but only if it's coupled with that of SMRR and the POA.

Incumbency helps. A lot. One might think, judging by the infrequency by which Santa Monica voters reject incumbents seeking reelection, that Santa Monica, not that theme park down the road, is the "happiest place on earth." Of course, we know that's untrue. Santa Monicans are unhappy. They must be—otherwise, the City Council wouldn't be so busy, burning the midnight oil, hiring code enforcers and traffic cops in the face of yawning deficits.

But Santa Monicans can't agree on their unhappiness: Everybody is unhappy, but since everybody can find at least one or two council members to agree with, come election day, our gripes cancel each other out. The smart money is always on the incumbents. We are happy in the aggregate.

Speaking as a Santa Monican who is happy to acknowledge my individual happiness, I wish our incumbents would derive more confidence from the power of their incumbency, and, instead of trying to patch every tear in the social fabric instantly, instead of responding to every complaint immediately, that they pondered a little before throwing

more money at a problem, making up some new rule or changing some long-charted course.

But then what do I know about Santa Monicans? I supported five measures on the local ballot, and only one passed. I opposed two measures, and only one failed to pass.

I am so out of step with the electorate that I am qualified only to be a columnist.

This was a dismal election that ran from the catastrophic (the failure of the parcel tax to get the necessary two-thirds vote) to the lamentable (the failure of the living wage ordinance), to the outrageous (the fact that a police union made up of city employees who don't live here, who make their choices in the metaphoric dark of night, who have no compunction about slandering elected officials, have so much influence on the electorate).

Until all the absentee ballots are collected and before the precinct-by-precinct data are available, it's premature to make definitive comments about what the results mean, but a lot of results—especially the failure of the parcel tax—seem best explained by low turnout among Democrats in the renter districts. The gubernatorial election was a turn-off [Note: Gray Davis, who was recalled a year later, was the Democratic candidate], and there was no Senate race this year, or even a sexy statewide ballot measure.

If Barbara Boxer were running with the fate of the Senate in the balance, results might have been different.

Still, it's a strange year when a school tax fails in Santa Monica and Malibu but a school bond passes with 68 percent of the vote in Los Angeles—and only eight months after the Santa Monica College bond passed in a spring election with 70 percent of the vote, on much lower turnout. The schools need and deserve more money—let's hope the District can figure out what went wrong and comes back with a proposal that works.

In the meantime, my favorite post-election comment came from Seth Jacobson, a spokesman for the hotels who opposed the living wage ordinance. As quoted in the *Lookout*, he said, regarding the aftermath of the hotels' victory: "Our attitude is we're here and we want to talk if they want to come to the table."

Wait a minute. I have the distinct recollection that the local living wage movement got started precisely because the hotels have done and continue to do everything they can to prevent the possibility that they might "come to the table" with a union representing their workers sitting on the other side.

Maybe I was wrong. Maybe it's because of the living wage ordinance that the hotels hire union busters, require their workers to listen to anti-union diatribes, and hassle union supporters. Maybe now that they have defeated the ordinance the hotels will "come to the table." But I doubt it.

Sometimes column writing makes for strange associations. In this column I linked Hall of Fame Dodger pitcher Sandy Koufax's early struggles as a bonus baby with the labor situation in Santa Monica.

DECEMBER 2, 2002

One aspect of having a child turning thirteen is that I'm starting to read books he recommends. Last week I read *Sandy Koufax: A Lefty's Legacy*, a new biography of the Dodgers' enigmatic icon (or iconic enigma?) by Jane Leavy, which my wife bought for our son. When he finished reading it, and pronounced it "good," his highest praise, I snapped it up.

I was fourteen when Koufax won 27 games in 1966 and then retired, and, even though I lived in Philadelphia, the name Koufax occupies an enduring place in an almost unconscious pantheon of my '60s childhood, somewhere in life when baseball was certainly more important than politics and even more important than sex. A few years took care of those priorities, but the fact that Koufax retired at just the moment when all hell was breaking loose must mean something.

Although then as now I lived and died with the Philadelphia Phillies, my "second favorite team" was, as I imagine was the case with a lot of Jewish kids, the Dodgers. My association with them, however, was not only based on Koufax's being Jewish, but also because my grandmother and a favorite aunt lived in L.A. We visited in 1961 and I remember getting a pack of Dodgers photos, probably at a Union 76 station. I remember how my older sister developed a crush on "Handsome Sandy," which is how Koufax was described on the back of his photo.

Part of the Koufax legend is that he is one of the few major league players who never played in the minor leagues. A fact that I learned from Leavy's new book is that Koufax never pitched in the minors not because he was especially good, although everyone recognized that at eighteen he had tremendous potential, but because the club owners had imposed a rule on themselves that required that clubs that paid "bonus babies" signing bonuses of more than $4,000 had to keep them on the major league roster for two years. Koufax signed with his hometown Brooklyn Dodgers for $15,000.

The purpose of the rule was to penalize any club that broke ranks with the other clubs and paid extravagant (!) bonuses to players whose only chance to negotiate in a free market was their first contract—after that, they were bound to whatever club "owned" their contract. If you consider how counter-productive it is to keep a good prospect on a major league bench when he should be getting experience in the minors, and if you reflect on the awkward space the bonus babies occupied on the bench, having taken a job from a veteran, you might start to understand why even today, when mediocre baseball players make millions, players are so suspicious of any efforts by club owners to restrict the market in salaries and bonuses.

Koufax played an important role as a baseball labor activist. Before the 1966 season he and Don Drysdale held out together, and by forming their "union of two" they were able to break the $100,000 salary barrier for pitchers. While their action broke no legal ground to emancipate the players from their perpetual contracts, the fact that Koufax and Drysdale challenged Dodger owner Walter O'Malley, the behind-the scenes ruler of baseball, encouraged the players' militancy and happened to coincide with the players' hiring of Marvin Miller to turn their players' association into a real union.

Needless to say, to this day the club owners declare that the demands of the players will drive them into bankruptcy, destroy the game, and end America as we know it. Meanwhile, the game has become much more popular and lucrative than it was prior to free agency, and the valuation of some clubs approaches a billion dollars. (Ted Turner paid about $10 million for the Atlanta Braves in the early '70s and everyone thought he'd been suckered.)

I expect that many of Santa Monica's hotel owners and managers are baseball fans, and I hope that they read this new biography of Koufax. They, like the baseball club owners, often say that they have the best interests of their workers at heart in resisting unionization. No doubt some of them are cynical, but others, like some of the old club owners, genuinely believe they know what's best for their workers.

There is a peculiar kind of self-flattery, mixed with self-justification, involved when people in charge believe they know what's best for those whose lives or livelihoods are within their control. The Walter O'Malley's of the world didn't lose money when the players organized, they made it, but they lost control, and that loss is what they regret.

S trangely enough, and with no connection to my column, within a week or so the Loews Hotel on Ocean Avenue agreed to a "card-check" election for its workers to decide if they wanted to unionize. I titled the following column, "Score One for the Grown-Ups."

DECEMBER 16, 2002

At a certain point during the news conference last Thursday at the Loews Hotel, the news conference at which hotel management, local and corporate, and the leadership of Hotel Employees and Restaurant Employees Local 11 announced their agreement for a new cooperative process to determine whether the hotel's employees want to unionize, I looked around and thought to myself, "Where's the guy in the Darth Vader suit?"

Lest we forget, the past several years of labor strife in Santa Monica owe a lot to the shenanigans that took place at the (formerly Sheraton) Miramar Hotel, starting in 1995, when management sought to decertify the union at what was then Santa Monica's only union hotel. New organizers had brought a more activist style to the union (then Local 814), which had been sleepy for years, and management responded by "encouraging" the workers, starting at the front desk, to seek decertification.

Ultimately, the hotel, among other things, required workers to attend "informational" meetings where the hotel's general manager donned a Darth Vader outfit to demonstrate to the workers the scariness of union leadership. In case Luke Skywalker's biological father wasn't scary enough, management printed posters depicting union leaders dressed up like Hitler.

Ultimately the decertification campaign became moot when Fairmont Hotels bought the Miramar. Fairmont had union hotels in other cities and saw no reason why they couldn't make enough money running a union hotel in Santa Monica. They quickly negotiated a new union contract. Score one for the grown-ups, but for every action, there is a reaction, and nothing energized the labor movement in Santa Monica like the effort to decertify the union at the Miramar.

At first the union made some missteps, trying to pressure the City not to allow Hotel Casa del Mar to take over the Pritikin site [on the beachfront], an odd tactic for a union that represents people who work in hotels, but ultimately the union hit on a better strategy. The strategy was two-pronged. On the political front, the union brought the living wage movement to Santa Monica to get the community behind the workers and show management that they could lose even if they prevented unionization. On the labor front, the union targeted key hotels—first Loews, then the Doubletree (and coming up, the

---

Four Points Sheraton)—where the union and their living wage allies could agitate and demonstrate. These hotels are owned or managed by nationwide chains that, like Fairmont, own or manage union hotels in other cities.

The union strategy has now paid off at Loews. Union and management have entered into a mutually respectful agreement that should lead to union recognition, collective bargaining, and a union contract.

I like *Star Wars* as much as the next middle-aged dad, but at the press conference it was a pleasure to be in a room full of grown-ups, with no Darth Vader in sight.

* * *

Congratulations to Richard Bloom on his election as our new mayor. I opposed his election to the City Council, and have opposed many of his votes, but on the dais Bloom rarely grandstands or goes rhetorical, and I won't deny that he's thoughtful. We should all wish him good luck—the next couple of years will be tougher for the City than the preceding several.

Council Members Ken Genser and Pam O'Connor told the *Lookout* before the mayoral vote that the council's votes for mayor did not reflect politics, but how the council members feel about each other, and about who they thought could best represent the City and run meetings. Specifically they said it wouldn't matter that Kevin McKeown, who expressed his desire to be mayor, was a Green Party member.

If who is mayor is not political, then why is the mayor always a SMRR member when SMRR has the majority, and not a SMRR member when SMRR is in the minority? In any case, I'm happy that we won't have another Green Party mayor the next two years. Not that I didn't think Michael Feinstein ran a good meeting—he did—but regardless whether O'Connor and Genser think it matters if our mayor is a Green, the Greens make a big deal about it, and that's enough to annoy me.

But perhaps annoyance clouds my judgment. Based on a bit of political theater that took place during nominations for mayor, it may be that not all Greens care whether a Green is mayor of Santa Monica. What happened was that when Ken Genser diplomatically suggested that the council split the mayoral term into two one-year halves, which would have allowed McKeown to have a turn, no one seconded Genser's motion—not even Feinstein, McKeown's fellow Green Party member.

Whoa. Word is that McKeown has said not-nice things about Feinstein in Green Party circles, and, of course, back in October 2001 there was that intra-Green Party spat when McKeown led the movement to scrutinize how Feinstein ran local Green Party finances through his back pocket. I expected that Feinstein and McKeown had buried

1917
Santa Monica voters prohibit alcohol sales in the city, 2,861 to 1,407,
and vote down annexation by Los Angeles 2,662 to 1,445.

the hatchet, given how chummy they were during the recent election, but now we know that there's room for good old political payback in the rarefied world of Green Party "grassroots democracy."

How reassuring.

O ne of the paradoxes of living in a city with left-wing government is that the business community, usually a town's fervent boosters, instead likes to talk the place down.

DECEMBER 23, 2002

Merry Christmas. The Chamber of Commerce was early by a week, but it gave Santa Monicans for Renters' Rights (SMRR) a big Christmas present—the chamber decided to break precedent and endorse candidates for the City Council. The decision is not surprising, as in the past few years more conservative members with more confrontational personalities have become more predominant at the Chamber.

On various issues, from preferential parking, to the homeless, to the living wage ordinance, to development, the chamber has been willing to take the City to the mat, which means opposing the political initiatives of the SMRR majority on the City Council. The rhetoric is not quite as vehement as that which characterized the battle over rent control, but the anger extends over many more issues.

The chamber seems to have forgotten how the City in the past twenty years, to a great extent under SMRR leadership, promoted the interests of local businesses and property owners, leading to the expansion of Santa Monica's economy, increased property values, more jobs, more retail sales, and ... a backlash against development. To an extent, this amnesia is understandable, as many of SMRR's more recently elected officials and appointed commissioners make it a point to insult business and property owners at every opportunity—to them, anything a business does is by definition not only motivated by "greed," but also inimical to the interests of "residents."

Particularly for developers, the City is a hard place in which to do business, but the chamber's rhetoric is overstated. The hard-liners in the chamber hyperventilate over issues—particularly the living wage and the homeless—that involve social issues far beyond the local business environment, while ignoring the nuts and bolts local matters where the City has bent over backwards to accommodate the concerns of local businesses.

For instance, the City is planning to spend a sack of money on more parking for downtown, mainly to benefit downtown businesses and property owners. The City has been eager to help the owners of Santa Monica Place to revamp their mall. The City has organized business improvement districts, the City has promoted itself as a tourist destination, and the City has organized major investments in infrastructure and facilities that attract customers. Even the transit mall, which some property owners later sued the City to stop, originated as a response to complaints from downtown businesses.

True, no-growthers SMRR elected in the '90s have managed to make life miserable for anyone who wants to build something, whether it be housing or a post-production facility, but in that context, the business community hardly agrees on what it means to be pro-business. Arguably the most anti-business decision the council made in recent years was the 5-2 vote against Target, yet the two votes in favor were SMRR council members—Pam O'Connor and Ken Genser. The crucial votes against the store were chamber favorites Herb Katz and Robert Holbrook.

If Katz and Holbrook, who complain these days about how long it takes to get developments approved, including the housing now planned for the Target site, had voted for Target, the store might have opened for this holiday season—bringing lots of business activity to Fifth Street, drawing pedestrians off the Promenade and sales taxes to the City.

Two of the chamber's least favorite council members are Michael Feinstein and Ken Genser. But who on the council is leading the effort to develop new zoning for the car dealerships? Feinstein. Who is leading the effort to "de-mall" Santa Monica Place? Genser.

Politics is a subtle art, and the chamber, particularly under the influence of the hardliners, doesn't seem to realize that it's a 365-day-a-year thing—not just a matter of elections. The chamber should be working to create a political climate that is favorable to business, to educate the electorate on the importance of continued economic progress.

Instead, the chamber prefers to "diss" the city at every opportunity, whether it's over the homeless, parking, traffic, or whatever. Luckily for business, the crowds keep coming—let's hope the customers don't listen to the chamber, or else they might decide Santa Monica's not a good place to spend money.

The chamber's move to endorse candidates will also be self-defeating, because it will play into the hands of the most anti-business elements within SMRR. The hard-liners pushing the chamber into politics don't seem to understand just how close SMRR came to electing all three council members this past election—just three hundred votes. The chamber might learn something from the police and firefighter unions. They regularly endorse SMRR candidates, such as Feinstein and Kevin McKeown, notwithstanding views on, for instance, the homeless, that are not an obvious fit. But by backing winners, the unions have benefited.

Judging by the current rhetoric, however, I wouldn't expect that kind of discernment from the chamber leadership. They seem hell-bent on an ideological confrontation—one they will lose.

1917/19
Pilots begin flying from Santa Monica Airport ("Clover Field"); the
airport is the oldest operating airport in Los Angeles County.

* * *

A while back I wrote a series of columns about design review. One point was how subjective it all is. In the "see what I mean" department, here's a quote from Planning Commissioner Geraldine Moyle from the commission's December 4 meeting: "To take as your measuring point what is really an ugly, abysmal, architecturally heinous piece of shit at the end of Wilshire Boulevard and to say that [yours] is only sixteen stories and that people can live there ..."

Moyle was responding to the owners of the Fairmont Miramar Hotel, who were presenting preliminary ideas for further developing their property at the northeast corner of Wilshire and Ocean, and who are seeking to enter into negotiations with the City for a development agreement. One of their ideas is to build a sixteen-story residential tower opposite 100 Wilshire, the twenty-story office building Commissioner Moyle referred to as "a piece of shit."

Moyle is entitled to her opinion of 100 Wilshire, even if the chair of the meeting should have asked her to apologize for her vulgarity. People on a dais have enough power without resort to the intimidating value of profanity. However, without agreeing or disagreeing with Moyle's opinion, or expressing any opinion about the new proposal, it's worth noting that the architect of 100 Wilshire was Cesar Pelli.

Pelli is one of the few "world-class" architects (to use a favorite Planning Commission adjective) to have designed a commercial building in Santa Monica. In fact, 100 Wilshire is one of only seven Santa Monica buildings of all types cited in *Los Angeles: The City Observed*, the architectural guide written primarily by noted architect Charles Moore. Moore and his fellow authors make the point specifically that the streamline moderne skyscraper "recalls the special character of the city."

One hundred years from now, Commissioner Moyle's opinion of 100 Wilshire, not architect Moore's, may be the generally accepted one. In the meantime, however, the dispute only underlines the care that the City's design arbiters—staff, ARB, and Planning Commission—need to take not to let their personal predilections prejudice them against someone else's architectural vision, assuming that vision can be executed in accordance with objective standards of quality.

The Christmas season turned out to be a good time to write about the homeless. After all, the nativity story celebrates a family seeking shelter. It's about the strangers in our midst.

DECEMBER 30, 2002

According to an article last week in the *L.A. Times*, cities all over the state and the country, starting with Los Angeles, are following Santa Monica's lead and enacting ordinances prohibiting sleeping in doorways. Los Angeles City Council Member Jan Perry introduced her ordinance the day after Santa Monica passed its ordinance in October, saying the "vast crush of homeless persons has exhausted our resources and strained our abilities to manage this problem."

"Exhausted our resources." Hmmm. The City of Los Angeles spends, on a per capita basis, a tiny fraction of what Santa Monica spends on homeless services. It seems that L.A.'s new policy of developing a residential downtown—admirable from a land use standpoint—has run up against its prior policy of using downtown L.A. as a last refuge, a.k.a. dumping ground, for the homeless.

The *Times* quoted the executive director of the National Law Center on Homelessness and Poverty as saying, with reference to Santa Monica's law, "there can be a domino effect, where city after city passes this type of ordinance." Funny that not too many other cities, least of all our big neighbor to the north, east, and south, have thought to imitate any of the programs Santa Monica has funded over the years to help treat and house homeless people, but they have jumped at the chance to replicate the one punitive program our City Council came up with.

The good we do is interred with the bones, of course, especially if it's expensive. The cheap, easy, and evil live after us.

* * *

When it comes to Christmas, I'm a thorough enjoyer, but as I'm Jewish, it's the secular aspects that I appreciate. I always make the rounds of friends' houses with Christmas trees, exchanging presents, and I adore Christmas lights. My wife grew up in a small western Pennsylvania town where the immigrants from all the different countries from eastern, central, and southern Europe had their own traditions, which they shared with

---

her Jewish family. To this day, she longs for the special lemon pasta the Sicilian families made.

One year we re-created a Sicilian Christmas Eve midnight supper, with about four courses of fish, including a big platter of fried seafood. That was great. A lot of work, but great. It's not just the food. Without, I hope, diminishing in any respect the religious significance the holiday has for Christians, let me express my appreciation for the message of tolerance and goodwill, home and family, that perfectly suits America's secular religion of equal rights under law and the dignity of all.

So, even if I do not celebrate Christmas, I am a great consumer of Christmas culture, although more of the popular than high variety. I have never attended performances of either *Messiah* or *The Nutcracker*, but every holiday season I listen repeatedly to the Phil Spector, James Brown, and *Hipster's Holiday* collections of Christmas songs.

This year, however, we had Philharmonic tickets for one of last week's performances of *L'Enfance du Christ*, Hector Berlioz's "sacred trilogy" about the childhood of Jesus. I had never heard of or heard this piece, but then, though I enjoy music immensely, what I know about music wouldn't fill an espresso cup. *L'Enfance* is a celestial work, and if it becomes a regular Christmas tradition at the Philharmonic, I will buy tickets every year. Berlioz's piece, which four soloists and a chorus sing, dramatizes moral issues that speak loudly to us today by telling the story of the state terror of the mad King Herod—the slaughter of the innocents—and the Flight to Egypt.

Mary and Joseph, escaping the terror with the baby Jesus, arrive in Egypt—strangers in the land. They knock on the door of an Egyptian house, and then the door of a Roman house, seeking shelter, and Romans and Egyptians rebuff them—"Away, vile Jews." But then they knock on the humble door of an Ishmaelite family, and they are welcomed as brothers and sisters. The Ishmaelite—not worrying that his resources would be exhausted—feeds them "milk and ripe grapes," and even provides Joseph with a job.

In short, *L'Enfance du Christ* is about homeless refugees, about a family that at that moment appears no more divine than a family of Central Americans who might have fled a dirty war to come to Los Angeles. It's about the strangers in our midst. After all, if the Ishmaelite had not answered the door, the Joseph family would have had to sleep in the doorway.

2003

In the aftermath of 9/11 and the dot-com stock market decline (which led to the City having to pay much more into the retirement fund for City workers), Santa Monica found itself in deep budget trouble. This was a shock for the City Council, which had increased the general operation budget 25 percent in the two boom years ending in 2001.

JANUARY 27, 2003

In an interview published in the *Mirror* recently, Santa Monica's new mayor, Richard Bloom, said that as mayor his "primary focus" will be the "economic picture." Last year when the City's budget crisis was looming, then mayor Michael Feinstein on more than one occasion cited the importance of the sales tax revenue the City receives from car dealerships, and how the City needed to develop zoning standards to keep them in Santa Monica.

I knew the City was in trouble, but if Richard Bloom and Michael Feinstein—both no-growth stalwarts—are talking about the economy, then we must be in trouble deep.

But it's hard to know what to make of this kind of talk. I would like to believe that the no-growth majority on the City Council—Bloom and Feinstein, along with Kevin McKeown and Ken Genser—have come to see benefits from economic growth, beyond balancing the City's budget, but I doubt it. Although they are aware that sales taxes come from sales, and perhaps aware that sales are generated by businesses that people invest in that sell to other people called shoppers using money they have earned at a job, my fear is that they only have a "cashbox" view of the economy.

By that I mean that the benefit they see coming from economic growth is strictly a matter of whether there is enough in the public till to cover the money they want to spend or, in the current situation, how much they have been spending. But the benefits

1920
Japanese village near Long Wharf condemned as unsanitary because
of sewage outflows; villagers establish new fishing village near San
Pedro.

of economic growth go beyond whether the City can hire more traffic cops and code enforcement personnel. The creation, accumulation, and investment of wealth, private and public, is what allows individuals to live better lives and what the public can marshal for public purposes.

In a region of have-nots and impoverished public services, in a city in which many live in poverty, economic development is a necessity, not a luxury. Previous city councils have understood this, but the current majority—until recently, at least—has taken the economy for granted, taking one action after another to frustrate investment in the city.

How might we know if they have changed their thinking? The first change might simply be rhetorical. If the no-growthers stop talking about "greedy developers," that would mean a lot. No-growthers use this kind of moral rhetoric as a smoke screen. The motives, good or bad, of developers and other entrepreneurs are irrelevant to the objectives of those opposed to growth, which are not to prevent developers from making profits, but to prevent developers from building new buildings to house new residents or new jobs.

Or sometimes, new students. Remember the no-growther opposition to Santa Monica College's bond issue? Since there are no "greedy developers" at the college, the no-growthers had to call the college a "bad neighbor."

Similarly, the council members (and planning staff for that matter) could lower the hyperbole by no longer referring to Santa Monica as "built out" when it clearly is not. Huge expanses of the city, in and along the industrial corridor, and up and down the boulevards, are lightly developed with buildings that in many cases look like they are ready to collapse.

Toning down the rhetoric would be nice, but rhetoric is not as important as how the City Council votes. Recently the council has given mixed signals. Although the council approved the Boulangerie site apartments and exempted certain affordable housing developments from discretionary review—actions that in any other town would be routine, but in Santa Monica were little short of courageous—when push comes to shove, the council tends to let fears about traffic trump the benefits of development.

The best recent example of this came back a few months ago when the City Council sent an excellent project, the expansion of the Lantana post-production studios, back to the drawing board, and possibly to oblivion, because of existing problems with cut-through traffic in the adjacent neighborhood. Still, the council's action was something of a "soft denial," and nearly all of the council members, in particular Feinstein, expressed chagrin that they could not bring themselves to approve a development that so ideally suited the light manufacturing and studio zoning the city had established for the district the property is in.

I hate cut-through traffic as much as the next person, but the way to deal with it is not by thwarting quality developments. Because so much of Santa Monica is zoned residential, it is inevitable that certain residential streets—particularly the few north-south streets that cross the freeway and go around the airport, and streets that feed them—will bear commuter traffic. But there are ways to deal with local traffic problems as traffic problems. Streets can be narrowed and blocked off. I live off Sixth Street, in Ocean Park, and to prevent traffic cutting through to Lincoln Boulevard, the City blocked cars from entering Sixth from Pico. The City narrowed Fourth Street and Ocean Park Boulevard. The impacts on the neighborhood have been reduced.

If we hold development hostage to traffic, the economy as a whole loses the benefits of development, yet traffic gets worse anyway because of sprawl.

F inancial problems or not, the eternal verity in local politics is always the squeaky wheel, and more often than not, it's the time-consuming, non-issues that get the grease.

FEBRUARY 3, 2003

Last week the City Council enacted an "interim" ordinance to prevent property owners in Sunset Park and the North of Wilshire area from building new houses, or expanding old ones, to the size permitted by current zoning. The interim ordinance applies in the two neighborhoods reduced zoning standards that the council enacted a few years ago, after a long process, for the North of Montana neighborhood.

According to the findings contained in the interim ordinance, the council had to pass it, instead of waiting for the results of a regular planning process (or, for that matter, waiting to see if the North of Montana down-zoning achieved its objectives), because "there exists a current and immediate threat to the public safety, health, and welfare should the interim ordinance not be adopted and should development inconsistent with the contemplated revisions ... be allowed to occur."

Okay, so what's new—the City Council declares an emergency to justify passing an interim ordinance. Big deal.

But according to the staff report, in the five years from 1997 to 2002, only sixteen homes in Sunset Park and fifteen in North of Wilshire were "redeveloped." That's just three per year in each neighborhood. There's no data, testimony, or other indication in the staff report that anyone found these "redevelopments" objectionable, let alone an "immediate threat to the public safety, health, and welfare."

The emergency down-zoning in Sunset Park and North of Wilshire is a perfect example of how our no-growth City Council dissipates the energies of planning staff by having them work on interim ordinances that address non-issues instead of real planning. What's even worse is that to declare these phony emergencies, the council forces planning staff and the lawyers in the City Attorney's office, who should have some professional standards (I hope they're being forced!), to validate this shameful junk-planning and to make law from these patently false findings, as if they're taking dictation.

The whole idea is to perpetuate a political culture of crisis and resentment—that we are under siege from "overdevelopment," that our neighborhoods need to be "saved," that change is to be feared—when the facts are quite the opposite. You would think the City Council would have learned after the "granny flat" debacle, when it had to pay out hundreds of thousands of dollars in legal fees because of similarly "cooked" findings, but then—who cares?

In the aftermath of the City's enactment of the ordinances prohibiting sleeping in doorways and restricting public "feedings" of homeless people in the parks, there was a lot of soul-searching in Santa Monica's left-wing community. Two stalwarts from the early days of Santa Monicans for Renters Rights, former City Council Member David Finkel and former City Attorney Robert Myers (who wrote Santa Monica's signature rent control law), gave a talk to the Democratic Club. The *Lookout* published the transcript, which engendered this column.

FEBRUARY 10, 2003

David Finkel's and Robert Myers' comments to the Democratic Club on the question of how progressive Santa Monica's government has been or might become weren't quite *Darkness at Noon* or *Animal Farm* material, but Finkel and Myers were there in the early idealistic days of renters' rights and it must be sobering for some people to hear how unhappy they are in year twenty-three of the revolution.

Finkel and Myers argue that leftists took power in Santa Monica on the basis of a progressive agenda—rent control—but then, once in power, winning elections became all important, and, ultimately, in Myers's words, they—Santa Monicans for Renters' Rights and the Democratic Club—elected a "bunch of technocrats" to run the city. Myers concluded by asking the Democratic Club how it could have endorsed Richard Bloom for reelection after he had voted for an anti-homeless ordinance.

What a town. If it's not the business and property owners complaining about how bad the homeless are for business (meanwhile, it's hello Levi's, hello Circuit City), it's left-absolutists complaining that Santa Monica's soul is in danger because the City wants to regulate how homeless people are cared for. And if you can't hear either the property owners or the lefties, it's because of the constant drone in the background about how our "sleepy beach town" is turning into a hellhole because of "massive overdevelopment."

All the complainers are wrong. Santa Monica is a better place than it was twenty years ago—both a better place to live and a place with a government that is more democratic and more attuned to social issues.

The problem with the Finkel and Myers argument is that their view of government is excessively "moral." Yes, one can judge the morality of a society by how it treats its most disadvantaged, but society is not the same thing as government, which needs to function for the benefit of the many, not just the deprived. To take just one example, both Finkel and Myers criticize SMRR's leadership in developing the Third Street Promenade. They

1921
Donald Douglas opens his first plant in Santa Monica in a defunct movie
studio on Wilshire Boulevard (the present location of Douglas Park).

may carp about the lack of community centers, or the sweatshop goods, but on any given night the Promenade is the most wide-open place in Southern California. All races and ethnic groups, all economic classes, mingle in peace—and have fun. Perhaps Finkel and Myers don't get outside of Santa Monica much, and they don't appreciate how extraordinary the mix on the Promenade is, but it's 180 degrees from where the rest of America went the past fifty years.

Finkel and Myers descend into silliness when they equate the progressiveness of a city with its foreign policy. Myers says that in the '80s Santa Monica was progressive, in part, because it opposed intervention in El Salvador and nuclear proliferation. Talk about window dressing. People who complain that Bush is distracting Americans from their economic woes by saber rattling in Iraq shouldn't then say that a city council that votes down jobs and housing is progressive because it opposes war.

But Finkel and Myers are right to this extent: Most of the good work in Santa Monica happened during the first ten years of left-wing rule (and the two years in the '90s when Paul Rosenstein was the swing vote on the City Council). In fact, I would agree with a lot of the Finkel/Myers critique if they would substitute the more accurate "no-growthers" for the misleadingly neutral "technocrats" in their identification of those the leftists elected to subvert their agenda. You can mark the decline of progressive politics in Santa Monica to the day in 1990 when SMRR endorsed Kelly Olsen for City Council.

After that, SMRR's most important swing constituency became people who think that traffic is not only a bigger issue than jobs and housing, but also the most important measure of civilization. SMRR's second most important swing constituency became the police union.

Whether Santa Monica is a progressive city depends on how it responds to the challenges it faces. While "progressive" is a word that has procedural connotations—civil liberties, for instance, or inclusiveness—ultimately, whether a government is progressive or reactionary depends on how it deals with substantive problems. In 1979, when various unusual market forces were conspiring to drive Santa Monicans of fixed incomes and limited means out of their apartments, it was progressive to use the regulatory powers of government to protect tenants.

Since then, whether Santa Monica has been progressive depends on how it has responded to the problems of the day—not the problems of twenty years ago. Between 1980 and 2000, the population of Southern California grew from approximately 12 million to approximately 17 million. The Southern California Association of Governments has projected, without controversy, that by 2025, or maybe 2030, our population will increase another six million, from 17 to 23 million.

If the current trend holds, most of this growth will come from what's called "natu-ral increase," the surplus of births over deaths, not immigration, meaning that most of these six million will be our children and their children. We can't stop the new Southern Californians from coming by not building them homes and schools, or by not investing in creating them jobs—they will already be here.

Dealing with this 35 percent population increase will be the great local issue of our time. Will we continue to sprawl and perpetuate all the problems—yes, including traf-fic—that we complain about? Will each city look after its own shortsighted interests, or will cities think, and act, regionally?

Whether we are progressive or reactionary will depend on how we respond to these questions.

So far, Santa Monica's response to these big problems has been reactionary. Popula-tion declined in Santa Monica from 1980 to 2000—in fact, Santa Monica was the only city of significant size in the region to lose population. While it was progressive to regu-late rents in 1979, it was not progressive to obstruct the building of new apartments after that, and we won't solve the problems of poverty by pumping up our police force.

At the core of progressive politics is the willingness to use government to solve prob-lems, but progressives must realize that taking that step is only the beginning. We must be constantly reexamining our premises. We must be thinking ahead.

We need government to solve big problems, to counterbalance private interests and to preserve fairness. Nonetheless, arguably our worst environmental catastrophe of the twentieth century, the damming and channeling of American rivers, and certainly the worst social catastrophe, the destruction of our cities and the building of segregated sub-urbs, originated in well-intentioned federal programs—the Bureau of Reclamation, flood control, hydropower, urban renewal, interstate highways, and the F.H.A.

The self-denominated progressive leadership of Santa Monica won't be progressive until it allows its own thinking to progress.

A s if on cue, the City Council ventured into foreign policy—the impending war in Iraq. Looking back, the fumbling the Council did on the issue is another sad reminder about how pathetic the national debate was before the invasion.

FEBRUARY 17, 2003

When people ask me if I'm against the oncoming war in Iraq, I have to ask first, which war? A unilateral, preemptive strike by the United States, without having persuaded anyone that Iraq has weapons that threaten us or its neighbors, with no plan for what to do with Iraq afterwards? (War #1.) Or a war under the auspices of the United Nations against a proven international outlaw, with an international commitment to follow through with Iraq's reconstruction, after having exhausted all peaceful alternatives? (War #2.)

I'm absolutely against War #1, but would I be in favor of War #2? Probably, although it doesn't look like I'll get a chance to support War #2, since War #1 is looking so likely.

Last week, a five-member majority of the Santa Monica City Council passed a resolution opposing a war in Iraq, but they were not exact about which one. Or, rather, they were clear that they were against War #1, but they were vague about War #2.

The title of the resolution was "Resolution of the City Council of Santa Monica Opposing United States Preemptive Military Action Against Iraq," implying that the City Council might support other than preemptive military action, and some of the council members who voted for the resolution made it clear that they were only, at this time, opposing a unilateral war.

However, when it came to the substance of the resolution, the "Be It Resolved" part, the council specifically declared its support for something called "House Concurrent Resolution 473." Council Member Pam O'Connor, who ultimately dissented from the resolution, asked that someone tell her what HCR 473 was before she voted, but no one did.

In fact, HCR 473 was an alternative Rep. Barbara Lee of Oakland proposed last September to the resolution Congress ultimately adopted authorizing President Bush's war-making powers. The operative language of HCR 473 called on the U.S. to "work through the United Nations to seek to resolve the matter of ensuring that Iraq is not developing weapons of mass destruction, through mechanisms such as the resumption of weapons inspections, negotiation, enquiry, mediation, regional arrangements, and other peaceful means." HCR 473, if it had passed, would have directed the administration to work through the U.N., but would not have authorized any alternatives that involved military force—U.N. authorized or not.

Ironically, the Bush administration did go to the U.N. as Representative Lee had suggested, "to seek to resolve the matter of ensuring that Iraq is not developing weapons of mass destruction." As a result, in November, two months after HCR 473 was buried in committee, the Security Council passed Resolution 1441, under which weapons inspections did indeed resume.

In other words, the City Council was so conscientious about opposing the war that it passed a resolution in support of a "House Concurrent Resolution" that was long out of date. (If council members had kept up with Representative Lee, they might have known that on February 5 she co-sponsored legislation to repeal Congress's authorization of the war.)

But the City Council's conscientiousness doesn't end there. The council resolution, which Mayor Pro Tem Kevin McKeown brought to the table, goes on to misstate HCR 473. According to the resolution, HCR 473 calls "for the United States to work through the United Nations to renew arms inspection, assure Iraqi compliance with United Nations Resolutions, [and] oppose unprovoked unilateral first-strike military action."

That's not what HCR 473 says. Compared to Representative Lee's original, the HCR 473 described in the City Council's resolution is more "hawkish," as, according to the City Council, HCR 473 expresses the desire that the U.N. assure Iraqi compliance, and only opposes "unprovoked unilateral" military action. The real HCR 473 contains no military option.

Perhaps this mischaracterization of HCR 473 means the City Council would support a War #2 after all. We may never know.

* * *

A week or so ago, there was a flap because someone at the U.N., so as not to have distasteful background images of wartime suffering embarrass the American diplomats arguing for war, covered the reproduction of Picasso's *Guernica* that hangs in the lobby of the Security Council. To me, nothing showed the emptiness of the Bush strategy more than this, although not for the reasons you might expect.

I grew up in a left-wing, anti-fascist household, in which the guiding principle for foreign policy was that in 1936 the western democracies failed when Hitler and Mussolini battle tested their weapons in Guernica. How many times did I hear my father say, "If we had gone to war in 1936 in Spain, then ..."

If the administration has proof that Iraq has weapons of mass destruction, or that Saddam Hussein is conspiring with Al Qaeda to attack us, then Colin Powell should be shining a searchlight on Picasso's painting, not covering it up.

Yet if the Security Council finds that Iraq has not disarmed, and if the Security Council has no peaceful means of ensuring compliance with its resolutions, and if the Security Council then authorizes military action, then there will be nothing immoral, or imperialistic, or racist in the world community joining together to rid itself and the Iraqis of a tyrant like Saddam Hussein, who has wantonly attacked the sovereign nations of Iran, Kuwait, and Israel; as well as Iraq's own populations of Kurds, Shi'ites, and the so-called Marsh People.

And if that happens, I hope someone brings a resolution to the Santa Monica City Council in support.

I n the spring of 2003 it was nearly impossible not to write about national affairs, as the juggernaut toward war picked up speed. In my own way of thinking, those of us on the left had our own measure of responsibility, because we had squandered the majority that should have been ours.

FEBRUARY 24, 2003

Last week, after I made fun of the Santa Monica City Council's foray into foreign policy, my wife accused me of being tougher on lefties than on conservatives. Maybe she's right. I am critical of people who call themselves progressive, but whose actions don't 100 percent fit my view of what progressive politics is or should be. Maybe they're right. Maybe I'm wrong. But in any case, why should I be hard on people who think they are doing good for the world, just because, for instance, they trivialize important issues—as they did last week with war and peace?

The reason is that I'm tired of losing elections.

I'm fifty years old. Until I was sixteen and watching the Democratic National Convention in Chicago on TV, I assumed that Democrats would always control Congress and that a Democrat would always be president. But then the Democratic Party self-destructed. Over a real issue, I'll admit, Vietnam, and after five years of assassinations and national turmoil, but since then Democrats have had a difficult time relating to the American electorate.

In 2004, when I turn fifty-two, of the thirty-six years since 1968, the Democrats will have occupied the White House only twelve. It's still inconceivable to me that Republicans control even one House of Congress—but now their control of both has become the norm.

Come on, guys, let's get this show on the road—I may only have twenty-five or thirty good years left.

Spare me the whining about the 2000 election. Sure Gore won it, but it should never have come down to five hundred votes in Florida. The real disaster was that in 1994, in the midst of peace and prosperity, our idiot savant Democratic President—still revered in many quarters—managed to lose control of Congress before the new Democratic era had barely begun.

Over the issue of health care! Our issue!

I'm still shaking my head.

By the way, after two years of Bush the younger, are we in agreement that there is a difference between Democrats and Republicans? Hello, are we? Already I can see the "true left" sitting out the 2004 election because John Kerry won't pour red paint on the capitol steps and chant, "No Blood for Oil."

What is most galling about the electoral fiasco is that culturally America has moved so far in the direction the Left wanted it to go. Five decades after the Blacklist, America—the people, not just the laws—are more tolerant, have fewer sexual hang-ups, have more respect for and give more protection to free speech and civil liberties than Lenny Bruce could have dreamed of.

I know, I know, it's all at risk because of Bush and his judicial appointments, but we also know that the crabbed and intolerant thinking of Bush's nominees—not to mention that of his attorney general—is out of sync with the culture at large.

Get this: in San Diego—San Diego!—they just elected a Jewish lesbian district attorney!

Even as the Right builds its political fortress in Washington, they are doomed to fight a losing rear-guard action against the expansion of personal freedoms throughout the culture. But how come, when the culture has gone our way, we leftists can't elect a government?

A couple of weeks ago, a friend forwarded me a speech the playwright Tony Kushner gave at an anti-war rally. Much of the speech consisted of calling George W. Bush names and equating the possible war in Iraq with the aggressions of Hitler and Mussolini. Here's a sample quote: "Most people, when they hear 'This Fratboy Plutocrat Blood-Grizzled schmuck of an inarticulate Rancher from Crawford Texas' say WAR WAR WAR, have a better idea, an answer, and now, all over the world, people are making sure that Bush, even Bush, hears their idea. And their idea, OUR idea, our answer to his WAR WAR WAR is PEACE PEACE PEACE."

What's the purpose of this kind of rhetoric? (And if I had a dollar for every useless "how stupid is Bush" joke I get by email I'd be rich enough to appreciate Bush's good points.)

Polls show that about two-thirds of Americans agree with Bush that it would be okay to invade Iraq, and that about 55 percent of Americans think he is doing a good job. But they also show that a good 60 percent of Americans—presumably including the one-third who don't think war is a good idea in any case—don't think we should invade Iraq without United Nations approval.

American opinion is not monolithic and Americans are open to argument, and if one's purpose truly is to stop the war, presumably by persuading the American people that war is not a good idea, does it makes sense, given that Americans tend to like Bush, or certainly, in these post-9/11 days, that they desire their president to succeed, to make

1924
The "Whirlwind Dipper," a bigger roller coaster, and the largest
ballroom on the West Coast, the La Monica, capacity 5,000, open on
the Santa Monica Pier.

insulting the President—and for that matter, attacking the whole of America's role in the
world—your primary rhetorical gambit?

What's the purpose—to score points for wit among left-wing friends, or to persuade
the rest of the country that you have a better idea? When Mayor Pro Tem Kevin Mc-
Keown floats an anti-war resolution before the Santa Monica City Council designed to
make him look like a good "progressive," and doesn't even know what his resolution
means, then if he is a representative of the Left, why should anyone take the Left seriously? Especially when, after 9/11, Americans have a legitimate worry about security?

These days, the Left must not forget, as it sometimes did during the later years of
the Cold War, that there are bad people out there. Yes, it was both stupid and wrong for
the U.S. to support right-wing regimes and subvert populist and leftist and democratic
nationalist regimes in the fight against communism, but if you don't believe it was good
that the wall came down, then what planet are you on?

It's not enough only to criticize the U.S. for the excesses of its policies—the Left has
to articulate alternative policies that will deal with the bad guys so that Americans believe
that the Left cares about the security of Americans. Those alternatives exist, but "PEACE
PEACE PEACE" is not enough.

N otwithstanding the action of the Santa Monica City Council, the United
States invaded Iraq.

MARCH 19, 2003

"In Berlin the Kaiser appeared on his palace balcony, dressed in field-grey uniform,
to address a tumultuous crowd: 'A fateful hour has fallen upon Germany. Envious people
on all sides are compelling us to resort to a just defense. The sword is being forced into
our hands ... And now I command you all to go to church, kneel before God and pray to
him to help our gallant army.'" —From John Keegan, *The First World War*

I don't generally accept seemingly easy historical parallels being drawn between the
history of others and the history of the United States. My belief in American exceptional-
ism, although not limitless, extends far enough to credit us, for instance, with international motives historically different from those that characterized our European historical
forebears as they extended their reach around the world with conquest and commerce.

However, after a cold peace of more than fifty years, not so many fewer years than
those between the last failed revolutions of 1848 and the failure of peace in 1914, I
wonder if September 11 will not be the Sarajevo of our time, as we seem bent on allowing events to carry us into an ever expanding conflict with our enemies in the Islamic
world.

I oppose this "preemptive war" on Iraq as immoral, and, partly because it is immoral,
because its goals, let alone the possible results, are so problematic and unpredictable.

That doesn't mean I oppose a war as immoral because it's preemptive. I would
approve a preemptive war waged under the authority of the United Nations. I wish the
U.N. had waged preemptive war in the early days of the Balkans conflict, or in Rwanda.
In this day and age, the only moral authority for waging a preemptive war must come
from international consensus, and, as cumbersome as the U.N. is, it's the only way to get
it.

"In this day and age," meaning a day and age when there is just one superpower and
we are it. It's not moral, nor is it prudent, to be us against the world.

Personally, I thought the saber rattling would lead to something good, like inspections that worked, or a tank commander in the Republican Guard who might grab his
main chance to end up on the victorious side and turn and drive on Baghdad. But the
Bush administration's timetable and the lack of nerve in the Iraqi armed forces have con-
spired against my naive optimism.

Now, what can—what should—we hope for?

We should hope for victory. Swift victory. We should not be embarrassed at the skills of our soldiers nor the force of our arms, even as we wish our leaders used them more wisely. The quicker the war, the fewer losses all around. While no one—pro-war or anti-war—has any special insight to predict the future, the range of possible outcomes skew much more toward the long-term good the shorter and more decisive the war is.

In fact, the future will to a great extent be foretold in the first few days of the conflict. If the Iraqi people rise up against Saddam Hussein and his regime, much as the Italian partisans took care of Mussolini themselves, or as the Romanians deposed Ceaucescu, then prospects for the future will be better. If, alternatively, the Iraqis resist our troops with anger and violence, or even merely greet them with sullen resentment, then the range of possible outcomes is bleak, and will become bleaker over time.

In that event, my prediction is that Americans will likely leave Iraq some years from now, the last of them lifting off by helicopter from the roof of our embassy.

Not having much influence on the president, I returned to my local beat and some regional issues.

APRIL 7, 2003

At a recent meeting of Santa Monica's Environmental Task Force (ETF), a representative of the Southern California Association of Governments (SCAG) presented the agency's projection that the population of Southern California will increase six million by 2030—the equivalent of "two Chicagos." Katherine Perez appeared before the ETF to encourage Santa Monica's participation in a series of "visioning" workshops SCAG will conduct over the next few months to gather ideas on what might be done to plan for this growth.

While "shock and awe" seem to be the most common reactions to SCAG's two Chicagos prediction, it should hardly be a surprise if the region's population increases by six million in twenty-five years, since it increased five million between 1980 and 2000. SCAG anticipates that at least half the amount of growth will come from "natural increase"— the excess of births over deaths—rather than from immigration. The 1990s were the first decade since the arrival of the Spanish that our population grew more from natural increase than from immigration.

This is important. Many Californians have railed for many years about how immigration has "ruined" the state, and this anger has increased as fewer immigrants hailed from Iowa and more from Mexico and points south and (far) west. I expect that SCAG hopes people will take planning for growth more seriously if they understand that most of the growth represents their children and grandchildren.

At the ETF meeting, however, Santa Monica Mayor Pro Tem Kevin McKeown took the argument in another direction. He suggested that advocacy of birth control should be part of the planning process. McKeown's point, as he subsequently explained it to me in an email, is that our planning efforts are based on the "supply side,"—i.e., we direct our planning energies to supplying enough infrastructure for whatever demand there will be, without trying, alternatively, to reduce demand by reducing population.

McKeown's ideas are misguided. There is nothing wrong with educating teenagers about sex and birth control and family planning. In fact, there is a lot that is right: the myriad reasons why young people should have the knowledge to make choices that will affect their own well-being as they become adults and raise families. But at the "macro" level, overpopulation is not the issue, neither locally nor globally. Demographers now predict that by the middle of this century, world population will be in decline. Already in

1924
World's first around-the-world airplane flight departs from Clover
Field on March 17. The four army pilots, flying Douglas World
Cruisers manufactured at Donald Douglas' Wilshire Boulevard plant,
return September 23 and are welcomed back by a crowd of 50,000.

Europe and Japan, the population is rapidly aging as births have declined below replacement levels. As the world urbanizes and develops, birth rates decline.

Locally, Southern California is one of the richest and most productive places on earth. Continuous population growth has presented constant challenge, but also constant opportunity. If you compare the problems we have here to the problems of cities that have stopped growing, you realize that the problems of growth are more manageable than the problems of decline.

For instance, traffic is terrible up and down the East Coast, where there has been little population increase, and they have the same urban and inner suburban problems we have—housing, schools, decaying infrastructure. At the same time, they have fewer economic resources.

While the Southern California megalopolis may appear chaotic and dystopic, the whole world looks here for inspiration. The wonderfulness of our urban life may be hidden behind the traffic, like the forest behind the trees, but we are the twenty-first century city, and it's because of our still dynamic growth. Complain as we all do, most of us wouldn't live anywhere else.

On a micro planning level, one has to ask what good it might do to include family planning in urban planning. What effect could these efforts have? If population increases five million rather than six, what difference could that have on planning? The only addition such thinking makes to planning is another rationalization for denial.

I do not mean to minimize the challenges continued growth will present. Just the opposite. Ever more people means that we must grow smarter—to manage our resources ever more efficiently, to manage growth so that it can be sustainable. Planning for growth used to mean subsidizing sprawl, with roads, schools, and other infrastructure.

Today our task is more difficult. In addition to resources that have traditionally been in short supply, such as water and clean air, we now face, in effect, a shortage of space itself as we choke on the cumulative negative effects of sprawl.

But there is no reason to throw in the towel and simply implore people to have fewer children. Instead we need to redirect investment to already built-up areas, so as to improve quality of life at the same time we make development more sustainable by increasing the efficiency by which we use limited resources. We can do it, although the obstacles, primarily political, are daunting.

Just consider the success of the long and ongoing battle against smog. There was the will, our predecessors found the ways, and nearly fifty years after the battle was joined, our air is much cleaner despite huge increases in population.

1925
Harry C. Henshey opens Henshey's, Santa Monica's local and independent department store.

We need to assemble our imaginations to devise solutions to analogous problems that only seem intractable, along with the will to make the decisions and investments needed to implement them.

Since writing my columns about Kelly Olsen's slandering the old Planning Commission and the planning department, I had tried to stay away from writing about the commission, but in April 2003 Olsen and the commission considered an issue that I couldn't ignore—the future of my Ocean Park neighborhood's corner markets. It's the kind of issue that defines local politics.

APRIL 14, 2003

"About six and a half years ago I entered this quiet and beautiful neighborhood, and operated this market in the past and I would like to operate it in the future." —Translation of the remarks of Hong J. Ahn, proprietor of the Mini-Mart at Seventh and Marine, at the Planning Commission meeting, April 2, 2003

As I have written before, it's always puzzled me how people who live in neighborhoods without corner stores typically panic at the idea of having them, while people who live in neighborhoods with corner stores panic at the idea of losing them. There is no good or bad here, no moral issue—it's just that people like what they are used to. Since my high school years, I've lived in neighborhoods with corner stores. I won't pretend to be objective. It's hard for me to imagine living somewhere where I can't walk a block or two to buy a gallon of milk or a six-pack of beer. When we have friends over for dinner, it's great to give the kids some money and send them out to buy ice cream.

I recognize the attraction single-use zoning has for people. People have an instinct for order, even if in real-life they rather enjoy chaos. This is not a progressive vs. conservative, or old fashioned vs. avant-garde issue. Modernists whose politics were radical liked the order of separating functions, as do traditionalists whose architecture is conservative.

Even people who live in and apparently enjoy neighborhoods made of diverse forms and functions can react negatively to the idea of more "disorder." For instance, neighbors who live on Second Street in Ocean Park, who acknowledge that they enjoy their proximity to the relative chaos of Main Street, insisted that developer Abby Sher, when she built the Edgemar complex on Main Street, include a big wall to separate them from the development.

What this separated them from was the charming "piazzetta" that Frank Gehry designed in the middle of the development. That sweet spot could have been part of their neighborhood, but now they have to walk around the block if they want to get a coffee from Peet's or an ice cream from Ben & Jerry's. What's the use of that? They still complain about noise from the parking lot.

When I moved to Beverley Avenue three years ago, the market at Fourth and Hollister became "my store." It's been in operation since 1925. That's fortunate, as it could not have been built even a few years later. In 1948 the City, following the trend to single-use zoning, decreed that stores in residential zones would have to close in twenty-five years. Fortunately by 1973, when the twenty-five years were up, something in the mindset had changed, and the City allowed markets to continue operation if they obtained conditional use permits.

My store, along with two others in Ocean Park, the Mini-Mart at Seventh and Marine, and the Fair Market on Fourth near Pacific, now need to have their conditional use permits renewed. For that purpose all three markets were the subject of the April 2 Planning Commission meeting. Planning staff wants to help the markets to survive, and proposed, among other things, amending the zoning law to give the Planning Commission and ultimately the City Council more flexibility in adjusting impracticable zoning requirements.

The hearing was interesting. The Planning Commission heard from about twenty neighbors. All of them wanted the markets to continue operation, without regard to zoning law limitations on store hours and the sale of alcohol. The neighbors were eloquent, speaking not only about the convenience the markets provided, but also the social benefits of having a place to bump into neighbors or to leave your keys for out-of-town guests to pick up.

The commissioners received a real lesson about how zoning rules enacted purportedly for the benefit of neighbors may in fact not benefit them at all. They initially had a hard time grasping the concept that sometimes actions taken and standards adopted in the past need to be revisited (as if that ever stopped them from voting down a development that was consistent with existing development standards), but ultimately came around and blessed the markets and sent them to the City Council for further proceedings

One issue was contentious, however—whether the City should allow the stores to remain open later, which they do now in violation of the zoning. Several of the neighbors mentioned this, and how convenient the late hours were, and this struck a chord with Planning Commissioner Arlene Hopkins. She asked staff the reasonable question whether there was any legal process available to fix the problem.

While usually commissioners treat each other with exaggerated courtliness, the same tone people use when talking to known psychotics, and allow each other to wander off in whatever tangents they want to go, something snapped in Commissioner Kelly Olsen.

He came down on Hopkins like a ton of glass block, accusing her, among other things, of not knowing the zoning code and wasting everyone's time by "thinking out loud."

This outburst came right after Olsen had ruminated for quite some time in a reverie of his own on an irrelevant "angels on the head of a pin" type issue regarding what theoretical change in the Fair Market's operation might be sufficient to trigger the need for a special permit for selling alcohol.

I'm not sure it was thinking, but it was out loud.

After the meeting, Hopkins confronted Olsen on the dais. Reliable sources report that they went at it, nose to nose, in the presence of other commissioners and staff, for more than five minutes. Hopkins let Olsen know that she didn't appreciate being lectured at.

Apparently Olsen forgot that the tone the commissioners use on staff, or applicants and their representatives, or members of the public they disagree with, is not appropriate to use on other commissioners.

As I wrote more columns, and learned more both about Santa Monica and urbanism, I began to see how issues in Santa Monica related to issues in the larger world. What I learned was not what I expected to learn. Like most people, I saw Santa Monica mostly through a lens of its specialness—the beach, the politics, etc. But the more I learned, the more I realized that Santa Monica and its history and experiences had a lot of relevance to other places looking for a "post-sprawl" future.

APRIL 28, 2003

The Southern California Association of Governments (SCAG) has begun its "Compass" process of envisioning what Southern California's future could be, taking into account a predicted six million increase in population over about twenty-five years. SCAG conducted one of the first Compass workshops last Tuesday evening at UCLA. Peter Calthorpe, the noted planner and "smart growth" theorist, led the workshop, and he began with a review of relevant demographic and economic data. A few numbers stand out.

While Southern California and its seventeen million people comprise the tenth largest economy in the world, meaning that, at that ratio of population to economic activity, we must be among the most productive people in the world, Southern California has much more poverty than other places. Our median income is about two-thirds that of the Bay Area, for instance. This explains our hugely unbalanced distribution of income and wealth, but the whole picture is not surprising in a region with so many hard-working but poor immigrants and first-generation Americans.

As these newcomers climb the ladders of skills, education, and income, they will become even more productive, and by accumulating their own wealth, the rising middle-class will create resources to solve the problems of growth. That is, if government organizes the infrastructure to make solutions possible and facilitates investment in those solutions, rather than, for instance continuing inefficiently to spend money subsidizing sprawl.

Another crucial piece of data is that fewer than 25 percent of American households now consist of two parents and children. What this means is that while the paradigm of the American Dream that still drives sprawl may yet be a detached house with a yard and a swing set, in fact there is a bigger market that could be sold on "urban living" if urban amenities were attractive enough.

After the preliminaries, workshop participants, who were seated at about fifteen tables, got to work. The task at each table was to distribute little stickers representing

1927
Ira C. Copley buys the Outlook along with fifteen other Southern
California newspapers owned by F.W. Kellogg. The local McClure
family later acquired the newspaper from Copley; still later the Copley
chain reacquired it

about three million new residents, about 1.4 million households, and 1.9 million jobs on big maps of the area running roughly from the northern Valley, down the coast through the central core to Ontario, and south through Orange County. It's not only that there will be six million more residents overall, but about half the growth in population and jobs will occur in the already most-highly developed areas, even if current patterns of sprawl continue. Contrary to stereotypes, the Southern California region is already one of the more dense in the country.

This is not surprising. Older cities that sprawl tend to "empty out," with little net regional population growth. Younger metropolitan areas such as ours and others in the Sunbelt and in the Third World, grow outward to accommodate net growth. But since the total cost of growth on the outskirts increases at the same time that raw land becomes scarcer, higher density development is inevitable as more growth occurs in older areas without vacant land.

What happens in Southern California the next several decades will be extraordinarily important, not only for us who live here, but for the world. Southern California invented the horizontal, automobile-based metropolis, and it's fitting that it is here that the model is first tending towards dystopia, at the same time that around the world newly industrialized countries are embracing the automobile and replicating our mistakes. Sooner or later they will be looking here for solutions to the problems they are now creating.

They may end up looking at Santa Monica.

People from outside enjoy characterizing Santa Monica and Santa Monicans as "latte liberals," and we Santa Monicans are prone to exaggerating whatever is the crisis du jour, but everyone may be missing the big picture. In the future Santa Monica may become best known as a livable model for the "post-sprawl city."

Events in Santa Monica presaged the trend of post-sprawl densification. The city densified in the '40s, '50s and '60s when apartments replaced single-family homes in many neighborhoods. Overall Santa Monica is comparatively dense for the region at 10,000 people per square mile, and, although that is not the region's highest density, there are neighborhoods in Santa Monica that are among the most dense.

Then Santa Monica evolved through many of the stages that marked urban decline in the post-World War II era, making the transition from small manufacturing town, to suburb, to decaying inner suburb in short order. Nor was Santa Monica spared the city-killing public works projects of the post-war era. The Santa Monica Freeway cut the city in half and displaced much of the African-American community, and urban renewal projects destroyed neighborhoods along the beach in the name of fighting "blight."

But Santa Monica not only survived densification, it thrived. In the '80s and '90s, Santa Monica developed a robust economy, converting from manufacturing to services

and retail. The City enjoys a rare triple-A bond rating, and has become a regional center of business and entertainment and an international destination for tourists.

Although we Santa Monicans complain as much as anyone else about all the indignities of life—i.e., traffic—our quality of life is such that our city has become one of the region's most desirable places to live. Real estate prices in some neighborhoods—significantly including dense areas where single-family houses coexist with apartments—are among the highest in L.A. County (and thus among the highest in the country). But Santa Monica is not an isolated pocket of affluence that has achieved its desirability by excluding the poor. Santa Monica's poverty rate is about the same as the national average, and 26 percent of public school children qualify for reduced-price lunches.

There is no downtown in the region that is more vibrant than Santa Monica's, and, significantly, in the past few years downtown developers have constructed or received approval to construct nearly one thousand apartments. Downtown could easily accommodate many times that number without exceeding a "European" height limit of five stories.

At the SCAG workshop, nearly all participants chose to place their growth stickers in already developed areas to preserve our remaining open space. Many low-density areas will need to grow to Santa Monican standards of density, and areas like Santa Monica will become even more dense.

As both "horizontal" cities around the world and first-generation sprawl cities in Southern California face the inevitability of higher densities, and as they look for something more, for an escape from sprawl, they could do worse than to consider how Santa Monica reversed the decline it faced in the '60s and '70s and achieved the success it has today.

A few weeks later, on vacation, I had the opportunity to travel to South Africa and see a little of the Third World. I also bought a digital camera and began illustrating my columns. I've included some of these photographs in the book.

MAY 27, 2003

Last year I wrote about how lucky I was that various relatives had houses in Italy where I could vacation at minimal cost. Well, my luck continues. After a visit to South Africa a few years ago, my wife's mother wisely decided that just what her extended family needed was to travel there together.

A couple of weeks ago I found myself on the world's longest non-stop flight, from New York to Johannesburg. We were only in South Africa for nine days, and five of those were at game preserves, so I can hardly claim to be any kind of expert. But it's a wonderful country. My mother-in-law travels a lot—Europe, Japan, Southeast Asia, China, you name it—but the only place she insisted her family visit was South Africa. That says something.

Nelson Mandela's cell on Robben Island

The South Africans we met—admittedly, not many, but they represented various racial, ethnic, and cultural groups—all seemed to share a quiet confidence about their future, even in the face of problems so huge that they make ours look trivial.

It's worth remembering that until forty or fifty years ago, America had its own version of apartheid. Restrictive covenants kept most neighborhoods white (and sometimes without Jews, either), and the FHA did not back mortgages in integrated neighborhoods. It's no accident that our suburbs are white and our cities are black and brown.

* * *

While I was gone there was news that was momentous, even epochal, in the history of Southern California. I'm speaking of the decisions by CalTrans, the MTA, and elected officials not to proceed with plans to widen the Ventura and Long Beach freeways. These decisions were so important that they escaped the California section and landed on the front page of the *L.A. Times*.

The decisions not to widen the 101 and the 710 mark the end of the freeway era in Southern California. CalTrans and the MTA are still spending millions of dollars to study the possibility of other freeway widenings and double-deckings—including for the 405. However, people are no longer willing to let freeways destroy their neighborhoods, as freeways destroyed cities throughout the country in the '50s, '60s, '70s, and '80s, to enable real estate development on the "outskirts of town." Nor are they gullible enough to believe that more freeway capacity will "solve" traffic.

It's hard to say what the alternatives to freeways will be. So far politicians and traffic engineers are planning to spend ridiculous amounts of money—hundreds of millions—on little fixes, to increase capacity at an on-ramp here or an intersection there. These will keep the highway bureaucracy and the paving contractors busy, but will do little or nothing to increase mobility, convenience, or quality of life.

The real future is for people to live closer to each other, so that they can both work and enjoy life without driving so much, and for us to invest more in public transit and freight rail to remove cars and trucks from the existing network of roads.

* * *

The most depressing news that I missed while I was on vacation was the resurgence of gang-related shootings in the Pico Neighborhood. Apparently, these shootings are racially motivated, or at least reflect the animosities between black and Latino gangs.

When we were in South Africa, one comment I heard more than once from whites was that the hostilities among the different black tribal groups, or between blacks and

the descendants of the slaves the Dutch settlers imported from the East Indies (the "Coloreds"), were as fierce as those between blacks and whites. While to a great extent this argument is a convenient rationalization and certainly ignores the "divide and conquer" tactics white colonists used for centuries, there was horrible violence between black groups in the years leading up to the 1994 elections.

What's important, though, is that although violent crime is still a big problem in South Africa, the communal violence—mainly Zulus against other blacks—more or less ceased after the first democratic elections in 1994.

While I don't mean to suggest too strong a connection between the politically incited violence of the pre-1994 years in South Africa and the atavistic violence between black and Hispanic gangsters in Southern California, maybe at the root of the crime and other problems that plague our disadvantaged communities is also a lack of democracy, or at least a lack of representation in the democracy we have.

It's hard to see much that government does in California—or anywhere else in the U.S.—that reflects the interests of poor people and their neighborhoods. For the most part, we have government of, by, and for them that's got, not them that have not. That's true in Santa Monica, too, where our elected officials are much more interested in discouraging "massive over-development" than encouraging investment in jobs and housing.

J une is budget-adoption time in Santa Monica, and in 2003, as in the prior year, the City was facing a big deficit.

JUNE 2, 2003

Americans dump on government, but we have an amazing tolerance for capitalism and all its brutal vagaries. I suppose this is rational, since on a macro basis capitalism has been successful at what it purports to do—create wealth—and specifically because it has been much more successful at doing so than those other more idealistic materialist systems that people have tried instead.

But the ups and downs of the "business cycle" show that those geniuses in the private sector aren't any smarter than the bureaucrats in government who bring us, day-to-day, a reliable product at a reasonable price. In some cases—public schools, for instance—the social return on the investment is better than that offered by the best mutual fund.

Some years ago, when I was more active in the film business, I used to invest occasionally in companies in the industry that I thought were well managed. I bought a little stock in New Line Cinema. A couple of years later, Ted Turner bought New Line—he liked the management, too. Turner was a capitalist genius who turned second-rate sports franchises into a media empire. He knew how to create wealth. Later, in another strategic move, Turner merged his company into Time Warner, and then things really started to click for my stock.

At one point my little investment had become serious money, and I appeared genius-like, too. The relatives who had bought New Line on my advice looked at me with new respect. Then Turner—the biggest shareholder in Time Warner—and the other genius capitalists there decided to sell the company to AOL, and did so based on the hugely overvalued price of AOL stock at the height of the tulip market, oops, I mean stock market. AOL Time Warner's stock price collapsed.

The most brilliant capitalists in America couldn't recognize a bubble when it was staring at them in the face.

I bring this up because at the moment capitalism is clobbering government. Governments at all levels except at the federal, where the government doesn't need to balance the budget, are facing huge deficits not only because of the "slowdown" in the economy, but also because of the stock market "correction."

Here in California, when the stock market was booming, governments increased their commitments to pay pensions to their employees. These commitments were easy to fund when stocks were up, but require hard cash now that the market is down. The biggest

Amelia Earhart and nineteen other female pilots depart Clover Field
for the first women's cross-country air race.

---

factor in the City of Santa Monica's deficit is not the slowdown in the economy. Tax revenues, in fact, are stable. The biggest hit is a $7.3 million increase in one year in the amount Santa Monica must pay into the state's public employee retirement system. The increase over two years is $11.4 million—about 10 percent of the City's annual general operating budget.

Santa Monica isn't alone in having bet on the stock market—the *L.A. Times* ran a story last week about how Orange Country has to come up with $734 million to fund its pension fund obligations.

I don't mean to let City officials off the hook for believing the good times would never end—I've reported before how the City Council irresponsibly increased the City's operating budget 23.4 percent between 2000 and 2002—but then if I had sold my Time Warner stock in 2000 my retirement would be more secure now, too.

A fter the school district's parcel tax failed to achieve the required two-thirds vote in the November 2002 election, the district came back to the voters with a smaller version on the June ballot. It passed—barely, but it passed.

JUNE 9, 2003

To appreciate how hard it is to get two-thirds of the votes in any election, consider that only on a couple of occasions has a presidential candidate even approached two-thirds of the vote. Sixty percent is a landslide. Nonetheless, until recently school bonds and parcel taxes passed easily in Santa Monica and Malibu, garnering up to 80 percent of the vote. Even in March 2002, Santa Monica College's bond issue passed with nearly 70 percent.

Then last November, EE, the $300 parcel tax, failed with 61 percent.

With a tremendous effort by supporters to identify "yes" voters and get them to vote, Measure S, the new $225 parcel tax, just passed with barely the required two-thirds.

It would be reassuring to think that the recent caution of local voters merely reflects the bad economy, or the anxious discontent that has overtaken the country since 9/11, but there's a local angle. Last week I received an email from a reader who thought that my arguments demonizing the opponents of Measure S were "one dimensional." This reader happens to be one of the more perceptive people in Santa Monica (i.e., he usually agrees with me), so I didn't take his words lightly. I won't identify him, because he works for an organization somewhat dependent on the City, but he's a renter and on a budget. This is some of what he had to say, after telling me he was voting in favor of the parcel tax:

> But I do understand what the 'NO' campaign is drawing on. ... I don't think its adherents should be written off generally as cold hearted.
>
> Imagine someone who loves renting in Santa Monica. They're gladly struggling to do just that, both tolerant of and at the same time overexposed to the homeless they perceive as surrounding them, working through nonstop city construction projects and dealing with these frustrations because this is nonetheless a very special place to live.
>
> Then they are hit with the argument that the city spends millions on homeless services that keep those people exactly where they are, right outside the door. They're told the city's social agenda has swallowed vast amounts of

money that could have been spent on schools. They're told the city spends endlessly on projects which in the end ... no one seems to want, again expending money that might have gone to the school district. ...

Finally they are told that "S" is going to divide the burden of supporting the schools equally by three, renters, the visually opulent businesses of Santa Monica and Malibu and the homes in the Malibu hills and north of Montana. It's suggested that if renters were to say no, 'I'm not cleaning up this mess,' that the city would have to reallocate funds from perhaps homeless services.

It's an easy argument to get caught up in. And it isn't going to go away with "S."

I'll stick to my guns about the cynicism of the right-wing nihilists who tarred the schools with the City's brush, but they would not have got so much traction if the perception wasn't out there that City Hall is out of control. I'm not going to bash every decision the City Council has made. Certainly their capital spending has been good, notwithstanding all the construction, and we'll ultimately be happy with the results.

But the City Council has done us liberals a great disservice, because they did just what conservatives blame liberals for doing—spending and taxing. It's hard to exaggerate how irresponsible the spending has been. The City Council thought the boom would never end—certainly not in Santa Monica, as if Santa Monica were separated from the rest of the world.

They increased the operating budget by nearly 25 percent in two years.

They hired myriad new employees to do useless tasks to make certain noisy constituencies happy. Sixteen, for instance, to direct traffic downtown.

The worst example is the Planning and Community Development Department. Its budget increased $5.24 million, more than 70 percent, between the 2000 and 2003 fiscal years. The City Council hired sixteen more planners and building and safety and code enforcement personnel.

Why? The City Council and the planners will say it's to keep up with "massive overdevelopment," but that's a myth. Since 2000, building permit fees in the aggregate have remained virtually the same, and the number of plan checks and the total value of plan checks have declined, respectively, 19 and 15 percent.

No—these new employees exist only to keep up with busy work City Council members create to flatter their own obsessions. All these employees have pension plans, too, and in the glow of the stock market, the council increased pensions, and now with the market down, we have a huge bill for that. All those employees need places to work, so the City needs to rent more office space.

As for anyone out there who blames the homeless and those who try to help them for the City's problems, be advised that the increases in the grants for human services over the same time period are relatively trivial—about a million dollars.

Another thing—the council fought development so vociferously that Santa Monica has lost forever the benefits of the investment that naturally accompanies a boom. The Target store alone would now be contributing at least a million to the budget annually.

Staff now proposes, among other things, that to balance the budget the City stop cleaning parks on weekends or holidays. In the midst of a gang war, the City will cut evening drop-off hours at the Police Activities League. Is it any coincidence that the City will cut the number of outside-contracted parks maintenance workers but not the number of regular staff? Is working for the City of Santa Monica a lifetime entitlement?

The consensus regarding the budget was that no one was at fault. The consensus did not include me.

JUNE 23, 2003

"Perhaps the greatest impact of the new economic and fiscal situation following a resource- and service-rich decade, will be mustering the discipline necessary to continuously and closely prioritize expenditures and services, to scrupulously evaluate the costs and benefits of current programs and to resist calls to throw money at problems."
—From Santa Monica's City Manager Susan McCarthy's message to the City Council transmitting this year's budget.

It's good someone in Santa Monica government sees the forest, but even the redoubtable Ms. McCarthy sees only part. The City's problem is not throwing money at problems; it's throwing money at non-problems.

The school district had a real problem—deteriorating schools. We voted twice to throw money at the problem, and now our school buildings are worthy of their purpose.

Our sewers are in bad shape. I'm happy the City is throwing money at them—even if I wonder why they repaved so many streets in recent years if they were just going to rip them up again.

Government needs to spend money, but the reason we have a huge budget deficit is that our City Council throws grease at squeaky wheels. I can't get over the fact—and I'm going to write about it again—that the City increased its permanent payroll about $800,000 to direct traffic downtown.

It's not easy to determine how much the City spends on directing traffic downtown. The amount is part of a general traffic services budget, which in turn is part of a $6.5 million piece of the police budget called "Office of Special Enforcement." To get an accurate number, I contacted Police Chief James T. Butts Jr., who informed me that the fourteen employees the City hired when the City Council voted to do something about downtown traffic—ten traffic service officers, two motorcycle officers, one communications operator, and one staff assistant—cost the City just under $800,000 in salaries and fringes.

Chief Butts also made a strong case that his department was spending the money the City Council appropriated prudently. For instance, to maximize flexibility, instead of hiring specialized employees only to direct traffic, the Police Department combined the new employees with the existing pool of parking checkers (there were originally twenty-

one), and trained them all to both give parking tickets and direct traffic. It was also the chief's view that by hiring new employees on a regular basis, the City was saving at least as much as it would otherwise be spending on police overtime to direct traffic on, for instance, busy summer days.

So what's my problem?

My problem is that the question is not whether the City is spending money well, but whether the money is well spent. Santa Monica doesn't have enough money to throw $800,000 at a problem that doesn't bother many Santa Monicans. What? Isn't traffic Santa Monica's biggest problem? Won't downtown customers and tourists stop coming if they see brake lights on Fourth Street?

Those are the reasons the City Council gave for spending the money, and the regulars at public hearings complain a lot about traffic, but as I have written before, when the City conducts its annual residents' survey, fewer than 20 percent of Santa Monicans mention traffic as one of the "most important issues facing the city." It's true that when asked specifically about traffic, most Santa Monicans, along with most people in the modern world, describe traffic as a serious problem. But when Santa Monicans complain about traffic, they usually complain about traffic in their own neighborhoods and along slow-going east-west arterials and north-south cross streets, not traffic congestion near the Pier on a summer weekend—something Santa Monicans know to avoid.

In the last residents' survey, as opposed to the eighteen percent who mentioned traffic as a major problem, 62 percent of Santa Monicans reported they use the parks. I suspect that if it came to spending $800,000 a year to direct traffic downtown or to maintain parks, most Santa Monicans would choose the parks.

What about downtown? Don't we need all those customers to pay for everything? Yes, but there's no indication that traffic scares customers away. All the popular spots in Southern California have lots of traffic. Even on a weekend, Santa Monica is relatively easy to get to, into, and out of—no worse, certainly, than Hollywood or Universal City. If you want to avoid traffic, you can spend your weekend in downtown L.A., but few people do.

It's dangerous for a columnist to make operational suggestions, but might this be where those twenty-one original employees of the traffic division come in? It was a great idea to cross-train them in directing traffic, as it's smart to have the flexibility to use them for both purposes. When confronted with the issue of what to do with weekend traffic, the City Council could have avoided hiring new employees by making do with the employees the City already had. ("Making do"—what a concept.)

1933
Long Beach earthquake on March 10 destroys many of Santa
Monica's schools.

There are many other examples of throwing grease on squeaky wheels, but my favorites involve planning. No wheel squeaks like the no-growth wheel. The City over two years increased the budget of the planning department by millions, and hired nearly twenty new employees, with special emphasis on code enforcement and to deal with the myriad new ordinances and emergency moratoriums and studies and discretionary reviews the City Council mandated to impede growth.

These are the reasons why Santa Monica's deficit is sixteen million dollars and Pasadena's is four and why it's annoying to hear city council members bemoan the economy and whine about how they wish they had more money for schools and other good things.

They spent it.

If you follow local politics anywhere in America, probably everywhere else, you know that nothing gets people going more than parking. In Santa Monica, one of the enduring issues is the battle over preferential "permit" parking districts.

JULY 7, 2003

I have ideas about preferential parking, but they're contradictory. Schizophrenic. My anti-car urbanista persona likes preferential parking because any limitation on parking is a disincentive for people to drive, and nothing encourages driving like the availability of parking. For instance, if because of resident-only street parking, employees must find parking farther away, or even, heaven forbid, have to pay for it, then some of them may find another way to get to work.

At the same time, however, my fairness persona thinks it's outrageous that residents can take over the streets for their own purposes—and for a measly fifteen bucks a year! Especially residents who already have garages and driveways.

I say no permits for anyone who has a garage full of junk!

Preferential parking also upsets my amateur economist persona, who is appalled by how many spaces go to waste on blocks with preferential parking. When my office was at Twelfth and Colorado, the streets nearby were residents-only, and half the spaces were empty during the day when local employees, clients, and customers couldn't find parking.

Then there is the shopper in me who gets angry when he can't find a place to park because the streets are limited to residents. (But then my urbanista personality gets indignant and tells the shopper he should have taken the bus.)

All these personas listened closely when the City Council, on June 24, debated a new plan for dealing with parking on the blocks on either side of the Montana shopping district. Five blocks in this area, all single-family blocks north of Montana, have already achieved preferential-parking status. The blocks are off-limits to nonresidents from nine to nine, except that on some blocks nonresidents may park for one hour. Predictably, the preferential parking on those blocks pushed traffic to other blocks, and residents on four of them, two north of Montana and two south, have petitioned for preferential status.

City staff came to the conclusion that this piecemeal process was not solving the problem, merely pushing it around. They examined the parking situation in detail and found that as a whole there is enough parking in the area for residents, employees, and shoppers although parking tends to bunch up in various "hot spots." Staff proposed to

make a preemptive strike against parking Balkanization and create uniform rules for the whole eighteen-block area. While residents on individual blocks would still need to petition to establish preferential parking on their blocks, the rules would be the same for everyone in the district, and the standards would be such that individual districts would not merely shift parking around.

At the core of staff's idea was that throughout the area residents in preferential districts would have priority only on one side of each street, leaving the other side open to everyone—residents, visitors, and employees. The concept makes sense because the demand for parking is fluid. Residents leave during the day for their jobs, employees arrive, customers come and go, then most of the employees leave by the time residents return. At all times, residents would have priority for half the spaces, which seems fair enough.

I am happy to acknowledge that the council member who "got" the concept better than any other was Kevin McKeown, normally the member most reactive to the most simplistic demands of residents. While the churlish cur inside me wants to say that even a broken clock is right twice a day, McKeown did his homework and deserves to be commended. McKeown had toured the area and concluded that staff's analysis of parking demand was accurate. He spoke eloquently about how preferential parking merely pushed parking demand to the perimeter, creating more demand for preferential parking.

Unfortunately, if he had been a little more persuasive, McKeown might have got Herb Katz, Pam O'Connor, and Michael Feinstein to vote for trying out staff's plan. Katz and O'Connor usually vote against all preferential parking, but this time O'Connor was open to the one-side-of-the-street proposal, and Katz might have voted the same way if it would have made a difference.

Michael Feinstein had good instincts, but instead of voting to give staff's proposal a try, he pushed a proposal for allowing employees to buy parking permits if parking were available. There is nothing necessarily inconsistent between the one side of the street plan and employee permits. Feinstein and McKeown ended up voting with Ken Genser, Richard Bloom, and Robert Holbrook on a compromise plan that mostly benefits residents. They rejected the one side of the street proposal, but allowed more liberal two-hour parking throughout the district.

The winners are residents, the survivors are shoppers (including movie-goers at the Aero, who presumably will be able to park at 7:01 p.m. and not get a ticket), and the losers are employees, who will need to park north of Alta. Again to highlight my own conflicting views, I have to admit there were arguments in favor of this plan, too. One

c. 1933
New Douglas plant adjacent to Clover Field produces DC-1's and
DC-2's for TWA. DC-3 leads to dramatic increases in production.
Number of workers at Douglas increases from 965 to 4,300 between
1933 and 1936

can imagine how, because of employee parking, the one-side-of-the-street proposal might not work, if employees arriving in the morning occupy all available spaces on the non-preferential side and keep them all day. The urbanista in me says that there is nothing wrong with employees having to walk a block to work, but I wonder if the residents north of Alta won't soon be petitioning for their own preferential district.

The root problem is that parking is a finite resource, not cheap to create, that people want for free. So long as residents can park on the street for free, or for fifteen dollars a year, they are not going to clear out their garages. So long as employees and customers can park for free, they're not going to park in the pay-lots or structures. London recently began to charge motorists five pounds a day for the privilege of driving into the city. This was controversial, but so far it's dramatically reduced congestion.

Michael Feinstein has the right instincts when he wants to develop an employee parking permit program: What we need to do is start charging a price for parking that reflects its value. If residents want to control all the parking on their streets, then they should pay for the privilege. Parking permits should be roughly equivalent to their value—say forty dollars per month. The same should go for employees, and, for that matter, customers, who want to park within a block of busy streets like Montana. You don't need cumbersome meters these days to do this. In Europe there are various systems in operation where motorists can buy parking in advance and then use it as needed, such as by displaying a card on the dashboard.

There was no rush to solve this problem—most blocks in the area have not yet petitioned for preferential parking. Given the complexity of the issue, and the high emotions, the best thing the council could do would be ask staff to research more options, including pricing options.

In July my family vacationed at my parents' place in Italy. The columns I write from Italy are fluff, but readers say they like them.

JULY 14, 2003

My parents live half the year in a farmhouse they fixed up down a dirt road from a village in the Umbria region of Italy. It's about two hours from Rome, two hours from Florence, but miles from nowhere in most directions. Some years ago my parents adopted a stray dog. They named him Lorenzo, as he appeared at their door on the feast day of San Lorenzo. Although not in any respect a "pet" person, I've always had some affinity for Renzo—I'm a lucky dog myself for having parents who decided to spend the summers of their retirement in Italy.

I have also appreciated that Renzo has the right idea about how to spend a day in the country—a walk in the morning, a walk in the evening, and lots of lying around in between.

Renzo

Renzo has appeared to be an average dog in all respects. His pedigree is indeterminate. Knee-high, his head a little small for his body, his mottled white fur not quite shaggy, not quite short, Renzo has always impressed me as the canine equivalent of a utility infielder. On the other hand, Renzo did learn, in middle age, a few words in what must have been

c. 1934
In the aftermath of the Long Beach earthquake, with Santa Monica
High School a tent city, the City permits the construction of rudi-
mentary gymnastics equipment on the beach for the use of Samohi
students.

a second language—"sit," "down," and "paw" in English. Not much worse than how much Italian I've managed to pick up in twenty years of sporadic learning.

Unfortunately, Renzo is aging fast. His eyes are misted with cataracts, his hearing is selective at best, and, worst of all, he recently underwent surgery for a tumor. Yet, late in his game Renzo has shown that he is some dog. We underestimated him from the start. In retrospect, the signs were there, if only—as with so many things—we better understood the locals.

When my parents first adopted Renzo, they were informed by Fausto, the village's *guardia della caccia*—guardian of the hunt—that Renzo was a hunting dog and that because of that, my parents could not let Renzo run free at any time outside of hunting season. The reason is to protect the young pheasants the hunters plan to shoot once the season starts. (During the season, dogs may run wild—apparently the pheasants are fair game for all species.)

The idea of Renzo—Renzo of the short legs and the little head—as a hunter has always amused me, but it is true that no dog ever lunged more viciously at a lizard or looked more ruefully at a startled bird rising from the brush by the side of the road. Yet, it turns out that Renzo has a skill that far surpasses an instinct for chasing pheasants or wild boar. Renzo is not a mere hunter, he is a gatherer.

Renzo is a truffle dog.

This part of Umbria is black truffle country. Truffles grow around the scrub oaks that grow in the *macchia*, the mass of weed-like trees and vines and thorns that takes over when the village farmers abandon rock-filled fields and olive groves to take jobs that pay cash. Where fields are marginal, as around our village, farming and raising sheep—after thousands of years—are on the way out. Italy has stringent laws protecting the rural landscape, and it's near impossible to build a new house outside of existing towns and villages, so farmland has no development value either. The local landowners are gradually selling their fields to vacationers—such as my parents.

My parents have acquired about fifteen acres of land, about half of which is *macchia*, and in truffle season about five every morning a car or two of truffle hunters and their dogs lumber down the dirt road past their house. Truffle hunters—as well as hunters of game—have free access to private property, as, under the law, one cannot own the products of nature. (Truffle hunters are, however, subject to other laws. For instance, the only tool they can use is a hand spade with a small blade—apparently designed to prevent a hunter from indiscriminately excavating the area around an oak tree.)

Occasionally—only occasionally—a truffle hunter will give a few of the precious fungi to my parents. This happened once during one of my visits, when I came to the

1935
In the depth of the Depression, the Santa Monica Amusement
Company, operator of the Looff Pier adjadent to the Municipal Pier,
declares bankruptcy. The La Monica Ballroom becomes a roller rink.

profound realization that no truffle tastes so good as a free truffle. Only when truffles are free does one feel justified in using them with the abandon that becomes them, because you really haven't tasted truffle until you've tasted a lot of truffle. True, as my father says, they taste like mud, but it's tangy mud and kind of addictive.

Which brings us back to Renzo.

A couple of months ago, my father took Renzo for a walk down to some *macchia* he bought two years ago and which he has been trying to clear, gradually, to free the old olive trees and grape vines that are now buried in brush. Renzo started sniffing the ground, intently, and scratching, and in a moment he was chewing on something. My father bent down and looked closer, and realized that Renzo was chomping on truffle.

That started it. Nearly every evening now my father takes Renzo for a walk in the *macchia*. Renzo keeps his nose to the ground, and when he gets serious, there's a race to see if the truffle will end up in the human's hand or the dog's mouth. You may have heard that the advantage of hunting truffles with dogs rather than the pigs the truffle hunters use in France is that you don't have to give the dogs any truffle to encourage them. Perhaps trained truffle dogs will find the truffle and simply "point," happy to wait for a dog biscuit or even just their master's approbation, but that doesn't go for Renzo. Given a moment's advantage, he'll eat the truffle himself.

After all, he's an old dog.

The first night we arrived on this visit I tried my hand at truffle hunting with Renzo. It's not easy. Renzo gets excited, and he likes to drag you through the brush. If you want to find truffles, you go along to the extent possible, which means squatting down to Renzo's height and doing your best Chuck Berry "duck walk" imitation, all the while trying to avoid the thorns. We found two truffles that night. There's nothing complicated about cooking with them. We chopped them in the food processor with olive oil and poured the "sauce" over pasta.

Of course, before we ate, we raised our glasses and toasted Renzo—Renzo of the unexpected tricks.

A few days after I wrote about Renzo, Santa Monica unfortunately was in the news even in Italy. An elderly man ran his car through the crowded Wednesday Farmers Market, killing ten people and injuring scores.

JULY 21, 2003

In one of my favorite books, Nathaniel Hawthorne's *The House of the Seven Gables*, there is a character, Clifford, who has been in prison for thirty years. When he is released, he learns about the telegraph from a man Clifford meets on a train. The man on the train tells Clifford that the telegraph will be a great help in catching bank robbers and murderers. This dismays Clifford. He tells the man that something as "immaterial and miraculous" as the telegraph should be reserved for the use of lovers, to "send their heartthrobs from Maine to Florida," or for purposes such as informing an absent husband that he had become a father, so that his child's "little voice" could echo in his heart.

Being nine time zones away from home, I thought of Hawthorne's telegraph, as Santa Monica's grief trickled to me by way of email and websites. As Clifford says, "Is it a fact—or have I dreamt it—that, by means of electricity, the world of matter has become a great nerve, vibrating thousands of miles in a breathless point of time?"

When I first heard about what happened Wednesday at the Farmers Market, after the initial horror, imagining the scene in a place I know so well, my concern was for the safety of my friends. Emails and phone calls went back and forth. Along with everyone back home, I waited for the coroner to release the names of the victims, and as I write this on Friday, I'm still waiting with dread to hear about the injured.

We all know this feeling. We would rather sympathize with someone else's grief than grieve ourselves, yet in our minds we know that the total amount of grief released by a tragedy will be the same, no matter who mourns.

As it turned out, I didn't know any of the dead, but then, reading of them and looking at their photographs on the Internet—vibrating thousands of miles away—I felt as if I knew them all, or at least had seen them around. It was as if a computer programmed to identify a random set of members of our community had selected a perfectly representative sample.

Surely, Santa Monica has never had a worse day.

Theologians and philosophers have long contended with the existence of bad things. Natural disasters and disease have made religious people question the benevolence of God, the evil deeds and moral evils of human beings have made everyone question the

c. 1936
Santa Monica builds a tumbling platform, rings and parallel bars
south of the Pier. Large crowds appear to watch gymnasts and bodybuilders, who include Vic and Armand Tanny, Joe Gold, Jack LaLanne,
Harold Zinkin, "Pudgy" Stockton, and Relna Brewer. By 1939 the
area is referred to as "Muscle Beach."

goodness of humanity. They all try—we all try—to get a grip on that question popularly posed as "Why do bad things happen to good people?"

In the Hebrew Bible, the basis of so much of the world's tradition, the prophets admonish their people to mend their own ways, to please an angry God. That attitude continues in many Christian churches as well, and in other religions, too, such as Islam, often coupled with the idea that since we cannot understand God, we don't know his bigger plan.

To me, this thinking has always seemed unfair both to humanity and to what in Hawthorne's day was often called Providence. Is it possible to believe that the victims of disasters, natural and human, have anything to explain about their lives? And what right do people have to project their human failings—anger, wrath, retribution—on the deity?

Certain philosophers have tried to shift the burden of evil to humanity, positing that however innocent humanity was in its natural state, the coming together to create civilizations unleashed social forces that caused bad things to happen. Another kind of philosopher says that we cannot explain the world and we should resign ourselves to that, and that any thinking beyond skepticism—any ambition to explain things better—will only make matters worse by leading us into superstition or fanaticism.

Let's face it, it's hard to understand such things as a man living a good, long life, only to make a wrong turn into a catastrophic moment of confusion, and equally hard to comprehend such things as a mass of people doing that most innocent and beautiful thing, shopping at a farmers market, only to be consumed by catastrophe. To me, there is no explanation beyond the horrible coincidence that if there are an infinite number of days of perfect happiness at, for instance, farmers markets, and an infinite number of people who are fallible, such as elderly drivers, then, sooner or later, there will be a disaster.

Solace comes from what we do. Do what we can to prevent future similar catastrophes. Heal those who are injured, and welcome them back to our community.

And remember the dead. Yes, grieve for the future that has been lost. But most of all, remember the joy they gave their friends and family in life, and the happiness they enjoyed themselves.

The Farmers Market accident was something like Santa Monica's own 9/11, without, of course, the murderous intention. Everyone was reeling. But sooner or later, you get back to everyday concerns. For me, that meant Kelly Olsen, but now I had the chance to gloat over his fall. In a 4-3 vote, the City Council did not elect Olsen to a second term on the Planning Commission. Michael Feinstein, who had supported Olsen four years earlier, changed his mind and cast the deciding vote. Although I doubt I had much influence over Feinstein, given that he had so often voted contrary to how I had hoped he would vote, I believe that my columns about the commission established a political context in which Feinstein could vote against Olsen.

JULY 28, 2003

I returned from Italy Wednesday night, so I missed the memorials and the reopening of the Farmers Market. I took my own walk down Arizona Thursday. For what it's worth, I agree that "the markets must go on," even if the sight of them in operation might trigger tears and anxious memories among the survivors and those who mourn.

But, as some farmer put it, the vegetables don't stop growing.

* * *

The removal of Kelly Olsen from the Planning Commission was a great day for the city, but now I'm going to find it hard to criticize City Council Member Michael Feinstein, since he cast the deciding vote against Santa Monica's demagogue of the discontented. I was in Italy when Olsen's ship ran aground—on vacation, relaxed, thinking only good things about the world. For a brief, mellow moment I considered that the classy thing to do would be to write another column about my parents' dog and leave Olsen alone.

As I said, the moment was brief.

I kicked Olsen when he was up. Don't I have the right to kick him when he's down?

Olsen and I now have something in common—we have both been un-reappointed to the Planning Commission. We could start a club of the "dis-appointed" with former commissioners Kathy Weremiuk and Anthony Loui. Come to think of it, it would be a lot more fun to go out to dinner with just Kathy and Tony and not tell Olsen what res-

taurant we're meeting at, and have a good meal and not worry about whether more than 25 percent of our tab is for alcohol.

There was much blather said and written about Olsen before and after the vote, starting with the assumption that he represents residents. I know a lot of residents, and most of them think Olsen is a loudmouthed hypocrite.

Did Olsen represent the residents who wanted their corner stores open early and late? The residents who wanted another Trader Joe's? The residents who wanted Target? The residents who want a residential downtown, or more apartments in Ocean Park, or the Madison Site Theater? Who don't think five stories equal "canyonization?" The residents who don't think Santa Monica is descending into hell on a flood of alcohol?

Even so, it wasn't Olsen's views that made him so terrible. There are many no-growthers in Santa Monica who wouldn't disgrace the city if they were on the Planning Commission. But Olsen is a bully. Throughout his tenure on the commission, Olsen accused the planning department—and the prior Planning Commission—of corruption, of making decisions "behind closed doors," of "rubber-stamping" the wishes of developers.

Olsen went out with a flourish, saying that the City Council's vote against him "sends a pretty clear message to the Planning Commission, the planning staff, and to residents that corruption and gross mismanagement in the planning department will be tolerated by the City Council."

Olsen never produced a shred of evidence for his charges. China was lost, so Joseph McCarthy made a career out of saying Reds controlled the State Department. Buildings were built in Santa Monica, so Olsen makes a career out of saying the planning department is corrupt.

After the vote on Olsen, I got an email from a friend expressing the hope that civility will now return to the commission and politics. My response was that in a democracy the presence of civility is important, but not as important as the absence of fear. As one of the few people willing to criticize Olsen in public, I can't tell you how often people thanked me for doing so, meanwhile expressing their reluctance to do the same, fearing retribution from Olsen or his political backers.

Over the past four years the planning department, petrified of Olsen's sneer, has stopped planning. They don't advise developers any more about how they could improve their projects—i.e., they don't do their jobs—because they are afraid Olsen will accuse them of connivance.

At the first commission meeting after Olsen's demise, Commissioner Jay Johnson moaned that the commission was losing Olsen's "institutional memory." What a joke.

1937

Sit-down strike at Douglas Aircraft plant ends when 340 sit-downers evacuate after police equipped with machine guns surround the plant.

True, Olsen took over a commission that had no institutional memory, because soon after his appointment Ken Breisch and John Zinner resigned, and all the other commissioners were new. But Olsen filled the void not with "memory," but with his own fantasy of how the planning system should work, namely that the process should revolve around the subjective judgments of the Planning Commission, rather than, for instance, the law.

Central to this vision was that the commission ruled staff and could treat them like dirt—an "institutional memory" that was appealing to his fellow commissioners but which had nothing to do with law or the mutual respect that had previously governed relations between staff and the commission. For all Olsen's piety about transparency, he continually tried to manipulate the process, whether by badgering staff, or encouraging appeals from the Architectural Review Board, or organizing opposition to projects on which he might later have to vote.

Weirdly enough, the people who seemed most in fear of Olsen were the other members of the Planning Commission. I wonder if their spouses and significant others have noticed lower levels of stress in their mates now that they don't have to share a dais with a ticking time bomb. The other commissioners were always glancing over their shoulders to see what Olsen would do next, and watching the Commission's current Chair, Darrell Clarke, trying to deal with Olsen was like watching an anxious grandmother trying to mollify the eccentric in the family so he won't ruin Thanksgiving dinner.

Three words come to mind: "battered commissioner syndrome."

Without Olsen badgering them, this commission could be good. For all the commissioners' happy talk about "consensus," Olsen lost many votes six to one or five to two. And don't forget that it must have been psychologically grueling to vote against Olsen, since whenever he lost a vote he would retreat into his patented condescending pout— sort of naked aggression on the verge of tears.

There is a potential good nucleus on the commission of Barbara Brown, Darrell Clarke, and Arlene Hopkins. They at least realize that the place is not Levittown and the time is not 1955. I don't know much about the new guy, Terry O'Day, but in his first action he persuaded the commission to let the Architectural Review Board do its job on a project, rather than micromanage the design, and that's a good start.

Jay Johnson often has his heart in the right place, and could be good if he ever read a book about urban planning. Even Julie Lopez Dad could be good if she recognized that her fellow humans sometimes make mistakes and/or sometimes have needs and concerns that are legitimate even if they are not hers. As for Geraldine Moyle, I'll say nothing and hope that she continues to skip as many of the commission's meetings as possible.

S anta Monica experienced a perfect NIMBY storm in August 2003 when the City announced plans to convert an empty commercial building near a freeway on-ramp into a drop-in center and housing for the homeless.

AUGUST 11, 2003

Although the Eskimo may have many words to describe "snow," we, as has been said before, have many words for lying. We can lie, prevaricate, dissemble, falsify, fib, perjure ourselves, deceive, equivocate, distort, obfuscate—and that's just a partial list of verbs. They all come to mind—and quite a few nouns—because the easiest way to get a handle on the controversy surrounding the plans of the City and the Ocean Park Community Center (OPCC) to convert the derelict building at 1751 Cloverfield—at the corner with Michigan—into a facility for housing the homeless and providing them with services is to examine the falsehoods and exaggerations that have been the fuel for so much hysteria.

1. Misrepresentation. The opposition to the new center comes mostly from the Pico Neighborhood Association (PNA), but PNA is hardly representative of the neighborhood. A couple of years ago I researched a column on neighborhood groups and learned that PNA had all of about 125 household memberships. The PNA board members who have most vociferously opposed the OPCC project—Peter Tigler, Don Gray, and the rest of the right-wing nihilists of Citizens for a Safe Santa Monica (CSSM)—are the same people who lead the opposition whenever the schools or Santa Monica College ask the voters for money, and the opposition to anything Community Corporation of Santa Monica tries to build in the way of affordable housing. Yet whenever the voters of Santa Monica have the chance, a majority votes in favor of the schools and the college, and in favor of building more affordable housing.

2. Distortion. Although the site is within the boundaries PNA claims for the Pico Neighborhood, the site is not in any "neighborhood" if you consider the common meaning of the word. The site is surrounded by commercial and industrial uses, the nearest residences are 800 feet away, about as far as one can get in Santa Monica from residences, and the freeway is between the site and the residences. The lies in the "public service" video PNA and CSSM produced to oppose the project would be comical if they weren't so vicious. Edison Elementary is not "around the corner," but on the other side of the freeway, a half-mile from the site. Grant Elementary is not "three blocks away," but at least five, and more than two-thirds of a mile. The Ralph's grocery store is, yes, "yards away"—about 300, and on the other side of Olympic. The site is not "a block"

211

1938
With WPA funds Santa Monica builds a new City Hall (still in use)
on land (the old train depot) acquired from the Southern Pacific in
what will become the Civic Center.

away from "your neighborhood park," but several blocks and about 1,500 feet, if you're talking about Virginia Avenue Park.

3. Obfuscation. Opponents of the project say that it will bring skid row to Cloverfield and bring homeless people into their neighborhood. But, as opponents of homeless services always remind us, our neighborhoods are already filled with homeless people. Santa Monica already has a problem with homeless people sleeping wherever they can find some shadows. The Pico Neighborhood has this problem and so does mine. But we're not going to do anything about it unless we build facilities like the one OPCC is proposing, which will provide long-term housing for homeless people working to get off the streets, and services for others making the transition.

4. Exaggeration. Opponents argue that the Pico Neighborhood has an over concentration of homeless services, but that's not quite the case. Most services that deal with homeless people directly off the street are located downtown, including three of OPCC's operations (including the one that has to move), the Salvation Army, and SAMOSHEL. Two service providers, Chrysalis, on Lincoln, and the Clare Foundation, on Pico near Lincoln, operate on the edge of the Pico Neighborhood, but neither of them deal primarily with clients coming off the street—Chrysalis finds jobs, and Clare works with both housed and homeless alcoholics and addicts.

OPCC operates transitional housing programs on Sixteenth Street north of Broadway next to its administrative offices, but even though this area is historically considered part of the Pico Neighborhood, the freeway and the industrial strip north of the freeway separate it from the Pico Neighborhood as generally understood. There are also privately funded mental health and sobriety programs that do not receive City funds operating in the Pico Neighborhood, but they do not deal generally with homeless people off the street.

5. Over-simplification. Opponents also argue that Santa Monica is once again spending its money to provide services to the homeless that the rest of government—other cities, the county, the state, and the feds—refuse to fund. There is some truth to this, in that other governments don't spend enough on services for homeless people, but it's not quite true that Santa Monica is spending its own money on this project. Most ($4.7 million) of the $7.4 million in housing funds the City is providing comes from bonds the City's redevelopment agency issued against incremental property tax revenues generated within two Ocean Park redevelopment projects that were created more than forty years ago.

These projects now include the Santa Monica Shores apartments and the Sea Colony condominiums. While the history of these projects is fascinating—involving the worst of 1950s-era "urban renewal"—the steady and sometimes spectacular appreciation in

1938
Tony Cornero's gambling ship, the Rex, operates off the Santa
Monica coast; 300 agents of the State of California close the Rex in
1939 in the "Battle of Santa Monica Bay."

the value of Ocean Park real estate, and in particular the recent sale of Santa Monica Shores, have led to a huge increase in the value of the "tax increment" the Redevelopment Agency diverts from the treasuries of the City, the County of Los Angeles, and the State of California.

While one can argue that it's terrible for redevelopment agencies to be able to skim all that tax revenue from other governmental agencies, particularly from the schools, the fact is that all the money that the Redevelopment Agency is using for the OPCC project is tax-increment money, and only a small amount of that would have gone to the City if the redevelopment projects didn't exist. Under the law applicable to those redevelopment projects, the City did not need to use the tax-increment money for housing, but awhile back the City Council made the reasonable and right decision to dedicate 100 percent of the money to affordable housing—a reasonable and right decision because so many low-income people lost their housing when those blocks near the beach were "urban renewed."

Seventy-five percent of the OPCC project will be housing—housing for formerly homeless people making the move from the streets to their own apartments. Some people have argued that a better use of housing money would be to build more low-income apartments. There are, however, other ways to build housing for people who can pay at least some rent, but no one other than service providers like OPCC is going to build housing for people who absolutely can't pay for it. That's why the OPCC project is an appropriate use of the Redevelopment Agency's housing funds.

6. Calculated hysteria. As all opponents of anything do, PNA and CSSM have raised the usual cry about the City trying to do something in the dead of night, without notice to anyone, without "process." Yet notice was given to everyone around the site, various commissions and the Chamber of Commerce have considered the project (albeit, hysterically), and now the City Council is going to conduct a wide-open hearing.

This is the process.

So what do I think about the OPCC project? My views are mixed. Cloverfield is a busy, even brutal street, with cars racing to and from the freeway. The site is not convenient to where most homeless people are, and I wonder if the location is the best imaginable from a therapeutic standpoint for people trying to get off the streets. But if John Maceri and the rest of the staff at OPCC, who know more than anyone else in town about how to deal with homeless people, are willing to use the site, if they feel it's the best available solution, then I'm not going to second guess them.

I don't consider myself soft on the homeless issue, unless believing that homeless people are human and deserve to be treated as such constitutes soft. I believe that it's inherently dangerous to sleep outside in an urban area, and since the criteria for civil commitment includes being a danger to oneself, I believe government should use its powers of civil commitment to get people off the streets.

Of course that would mean spending money that most people in our "greatest civilization of all time" and certainly all right-wing nihilists don't want to spend.

We have seen fit to tear down the flophouses that used to house the binge drinkers who did much of the menial and seasonal labor that no longer exists, we've closed the mental institutions, we've not built enough housing because we're afraid of urban life, and we've built nothing to take the place of all those beds. We don't like the situation, but it's our own damn fault.

No site is going to be perfect for providing the kind of services OPCC provides to Santa Monica's homeless population. But it's important to realize that all of us who believe the homeless are a problem are OPCC's clients, too.

About ten years after I first involved myself in Santa Monica politics, in connection with the City's plans to redevelop the Civic Center, a milestone was reached when the City opened its new Public Safety Building.

SEPTEMBER 2, 2003

In *Brunelleschi's Dome*, the author Ross King detailed how the city of Florence marshaled the engineering and artistic genius of Filippo Brunelleschi to build *Il Duomo*, the great dome of its cathedral. No one had constructed anything like the dome since the ancients had built the Pantheon in Rome and Santa Sophia in Constantinople. Brunelleschi, starting in 1418 when he won the competition to design the dome, had to invent, or reinvent, how to build it.

Brunelleschi's incredible accomplishments were not what impressed me most when I read the book. What knocked me out was that the city authorities way back in 1367 had decided to build the dome—which would be the world's largest—neither knowing how to build it, nor having the technology to do so. And the voters of Florence—the population of which was less than that of Santa Monica today—approved the plan in a referendum.

I bring this history up to give some perspective on the nine years it has taken from the passage of the Civic Center Specific Plan to last week's opening of the Public Safety Building. On one hand, compared to the time it took medieval Florence to build the Duomo, nine years is quick. On the other hand, Santa Monica didn't have to reinvent the dome.

I got my start in Santa Monica politics as a citizen participant in the Civic Center planning process. That was in 1992. A few years after that I was a co-chair of the campaign for the Public Safety Building bond issue, which garnered almost—but not quite—the two-thirds vote needed to pass. So I have a lot of personal history with the Civic Center and the Public Safety Building, and it felt good to attend the building's opening. The planning process now seems long ago, and the original plan underwent revision after the City purchased most of the Rand property. Yet things get built, and it's fascinating to see the area take shape mostly "according to plan."

The main question for me is whether the low densities of the buildings in the area, including the Public Safety Building, the Maguire Partners building on Ocean, Rand's new offices, and the housing that is planned—will be enough to animate the area. Although the densities are much like those of a suburban office park, I am hopeful that the Civic

1942
In the aftermath of Executive Order 9066, Santa Monica's Japanese
and Japanese-American population is interned at Manzanar in the
Owens Valley.

Center will become a lively place and a worthy center of civic life. I am hopeful for two reasons.

One is the mix of uses. The public buildings—City Hall, the Public Safety Building, and the courthouse—will always be a draw for the many people who have business with government, including at night, when the City holds city council and commission meetings. The private office buildings—Rand and Maguire Partners—will draw daytime workers and visitors. The Civic Auditorium is intermittently a big draw, and someday there will be a big park with a soccer field at the corner of Pico and Fourth, ensuring lots of people on weekends. The housing, even at the reduced scale of the revised plan, will one day provide a twenty-four-hour presence.

The other reason I'm hopeful about the area is the design. While up until now the buildings in the Civic Center area have been notable for how isolated they are from street and sidewalks, the new buildings emphasize connections to the street. The Public Safety Building is accessible to the public from the street, not from a parking lot. When built, the new parking structure across Olympic from the Public Safety Building will bring retail— stores and cafes—to an area that now is devoid of any kind of public amenity.

The esplanade and Olympic Drive facing west: waiting for the trees to grow.

Good urban design just doesn't happen. Everyone in the city except the no-growthers who obstinately opposed the Civic Center plan should be proud about the product of a very public process.

1939
Santa Monica voters prohibit oil drilling in the city.

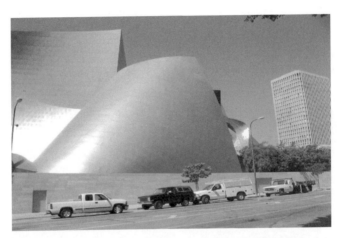

The First Street side of Walt Disney Concert Hall, facing the Music Center

If you want to see the alternative to good urban planning, take an architecture trip to downtown Los Angeles, something I did few weeks ago when my mother-in-law was visiting. She's a big fan of Frank Gehry's Guggenheim Museum in Bilbao—she's been there twice. We decided to spend a day being tourists in L.A. so that she could see Gehry's new Walt Disney Concert Hall, as well as the new cathedral, designed by José Rafael Moneo.

These are two fantastic buildings that are, in the architectural context, something like the Duomo in Florence, at least for our time and place. But what the Florentines could do six hundred years ago that our greatest architects seem incapable of is to design big buildings that connect with the street on all sides. The Duomo, of course, has been the center of life in Florence since it was built. It is surrounded by intersecting, densely developed streets, and by pavements that are always full of people. Although Los Angeles is rebuilding Grand Avenue to create what looks like good open space in front of Disney Hall, and the cathedral's wide open plaza is wonderful, both Disney Hall and the cathedral present blank walls to the public along most of their perimeters.

When it comes to creating a real city, Disney Hall and the cathedral are little more than the false fronts of a movie set. After showing my mother-in-law the new architecture of downtown L.A., we parked near Union Station and took the new Gold Line to South Pasadena for lunch. Then we grabbed another train to Pasadena. We had a delightful time walking around Old Town, eating ice cream. As is happening in downtown Santa Monica, lots of people are moving into downtown Pasadena.

Santa Monicans, count your blessings. In the future, when you drop in at the Public Safety Building to pay a ticket you'll be able to walk off some of the annoyance on the esplanade, or maybe bump into a neighbor or two, and sit outside and have a coffee.

The Temple Street frontage of the Cathedral

A nother murder in the Pico Neighborhood and I turned my attention back to childrearing.

SEPTEMBER 8, 2003

Another young man, Jalonnie Carter, 19, is dead, in Santa Monica's ongoing, simmering, gang war. With all the shots and near killings this summer, it was inevitable that someone would soon die. Okay, so our local saga of meaningless death can't hold a candle to all those people around the world killing each other for principle, but after all—this is Santa Monica, wealthy and progressive. Shouldn't we have solved this one by now?

What makes a young man "drive by," or "lie in wait" to shoot down another young man in the street? Can we dismiss gang violence as atavistic and throw up our hands? There are many places in the world where young men don't kill each other for turf. Why can't Santa Monica be one of those places? I agree that it's important to solve the ficus tree problem on Yale Street, but let's have a sense of proportion: young men killing each other is our biggest civic problem.

Freud wrote, "civilization (was) created under the pressure of the exigencies of life at the cost of the satisfaction of the instincts." When I had a toddler, what impressed me most of all was just how hard it was to get this civilization thing across to him. No, no, and more no, for about five years steady. Now he and his friends are thirteen. It seems that no matter how civilized your six year old is, you start over at puberty. How could the young men who are killing each other now in Santa Monica and Venice and Culver City have been thirteen only six years ago? Didn't we know enough then not to let this happen?

In our community, the people most in charge of channeling excess adolescent hormones into civilized behavior are the teachers and administrators of the school district. Two years ago John Deasy arrived and promised that the district would increase the academic performance of our disadvantaged students. At least according to the latest standardized tests, the district is making significant progress. The ultimate test will be if today's gains at the elementary level can be sustained through middle school and into high school, but the big point is that concerted effort and targeted interventions will lead to results.

Meanwhile, the scores show that as the scores of the historically lower achievers increase, so do the scores of the historically high achievers. For instance, as the percentage of black and Latino students who were proficient in English increased to 48.6 and

48.2 percent from 29.6 percent and 26.4 percent respectively, the percentage for white students increased to 83 percent from 70 percent.

Speaking as the parent of a middle-school student who has all the educational advantages from two parents with advanced degrees to his own desk and computer, it's important to say what should be obvious but which is sometimes forgotten, namely, that the best way to give high achievers the means and the challenges to achieve even more is to raise the overall level of achievement.

Other adults in our community who have a lot of contact with raging hormones are the volunteers who coach youth sports. Saturday was the start of Santa Monica's American Youth Soccer Association (AYSO) season.

I never played organized sports when I was a kid, but I've become a believer as a dad. You've heard all the horror stories about obnoxious parents and coaches, but you know what—you can find more boorish behavior in a random sample of freeway drivers than the same number of people at AYSO or little league.

But let's face it—even adults who aren't violent are screwed up. The youth sports experience is partly about burning off excessive youthful energy and partly about giving kids experience dealing with adults and all their inconsistent and irrational behavior. I coached soccer for six or seven years and I shudder to recall how many times I told defensive players in one breath to spread out and play back and give ground, and in the next to be aggressive, and go for the ball. Sometimes I'd tell the offensive players to make long passes. Sometimes I'd tell them to make short passes.

Oh, and by the way, I yelled at them a few times. Really blew my top. It's amazing how difficult it is to persuade a dozen thirteen-year-olds to stand in a straight line.

The good thing about sports is ultimately the kids learn that they have to go out and make their own judgments about when to give ground, or go to the ball, or when to kick it long and when to kick it short, and that there are consequences if they make the wrong decision.

My problem with youth sports is that the programs stop too soon. Somehow we think that when kids reach age sixteen, unless they are on the high school team, they don't need sports anymore. Participation in sports leagues drops off precipitously after age fourteen—just when kids most need an environment to compete harmlessly and a place to burn off that excessive energy.

Or they will, literally, start killing each other.

Could Santa Monica and other local cities organize "town leagues" of local young people between, say, 17 and 25, to compete for their cities or neighborhoods in soccer, basketball, and baseball?

When the economy declined after the dot-com boom, California, which had been rolling in money, suddenly found itself in budget trouble. Gov. Gray Davis found he had little political capital after a narrow reelection victory in 2002, and the recall was born. Arnold Schwarzenegger became governor. I wrote some bigger picture columns in response.

OCTOBER 13, 2003

"Schwarzenegger's overwhelming victory quieted previous speculation that Democrats might immediately launch a recall campaign against the new governor." —L.A. *Times,* October 9, 2003.

Please, no more recalls, but ... an "overwhelming victory?"

As of Saturday, with 100 percent of precincts reporting, the No votes on recall—the equivalent of voting for Gray Davis—totaled 3,668,076, or 44.7 percent of the 8,204,338 cast. On the second part of the ballot, Arnold Schwarzenegger had 3,850,804 votes, or 48.7 percent, of the approximately eight million votes cast for whom should succeed Davis. That's a difference between Davis and Schwarzenegger of only 182,728 votes, less than 2.5 percent of the total number of voters who chose either Davis or Schwarzenegger.

Or consider this: 4,536,262 voters voted Yes to recall Davis. If you assume—and it's a reasonable assumption—that at least 95 percent of Tom McClintock's 1,053,907 voters had voted Yes before they voted for him, and you subtract that 1,001,211 from the total Yes vote, that leaves only 3,535,051 Yes votes available to vote for Schwarzenegger. Even assuming all 3,535,051 voted for Schwarzenegger, that means more than 300,000 of Schwarzenegger's 3,850,804 voters originally voted for No on recall—meaning that more than the margin of difference between the once and future governors preferred Davis.

It's true that the 55-45 vote against Davis was within the realm of what in American politics is considered a decisive, if not landslide, margin. But before Karl Rove decides to pump lots of President Bush's 2004 resources into California, I expect he will reflect not only on Schwarzenegger's equivocal results, but also that the same voters who rejected Davis rejected anti-affirmative-action Prop. 54 by nearly two-to-one.

Aside from an overwhelming sense that Gray Davis was a political lifer who deserved to be paroled, I don't see anything overwhelming about the election. If anything, I see more mixed signals. California is still a Democratic state, but only because the Republican Party rejects the social values of Californians. If the Republicans ran more candidates who were pro-choice, pro-gay rights, reasonable on gun control, and spoke passionately

1944

Employment at Douglas Aircraft in Santa Monica reaches 33,000.

---

about education and opportunity—assuming they could find any such candidates outside of Brentwood—then California would be a Republican state.

Because as it is now, those people the Democrats consider themselves as representing, don't consider the Democrats to be their representatives, except when it comes to issues of personal freedom and general fairness. People who believe the biggest problems in California are the problems of working class and poor people currently dominate the California Democratic Party. I agree, but the decisive voters in California don't.

This might not matter so much politically, but the party has done a poor job of inspiring any great number of those who presumably do agree—i.e., working class and poor people—to vote and to vote for Democrats. If Democrats want to continue to define themselves as the party of the underprivileged, then they need to persuade the privileged that investing in the infrastructure that benefits the poor and working class—education, housing, transportation—also benefits them.

Voters want advocates. Consider Davis. During the electricity crisis, he was "responsible." He did everything he could to keep the electricity flowing. Which he did.

Gee, thanks Gray.

Imagine if instead of being responsible, Davis had acted like an outraged populist. Imagine if he had refused to pay extortionate prices for power and had let the lights go out? That's right, rolling blackouts every day, but no bonds to pay the price for those extra kilowatts. Sure, everyone would have said he was destroying California's business climate, but today, given what we know about Enron, he'd be a hero.

He'd be the terminator.

So now what? Schwarzenegger, like Davis, has been elected with less than a majority. While a new recall is unlikely, what is Schwarzenegger going to do to get reelected, with a majority, in 2006? By then, if Schwarzenegger hasn't accomplished some reasonable percentage of his goals, his celebrity will have worn thin. He has a lot of motivation to become a successful governor. To do that, he needs to get the wheels of government turning. He needs to make Sacramento relevant.

It may turn out to be significant that the electorate that voted Davis out and Schwarzenegger in turned down Prop. 53, the latest attempt to handcuff the governor and the legislature from governing. Maybe the voters have realized that all this ballot box government has been a bad idea. In that case, perhaps the mood is right for Sacramento to take back its birthright and start governing.

All the parties up there should be motivated to cooperate with each other and make the system work, so that when they go back to the voters, they can fight about who should get the credit for success, rather than the blame for failure. Democrats, with

1945
World War II ends. During the war, 10,000 men and women from the
Santa Monica Bay area served in the armed services; 500 died.

their big majorities in the legislature, need to show they are relevant. Republicans need to show that they are more than mere obstructionists, and that moderates are welcome. They also owe Schwarzenegger a lot more than he owes them. And, as mentioned above, Schwarzenegger needs to succeed. To do so, he will either push a few right-wing Republicans to the center and cooperate with the Democrats, or entice a large number of Democrats over the center line to join the Republicans.

There are lots of reasons everyone should cooperate. Why am I not optimistic?

In the context of Arnold Schwarzenegger's triumph and two big strikes taking place in the region, I found more reasons to be tough on my compatriots in the Left, who so often seem to do everything they can to alienate their rightful constituency.

OCTOBER 20, 2003

Perhaps someday I will get over the opportunity the City lost when it rejected Target's proposal to build a department store at Fifth and Santa Monica. But sometimes events survive as metaphors, and there was news this week that reminded me of Target. What jogged my memory was City Council Member Kevin McKeown's well-intentioned proposal that the City develop a jobs program for youth in the Pico Neighborhood.

What's the connection? When McKeown spoke about the need to create jobs for young Santa Monicans to keep them out of gangs, I couldn't help but recall Planning Commissioner Julie Lopez Dad's response when Target's supporters touted the four hundred jobs that the store would create. Dad's response was that she didn't think many in Santa Monica would want to work at Target, because Santa Monica had become, in her words, "more and more and more an affluent community."

McKeown and four other members of the City Council voted against Target. As you'll recall, stupid, it was the traffic. The jobs didn't matter, even though if the council members had read the City's own data, they would have known that 22 percent of the residents of the 90404 zip code lived beneath the (absurdly low) federal poverty line. McKeown now acknowledges that there are unskilled and semi-skilled people in Santa Monica who need jobs.

He wants the City of Santa Monica to hire them.

McKeown's jobs proposal wasn't the only recent event that brought the Target debacle to mind. The Democratic Party lost, to its great embarrassment, the governorship of California when great numbers of low-wage workers and poor people, as is typical, either neglected to vote, or—even worse—voted against the Democratic governor. Even the numbers for union workers and their families weren't good.

How could this be? Would it explain anything about the Democrats' problem to know that the president of the Santa Monica Democratic Club is the same Julie Lopez Dad who three years ago didn't know there were working class people in Santa Monica who might want to work at Target?

Would it explain anything about how organized labor has such trouble organizing workers to know that the local leadership of the United Food & Commercial Workers union, headquartered in downtown Santa Monica, testified against Target and its four

1945-47
Douglas Aircraft Company receives federal contract for "Project
RAND" ("research and development"); in 1947 Rand moves to sepa-
rate offices in downtown Santa Monica.

hundred jobs because they said the store would make traffic worse? Nearly all Target stores are not unionized, and no doubt that annoyed the union, but what can you say about a union leadership that valued the ease of their own commutes higher than having, three blocks from their office, a store with four hundred workers they might organize?

Surely the world has enough problems with right-wingers who sling around so much garbage about the Left in America, but do we have to help them? Because somewhere between limousine liberals like Dad, "environmentalists" like McKeown who think that traffic is more important than jobs, and labor leaders who haven't organized a new shop in years, is the reason the Left has failed to mobilize the working class.

At the moment, there are two big strikes going on in L.A. One, by the very same United Food & Commercial Workers I chide above, is a good fight. The UFCW is striking to prevent an industry—supermarkets—from turning real jobs people can stake their lives on into the junk jobs that characterize so much of America where unions are weak. The issue is health care. Fortunately, the legislature recently passed legislation that Governor Davis signed a couple of days before the recall election that aids the unions in this struggle by leveling the playing field, on a higher plane, between unionized businesses that provide medical insurance and big employers that don't. The legislation requires companies with fifty or more employees to provide health insurance for their workers. [See note below.] (As for why it took a Democratic governor and a Democratic-controlled legislature five years to enact this legislation, see above.)

The striking UFCW workers deserve everyone's support, because it if weren't for unions that fought for health insurance, no other workers would have it.

The other strike, by a small union of 2,400 mechanics against the Metropolitan Transportation Authority, is ridiculous. I'll grant that Zev Yaroslavsky is not an impartial observer since he is the chairman of the MTA board, but he was right to call the strike an embarrassment to organized labor. Beyond the egoism of the union's leader, the dispute involves mostly a deficit at the union's health plan, which the MTA was willing to fund. The parties were not that far apart when the union struck, after the end of a court-mandated cooling-off period.

Now the lives of 400,000 mostly poor and working-class commuters are upended, another seven thousand employees of the MTA are out of work, and the retrograde image of today's typical union as having no sense of the bigger picture has been reinforced.

[Note: Business interests put the health insurance bill on the 2004 ballot, and with Schwarzenegger's supporting business, the initiative voiding the law passed.]

M eanwhile, I had some family news to report that was actually relevant to the topics I had been writing about.

OCTOBER 27, 2003

Something over a year ago I wrote about how I was surprised to see a billboard on Lincoln Boulevard advertising apartments for rent in a new building in downtown Santa Monica. The developer was offering a month's free rent, a sure sign that after decades of a short supply of apartments, there was now competition for tenants.

My most loyal reader, who happens to be my father, was in Italy, but he called me to ask me to find out just what those apartments were going for. To cut a long story short, this past Thursday night I picked up my parents at LAX and next month they are moving into a new apartment on Sixth Street. They gave up their apartment in Philadelphia, and now are Santa Monica's and California's latest immigrants.

It's interesting to see big social movements in little pieces. My father is the sixth of seven siblings from Akron, Ohio, to move to the West Coast. My mother is the second of three from Texas. My parents represent two of the six million new Southern Californians, most of them to be born here, who will be looking for houses and apartments in the next twenty-five years. They also are two of the people continuing to exit Philadelphia, which has lost about 40 percent of its population in a few decades.

My parents haven't only removed themselves from Philadelphia, but also a lot of economic activity. They paid rent there and bought groceries, went to movies and concerts, and paid for cable television. Although they are, knock on wood, in reasonably good health, between doctor visits and prescriptions, they are not insignificant contributors to the health care sector of the economy. Or rather, Medicare and the health plan my father's employer in Philadelphia funded do most of the contributing.

You can see that the shift of these two retired people represents a significant shift of economic activity from Pennsylvania's account to California's, and why for all the problems of growth, people are more prosperous where economies grow than where they don't.

Every locality has its share of characters involved in politics. One universal type is the NIMBY activist who just won't let go. In Santa Monica, the best-known chronic testifier at city council, board, and commission meetings was Stephanie Barbanell. Her specialty was to oppose liquor licenses, but she was eclectic enough to oppose nearly any kind of commercial or residential project. In November 2003 I learned that Ms. Barbanell herself, the great opposer of zoning variances and the like, was seeking a variance for her own property on a walk street near the beach. This triggered a series of columns that may not rank high in cosmic importance, but which were among my most popular. Their popularity was probably based on the personalities involved, but anyone who has ever dealt with a local planning issue will relate to the saga of Seaview Terrace.

NOVEMBER 3, 2003

Of all those who protest whatever their neighbors and developers want to build in Santa Monica, perhaps the most tenacious is Stephanie Barbanell. A neighbor of hers told me that Barbanell had protested twenty-nine projects over the years, and after "Googling" "Stephanie Barbanell" and "Santa Monica" I have no reason to doubt that number.

Barbanell lives on Seaview Terrace, a walk street north of Pico near the beach, and she has sought to obstruct the building of nearly everything in or near her neighborhood. On a citywide basis, Barbanell's obsession is drinking. She believes Santa Monica is drowning in alcohol, and she protests nearly every permit for selling the stuff, often to absurd lengths. She ran a little wine store on Montana through the regulatory wringer because the owner wanted to host wine tastings.

What has characterized Barbanell's tactics is an obsession with the details of ordinances, codes, permits, licenses, etc., and a relentless drive to see that the authorities enforce every detail—every detail, that is, consistent with her interpretation. Woe to anyone who might seek a variance, or an approval with conditions.

So, it was with some interest that I read the agenda for the November 11 hearing of the City's Zoning Administrator. Jerry Bass, Barbanell's husband who frequently joins in her appeals and protests, was seeking a variance for a six-foot fence and fourteen-foot hedge in the front-yard setback of the couple's house. Barbanell and Bass need the variance because the City's height limit for a fence, wall, or hedge in a front-yard setback is forty-two inches.

A little background. Although the forty-two-inch rule has been on the books for many years, and the City typically grants only six-inch variances to the rule, many illegally high

1946
Santa Monica voters approve, 14,206 to 6,161, a new City Charter,
providing for a City Manager and a seven-member City Council.

fences, hedges, and walls exist in the city because the planning department only enforces the law when someone files a complaint. This is not something that happens often.

City Hall was closed Friday and I wasn't able to view the planning department's file on the Barbanell/Bass fence. I did speak, however, to some others who live on Seaview Terrace about the course of events that preceded Bass's application for a variance.

For good reason, the City keeps the identities of those who file complaints secret, and no one knew for certain who had filed the complaint against the Barbanell/Bass fence. But the neighbors were quite aware of what happened as a result of it, because in response to the complaint, the City cited not only the Barbanell/Bass fence and hedge, but also all the other illegal fences on the block. Apparently, that is City policy, so as not to be accused of selective enforcement.

Newly shortened wall on Seaview Terrace.

What happened is illuminating. After discussing the matter with planning staff, all the other property owners on Seaview Terrace agreed to comply with the code, and about a month ago they cut their fences and walls down to forty-two inches.

The only people on the street who are seeking a variance are the Barbanell/Basses.

On Saturday I went over to Seaview Terrace to take photos for this column. While I was photographing the Barbanell/Bass fence and hedge, the gate opened, and out popped Barbanell and Bass. I introduced myself and we talked a little about their variance application. I asked Barbanell if she thought it ironic that she was asking for a variance given all the variances she had previously opposed, and she told me she thought it was ironic

that the City hadn't allowed her and her neighbors to fence off Seaview Terrace because of high crime near the beach. Barbanell was carrying a three-ring binder, and she pulled a letter from it from Police Chief James Butts Jr. that she said supported their position that she and Bass needed the high fence and hedge for security.

That was the end of my conversation with Barbanell, however. Apparently she and Bass had exited their house to meet someone, because Barbanell looked past me toward Ocean Avenue and said, "Here's Julie." Leaving Bass to continue the conversation with me, Barbanell walked up the street to greet Planning Commissioner Julie Lopez Dad. The two of them walked back toward Ocean Avenue to have their own conversation.

Bass is affable and he doesn't answer questions with questions, and we talked for about ten or fifteen minutes about his rationale for the variance. Then I left Seaview Terrace by the beach side. As I did, I met up with Barbanell and Dad, who were completing their walk around the block. I asked Commissioner Dad whether she was meeting with Barbanell to discuss her case for the variance. I told her I thought it was odd that a planning commissioner would meet with an applicant before the matter had reached the commission level.

Dad told me that she was meeting with Barbanell to get data on code enforcement issues. I was about to ask another question, but Dad said she had no further comment.

The six-foot fence and fourteen-foot hedge in front of the Barbanell/Bass house on Seaview Terrace.

The saga of the fence on Seaview Terrace continued. It turned out to involve not only the Barbanell/Basses, but also their neighbors and the most prominent land-use lawyers in Santa Monica, who advertised on my webpage presumably because they liked what I had to say in favor of the kind of projects Stephanie Barbanell typically opposed.

NOVEMBER 10, 2003

Mr. Gorbachev, tear down this wall. —Ronald Reagan, 1987.

Last week I found out that Stephanie Barbanell and Jerry Bass, two residents who are among the city's most heavy-duty code-enforcers when it comes to other peoples' properties, were themselves seeking a variance to the City's rules against overly tall front-yard fences and hedges. As if that weren't enough irony, this week, when I went into City Hall to look at the file on the variance application, I found out that Barbanell and Bass have hired the law firm of Harding, Larmore, Kutcher & Kozal to represent them in the matter.

That's right, the same Harding, Larmore, Kutcher & Kozal who are the bêtes noires, the veritable ogres, the princes of darkness, etc., of Santa Monica's no-growthers. The very law firm that advertises on this page! (And what better advertisement could there be for a law firm?) The very same law firm that includes on the front page of its website, a picture of Le Merigot Hotel, the Ocean Avenue hotel near their Seaview Terrace home that Barbanell and Bass fought for so many years.

This is great for me. Now if anyone says that I'm in the thrall of the HLKK firm because they advertise on this page, I can just smile, and say, "of course I'm in their thrall—they're Stephanie Barbanell's lawyers."

Oh well. Barbanell and Bass are going to need all the high quality lawyering they can get if they're going to win their variance, as the law is clear about the forty-two-inch limit on front-yard fences, and significant variances are unheard of. When I was on the Planning Commission, 1995-1999, we had a few fence cases and no one from the City could remember anyone getting a variance of more than six inches. Moreover, this is an issue on which the "new" Planning Commission that took over after 1999 agrees with the old one. The otherwise unlamented Kelly Olsen, for instance, took a strong position in favor of preserving the open vistas the forty-two-inch rule is designed to protect. The City favors open, pedestrian-friendly streets, and from a security standpoint, the police have always been in favor of open sight lines and neighborly "eyes on the street."

Fact is, it's hard to obtain any variance. To get one, a property owner has to persuade the Zoning Administrator, or the Planning Commission on appeal, to find all of a long series of facts. These findings must include that there are exceptional characteristics of the property that distinguish it from other properties in the vicinity, and that the variance would not conflict with the general intent and purposes of the zoning law or the City's general plan.

In practice, unless there are unusual topographical features, such as a hillside, it's hard to make a finding for exceptional characteristics. As for fences, since the general plan is full of paeans to pedestrian-friendliness, and, specifically in the residential part of the land-use element of the plan, to the "continuity of street frontage," variance seekers have had a hard time showing that walling in their front yards is not in conflict with public policy. Barbanell and Bass may have an even harder time than usual, because their house is in the Oceanfront District where the general plan says the goal should be to "enhance east-west streets, view corridors, and pedestrian access-ways to the beach."

Not that I want to obsess particularly on the Barbanell/Bass application for a variance—okay, maybe I do—but sometimes particular cases provide, in addition to juicy gossip, a lens for viewing issues of general interest.

One of Robert Frost's most quoted lines is, "Good fences make good neighbors," but what most people who use the quote don't mention is that Frost, as the writer of the poem, is skeptical about fences. After quoting his crusty neighbor on fences and neighbors, Frost goes on to wonder:

> Before I built a wall I'd ask to know
> What I was walling in or walling out

Seaview Terrace is a special street. It's a walk street that connects Ocean Avenue to a flight of steps that leads to the beach. Whoever developed it obviously did so with some care, with the idea of creating a little community focused on the narrow path. The very name, "Seaview," bespeaks openness and transparency. Yet at some point people started fencing themselves in. One property owner built a six-foot-high cinder-block wall. But the fencing in didn't stop with physical walls. The residents, under Barbanell's leadership, fought every development in the area, from hotels and restaurants to a new apartment building that a developer planned for the vacant lot at the beach end of the block.

For what purpose? At the same time the residents were complaining that their run-down neighborhood was overrun with vagrants and criminals, they were complaining about anyone who wanted to invest in the neighborhood to make it better.

1950-51
Santa Monica sells eight acres of land opposite City Hall to the Rand
Corp. for $250,000; the City uses the money to condemn and acquire
houses and lots in the Belmar Place Triangle, an African-American
neighborhood south of the new courthouse, for the site of the new Civic
Auditorium.

The file on the Barbanell/Bass application contains letters opposing the variance from the next-door neighbors, Sally Frautschy and Greg Cole. The letters dispute the specific reasons Barbanell and Bass have advanced to support their application, namely, their concerns about privacy and security, but the paragraphs that mostly interested me were a couple that eloquently addressed the bigger, Frostian "walling in or walling out" issue that lies at the heart of why cities like Santa Monica try to foster community by restricting the height of fences.

Apparently, Frautschy and Cole used to join with Barbanell and Bass in their obsessions about development and crime. But they were among the Seaview Terrace neighbors who complied with the City's order to lower their fences last month, and already this has caused something of a change of heart.

To quote from Frautschy's letter: "Having properties walled, fenced and hedged off has grossly diminished the beauty of [Seaview] Terrace according to the older residents we talked to (Mrs. Estelle Seeger, Cora of Cora's coffee shop fame, our neighbor Elaine Anderson) who knew it in its former splendor. ... Having this issue forced upon us and taking the fences/walls down has caused many of us to readjust our perspective. The older residents are right. The high fences, hedges and walls should come down."

I can't say it any better than that.

W hat was fascinating about the controversy over the Seaview Terrace
fence, and how it spread to the neighbor's addition, was how this one
small place came to embody just about every frustration people have about
planning.

NOVEMBER 17, 2003

I don't know if the best metaphor would be the layers of an onion or those nesting
Russian dolls that symbolize enigmas wrapped in riddles, but the more I look into the
issue of the Barbanell/Bass fence and hedge on Seaview Terrace, the more interesting it
gets. As *Lookout* readers know, local no-growth and anti-alcohol activists Jerry Bass and
Stephanie Barbanell have applied for a variance to keep the six-foot fence and fourteen-
foot hedge that separates their front yard from Seaview Terrace. Barbanell and Bass had
their hearing before the Zoning Administrator last Tuesday. It will be a month or so
before the Z.A. gives her decision, but that doesn't mean that Seaview Terrace will be
unheard from during that time.

Which is not surprising: Seaview Terrace has never been, during the past fifteen years,
a quiet place when it comes to planning. With instigation from Barbanell, the residents
of the little street have protested nearly anything being built nearby, including hotels and
restaurants (and their liquor licenses), the rebuilding of the Sea Castle apartments after
the earthquake, the remodeling of nearby houses, and, perhaps most tenaciously, a condominium project on the vacant lot at the corner of Seaview and Appian Way that is now
being developed as apartments.

During that time—and I am writing this as a former member of the Planning Commission who heard some of these matters in various stages—one could always count
on Barbanell and ten or twelve of her legionnaires showing up at a hearing to make
whatever argument they could to stop or slow down whatever the plan was. What has
been consistent were the group's loyalty to each other and their inventiveness in devising
subjective arguments to counter plans that objectively satisfied all legal criteria. When I
say "subjective," I mean vague and generalized complaints about "scale and massing,"
views, and sea breezes, as well as amateur hunches about soils, anecdotal accounts about
crime, and hysteria about drink.

Barbanell hasn't been alone, but she's exemplified a type that is familiar to anyone
involved in Santa Monica politics and planning. Rating their own convenience above
everything else, they are SMFCs—"Santa Monicans Fearful of Change"—and they have
had a huge impact. When certain city council members and planning commissioners talk

233

1950

L.A. County constructs courthouse on former brickyard site immediately south of Santa Monica City Hall.

about how they represent the "residents," it's the noisy SMFCs they are talking about, not your typically reasonable "live and let live" Santa Monican.

Back to Seaview. The unanimity among the Seaview residents is no longer. I found this out when I first started to talk to residents about the fence issue. Several broke with Barbanell over the issue of the Viceroy Hotel's liquor license. Barbanell has pursued the Viceroy relentlessly since it opened, protesting that they didn't have a license or the proper city permit to serve alcohol around the pool. But Barbanell went too far on this one. The residents I talked to thought it was ludicrous to pursue the Viceroy, as if apple martinis at the pool had anything to do with the residents' problems with inebriates on the beach. When Barbanell persisted in representing herself as representing Seaview residents, one resident told me she sent the planning department a letter saying that Barbanell did not have her proxy. When in August the Planning Commission granted the Viceroy's request for a new conditional use permit, Barbanell was the only resident to speak in opposition.

Various residents of Seaview may have disagreed with Barbanell about the Viceroy, but that wasn't personal. What's happening on Seaview now is. As I wrote last week, the next-door neighbors of Barbanell and Bass to the east, Greg Cole, who previously joined with Barbanell in her activities against the multi-unit building at the corner of Seaview and Appian Way, and Sally Frautschy, have written letters to the planning department opposing the fence variance. Other neighbors and property owners are supporting the Barbanell/Basses.

But Seaview Terrace solidarity has crumbled completely over an addition the Cole/Frautschys want to build in the backyard of their property. While this project—to add a garage and about 1,000 square feet of living space to a single-family house in an R3, multi-family, zone—did not need discretionary development review, it does need design review. When the Cole/Frautschys presented the project to the Architectural Review Board last August, Jerry Bass led the opposition.

The arguments against were the usual hyperbolic generalities over "size, scale, and massing," and "air, sky, sunlight and ocean breezes," even though the project is considerably smaller than what could be legally built, and—and this is classic—the addition will not be as tall as the second story Barbanell and Bass added to their house several years ago. Bass argued that the Cole/Frautschy addition would violate view corridors, yet he and Barbanell want to keep their fourteen-foot hedge, which interferes not only with the view as one walks toward the ocean, but also a fifteen-foot-wide easement for "walk and park purposes" that runs along the center line of Seaview Terrace. This easement, and a parallel one on the other side of the street, indicate that the historical plan for Seaview Terrace was to have thirty feet of clear, unobstructed space between the houses.

1952
In the midst of the baby boom, 3,411 babies are born at St. John's
Hospital in Santa Monica and 2,321 are born at Santa Monica
Hospital.

Despite Bass's pleas, the Architectural Review Board approved the Cole/Frautchy addition—on its first viewing, which these days is highly unusual and a real testament to the quality of the design. But the indefatigable opponents have appealed the approval to the Planning Commission. The appeal, nearly four months after the ARB approval, is on Wednesday night's Planning Commission agenda.

And that's why people are frustrated with the planning process in Santa Monica.

I took a break from Seaview Terrace and wrote about L.A. and the bizarre myth that Southern California has a cultural inferiority complex.

DECEMBER 1, 2003

A couple of weeks ago I attended my first Los Angeles Philharmonic concert at the new Walt Disney Concert Hall, and I found myself reflecting on all the nonsense I read in October when the Phil opened its spectacular new home. Not that the house Frank Gehry built doesn't inspire awe. Nor was the concert anything less than wonderful. The Phil, the Los Angeles Master Chorale, and five talented singers performed Haydn's *The Creation*, and they and the room did make you believe you were "in the beginning."

But thinking back to what the critics and civic leaders and others wrote and said at the opening, I wondered if anyone knows anything about this "island on the land," as Carey McWilliams described Southern California. Or is it just that much easier to recycle conventional wisdom?

You know what I'm talking about: the old "real city" question, as in, "are we one?" As screenwriter Naomi Foder, quoted in the *L.A. Times*, ineffably expressed it, "Speaking as a New Yorker, this is beginning to feel like a real city." Or, in an alternative formulation, stories datelined Los Angeles couldn't fail to mention those peripatetic suburbs, sometimes sixty, sometimes more, but always wandering, wandering, "in search of a center" (Bernard Weinraub, the *New York Times*). Then there were the obligatory references to the Hollywood sign as symbol of our ephemeral culture, as in "a civic triumph for [Los Angeles], which now has something other than the sun bleached white letters of the 'Hollywood' sign to flaunt on postcards" (Blair Kamin, *Chicago Tribune* Architecture Critic).

It's not only the outlanders who have no idea. John B. Emerson, chairman of the Performing Arts Center of Los Angeles County, found a way to touch every base in just a few sentences: "When people think of Los Angeles, they think of the entertainment industry. They don't think of culture. They think of sprawl and a place that doesn't have a core. ... When people think of Los Angeles (post-Disney Hall), the first image that pops into their mind won't be just the Hollywood sign."

That poor sign.

And wait a minute—I thought the Getty Center already put us on the cultural map. Or was it the Museum of Contemporary Art? I don't mean to be unappreciative of the facilities, but was anyone asking to be validated?

I like living in a city that is defined not by the culture it consumes, but by the culture it creates.

Maybe the most ironic comments about Disney Hall and its sociological impact came from Eli Broad, the philanthropist who made his billions the old-fashioned Southern California way, by building sprawling housing developments. He told Mr. Weinraub, the *New York Times* correspondent, that no one in Los Angeles traveled from the Westside to the Eastside, and that now, post-Disney Hall, "we can all unite in the center."

Apparently Mr. Broad doesn't eat Chinese in Monterey Park—and I feel sorry for him about that—but I would like him to explain (i), who are all those people on the 10 Freeway, and (ii), how nineteen million Southern Californians, with all their different languages and cuisines, musical traditions, and arts, can fit "in the center"—even with the new wide sidewalks on Grand Avenue?

Pardon my arrogance, but the idea that Southern Californians have a cultural inferiority complex—particularly because downtown L.A. offends every urban instinct—is hilarious. It's like the idea of a rivalry between L.A. and San Francisco, or that old William Hamilton *New Yorker* cartoon: A couple is removing their winter coats in the foyer of an upscale apartment. The woman says to the man, "Be sure to tell them how much you miss the seasons."

Here's another quote about Disney Hall, from Paul Goldberger, the *New Yorker's* architecture critic: "It is a serene, ennobling building that will give people in this city of private spaces a new sense of the pleasures of public space." The building is serene and ennobling, but contrary to the experiences of literati on safari, the quintessential L.A. experience is not a salon in Brentwood.

If Mr. Goldberger wants to sense the pleasures of public space, he might join a million or so people on the beach, or fifty thousand people at Dodger Stadium eighty nights a year, or stroll the Promenade or Broadway in downtown L.A., or eat lunch at the Farmers Market in Fairfax.

Or consider this, from Herbert Muschamp, *New York Times* architecture critic: "What is being reborn is the idea of the urban center as a democratic institution: a place where voices can be heard." As much as I cherish my opera and Phil subscriptions, as proud as I am that Schoenberg and Stravinsky exiled themselves here, I doubt that a hall with 2,265 seats, at symphonic prices, is going to turn downtown L.A.—home of the glass tower and the viaduct—into a democratic institution, or even the idea of one.

If culture plus public plus democracy equals city, then L.A. doesn't have much to worry about, and for that matter anyone who has ever seen the roof of a Ship's restaurant or the Cinerama Dome knows that when Mr. Gehry designed Disney he drew from the cantilevers, parabolas, and ellipses of an earlier local architecture.

Southern California is too busy creating culture to worry much about how and where we consume it. It's not just the obvious stuff, television, music, and movies, although as for the last it means a lot—regardless of the condescension to Hollywood and its sign—to be the center of the universe for the art the world most universally understands, the one art that appeals to all social classes in nearly all nations.

It's all the other stuff, all the influence Southern California has, culture in the anthropological sense. Fashion, styles, design, politics, mores and morals, technology. Skateboarders and surfers, low-riders and Valley girls. The products of a wide-open society of immigrants and exiles.

If we could just let everyone know that the whole place didn't burn down last month.

W hat I like about my column is that I can write about Disney Hall one week and Seaview Terrace the next.

DECEMBER 8, 2003

Okay, okay, after taking so many shots at the Planning Commission, I am obliged to admit that they—or at least the four who were present—did the right thing Wednesday when the commission finally got around to looking at the addition to the Cole/Frautschy house on Seaview Terrace. The four unanimously denied the appeals of last August's Architectural Review Board approval.

It did take them a while—three hours—and there were some bumpy moments, but in fairness to the commissioners, and even to the appellants—let me see how far I can take this fairness thing—a lot of the time that was wasted at the meeting would not have been wasted if the City's ordinances were more clear.

One appellant, John Oursland, based much of his appeal on whether planning staff, in approving the project's zoning compliance, had properly measured the site's "average natural grade" (ANG). Mr. Oursland's point, briefly, was that the low point of the site should have been determined with reference to the property's southern edge in the alley in the back, not, as the City's policies determine it, within the site where the buildable part of the property begins. Mr. Oursland contended that the property had been filled in, unnaturally, to be level with the higher elevation of Seaview Terrace, and that if the ANG were lower, the two-story addition on top of a garage that property owners Greg Cole and Sally Frautschy want to build would be too high.

Although Planning Commission Chair Darrell Clarke ultimately made some calculations to show that even if Mr. Oursland were correct, the proposed structure would not be higher than the zoning allowed, the issue led to a tense exchange between Planning Director Suzanne Frick and two commissioners, Arlene Hopkins and Jay Johnson.

Ms. Frick quite properly admonished the commissioners that an appeal of an ARB decision is not the proper venue for either an appellant to raise zoning issues or planning commissioners to question the meaning of ordinances, but Hopkins, Johnson, and Oursland had good grounds for being confused as to the meaning of ANG and how it applied to the Seaview Terrace site. The reason is that the zoning ordinance's definition of ANG bases it on the "natural state" of a parcel's ground level. As it happens, though, after a century of cutting and filling, in a town where even the sand on the beach owes more to man than God, the City would need a forensic geologist to determine consistently what the "natural state" of the land is.

1954
Santa Monicans vote to prohibit oil drilling in the bay and to issue
bonds to build a Civic Auditorium.

For this reason, when the ordinance says average "natural" grade, the City has always interpreted this to mean average existing grade. Existing, that is, before new work is done—a planning staffer told me that a few years ago a property owner on Sixth Street tried to get away with doing his grading before his survey. As evidence for how the City determines ANG, the City Council adopted a different standard for the hills of Ocean Park—"theoretical grade." Theoretical grade was, paradoxically, an attempt to compute what Mr. Oursland might call "natural" grade.

Who can blame people for being confused in a city where the natural is the existing and the theoretical is the natural?

I admit to having become fascinated by Seaview Terrace. Next February the Terrace celebrates its ninetieth birthday. The neighborhood disputes raging about it today encapsulate ninety years of conflicting desires for both community and personal space and conflicting attitudes toward neighbor and neighborhood.

Seaview Terrace was founded on communitarian principles. The developer who subdivided it created an easement running thirty feet wide down the middle of the parcel for "park and walk purposes." The developer believed that this mandated shared space would be an amenity that would make the little vacation lots he was peddling more valuable. More than any structure, that impulse for and faith in community is the historical legacy of the Terrace and something to ponder in our day of gated communities.

Opponents of the Cole/Frautschy addition spoke extravagantly about how the modern addition would "destroy" the historical character of their beach community. Commissioner Hopkins, an ardent preservationist, several times asked them if they had done anything to create a historic district. The expressions she drew were blank. Ms. Hopkins made a telling comment about preservation; she said that there is no conflict between modern design and preserving old structures. Modern design in a historical area serves history by highlighting it, as opposed to faux historical additions that debase it.

For a long time the property owners and residents of Seaview Terrace thought they were part of history because their old buildings were crumbling around them. Did anyone on the block care much about its history except as it provided a tool for interfering with the plans of their neighbors? They walled themselves off from each other. They opposed anyone who would invest in the area. Now they are shocked to find themselves unable to communicate with each other outside a hearing room in City Hall.

As if we were archaeologists, we tend to judge human settlements based on the hardscape, but it's the soft tissues that are more important.

2004

Only a few weeks later, however, I was reflecting on the hardscape that people created to aid memory. And what better chance to do so than at Gettysburg?

JANUARY 12, 2004

In an age of media and information, when emotion is the subject of instant audio-visual dissection, when our critical faculties are more developed than our sentiments, when mourning is brief and to the point, when we can rationalize anything, and are skeptical of everything, memorials are a challenge. But maybe nothing has changed. For the innumerable monuments to the heroic or tragic dead, for all the speeches at their dedications, precious little of the art approaches the level of a Pieta, and only two dedicatory speeches—Pericles' funeral oration for Athenian dead of the Peloponnesian War and Lincoln's Gettysburg Address—have survived as part of the canon.

In his case Lincoln turned out to be wrong, but he was on safe historical ground when he predicted that people would little note, nor long remember, the words said at the dedication of the Gettysburg National Cemetery. At least in Pericles' day, though, and in Lincoln's there were certain rituals that were meaningful. Now in the face of tragedy, we hardly know what to do. For the first annual commemoration of 9/11 the mayor of New York didn't trust anyone to say anything new about the event and had someone read the Gettysburg Address instead.

We've perfected the "life must go on" rituals of mourning but lost the others. You wouldn't know it by reading the papers, but the biggest hurt of 9/11 was not what it did to the economy. .

Over the holidays I spent a lot of time looking at memorials. This wasn't planned. My wife had a conference in Washington, D.C., and before going there we visited her family in Pittsburgh. That meant that we drove from Pittsburgh to Washington, which meant we could stop and spend an afternoon with our eighth-grader son in Gettysburg.

I had never been to Gettysburg before and the next time I go I'll give myself more time. We arrived with about three hours of daylight remaining and set out on the Park Service's "two-hour" self-guided auto tour. At dusk we had only made it to the end by skipping most of the Confederate memorials. If you go to Gettysburg give yourself a day and rent a bicycle. That's how to see it. You want to read every name, you want to imagine what happened, you want to think about what did not perish from the earth those three days in July 140 years ago.

The memorials are unique, the quantity of them overwhelming, and their communicative power immense. Nearly all are related to place. States, regiments, brigades, cities, even individual artillery batteries, erected monuments to remember the sacrifices their sons, husbands, fathers, and comrades made at specific locations. The monuments tell the story of the battle, sometimes with words, sometimes with sculpture, often with both. Names are everywhere.

Gettysburg: the copse of trees at the "high water mark" of the Confederacy.

The memorials are personal, idiosyncratic. One unit, the 11th Pennsylvania Infantry Regiment, included its dog, Sallie, in its monument—Sallie had guarded their dead and dying for two days during the battle. Another monument consists of an undressed "puddingstone" boulder from Roxbury, Massachusetts. This was the kind of boulder that the

c. 1957
Douglas Aircraft begins shifting manufacturing operations to Long
Beach from Santa Monica because Santa Monica will not expand the
airport to accommodate Douglas's DC-8 jet. Research and develop-
ment, missile production, and sub-assembly work continue at the
Santa Monica Airport plant.

men of the 20th Massachusetts played on together as boys, and they thought this was a
fitting memorial to how they fought together as men.

The monument to the 140th New York Regiment, where Patrick O'Rorke fell.

This week the Lower Manhattan Development Corporation will release details of the
design its memorial jury has selected for the principal memorial for all the 9/11 attacks.
The memorial will not only commemorate the attacks on the World Trade Center, but
also the attack on the Pentagon and the people who died on Flight 93. Based on an
earlier version of the design, we know that its dominant elements will be two reflecting
pools occupying the footprints of the twin towers, but we won't know until the unveiling
this week of the revised plan what the iconography of the memorial will be. The jury has
shown itself to be conscientious and capable, and I am hoping for the best.

One of the disputes that has dogged the process for selecting a design for the 9/11
memorial has been an unfortunate one between some of the families and surviving comrades of the fire and police personnel who died trying to rescue people and some of the
families and survivors of "civilians." The dispute is whether the names of the rescue

1958
Santa Monica creates the Ocean Park Redevelopment District;
ultimately in the name of redevelopment the City destroys the Ocean
Park beachfront of amusements, hotels, and residences, displacing
316 families, 502 individuals, and 212 businesses, and builds high-
rise apartment towers in their place.

personnel should be listed apart from the names of the civilian victims. While those who want to list all the names together say that there should not be two different "classes" of victims, I would say, respectfully, that the more detail the memorial employs, the better it will allow future generations to remember all the victims and comprehend the tragedy of the day.

The monuments at Gettysburg are living memorials because they tell the story of what happened. More than a century later it means something to know that the "Philadelphia Brigade" held the line at the "Angle," or that Patrick Henry O'Rorke—born in Ireland, first in his class at West Point—died leading the 140th New York in repulsing the rebels' last attack on Little Round Top

Gettysburg: Cemetery Ridge.

While it would be easy to analogize to the Gettysburg monuments a monument, for instance, to the five fire fighters from Engine Company 55 who died in the north tower, or to the thirty-seven Port Authority police who died, or to the heroes of Flight 93, I would go even further. I would list the names of all the victims of 9/11 in such a way that we know just what they were doing that day. I would group together the names of the seventy-nine workers at Windows of the World who died, just as I would group together the business people who were attending the Risk Waters seminar. I would memorialize as a group the three hundred people who were working at Marsh & McLennan, the

insurance brokers whose offices on the ninety-sixth floor of the north tower were struck
by the first plane. I would build a monument for all the people who were just visiting,
and another to passengers and crews of the planes.

When you get down to it, if Gettysburg was a clash of armies, what we want to
remember about 9/11 is that it was an attack on the unsuspecting.

J anuary 17, 2004, was the tenth anniversary of the Northridge Earth-quake, which hit Santa Monica hard, particularly downtown.

JANUARY 19, 2004

My memory of 4:31 a.m., January 17, 1994, is probably similar to that of other Santa Monicans—i.e., suddenly my bed turned into Mr. Toad's wild ride. My wife and I leaped out of it, we ran to our four-year-old's room, and we grabbed him and stood under a doorway for five minutes. I'd lived here fifteen years and experienced quakes before, but this one I knew was different. I was sure the fault was about ten feet underneath our floor.

As it happened, our house, in Ocean Park, sustained no damage. But when the sun came up, and communications got going, we started to comprehend what had, so to speak, "gone down." We walked over to some friends' house. Kevin and Dana were also okay, but when we heard that the freeway had collapsed, Kevin suggested that we go to the grocery store and buy some supplies before the food riots started.

We drove over to Lincoln Boulevard, and we started to see real destruction. The gro-cery store was closed because all the stock was on the floor. At that point Kevin, who's an architect, started getting nervous about an addition he had recently designed for a house north of Montana that had a big picture window. We drove over there to check it out.

We drove up Fourth Street—we were stunned to see all the bricks piled on the side-walks. Then we turned on Montana. Nearly all the shop windows were shattered. Up ahead we saw a long line. What could it be? An emergency aid station? A store with bat-teries? Looters?

No—the line was outside a coffee bar. People were lined up for cappuccino. I knew Santa Monica would pull through.

O ne of my missions since starting the column was to investigate the history of Santa Monica. Local politics reflects local history. Often it is a slave to conventional wisdom about local history. With a transitory population, many people know little about where they live, and, as is the case with local news, local history is hard to find.

FEBRUARY 16, 2004

"Santa Monica had a lot of the same positives and negatives as other cities, but everything was just smaller." —LeVert Martel "Marty" Payne, speaking at the Santa Monica Historical Society Museum, February 8, 2004

I attended the recent talk by Marty Payne at the Historical Society Museum about what a trunk full of documents meant to him and to Santa Monica. I arrived a little early and as I waited for Mr. Payne to begin his enlightening stream of associations about African-American life in Santa Monica in the '40s, '50s and '60s, I looked over the museum's current special exhibit, a selection of old Santa Monica postcards from the collection of (Landmarks Commissioner) Roger Genser. What struck me from perusing Mr. Genser's century-old postcards and listening to Mr. Payne is how the history they explicated was so different from the prevailing sense of what Santa Monica's past was.

For instance, one common complaint is that tourists are overrunning Santa Monica, that we've turned our downtown into Disneyland. But Mr. Genser's postcards illustrate that when Santa Monica was young it was a resort more than anything else. Being a magnet for tourism has always been a crucial part of the city's identity. We were Disneyland before there was Disneyland.

Along the same lines, a common criticism of any efforts to develop business and jobs in Santa Monica is to say that Santa Monica was historically and should ever remain (i) a sleepy beach town, or (ii) a suburb. Yet Mr. Payne's main point was that black people came to Santa Monica not to hang out around the beach (which was segregated), or to live in a bungalow and commute to Los Angeles, but to work, and they came because there was work, specifically industrial jobs (40,000 of them) at the Douglas plant during World War II.

What was true for minority blacks was also true for majority whites, as I learned after Mr. Payne's talk, in a conversation with two men who know as much about Santa Monica as anyone—former Mayor Nat Trives and former member of the City Council Bob Gabriel.

1958
Santa Monica opens its new civic auditorium; for a few years it hosts
the Academy Awards, but within twenty years it is called a white
elephant.

I had always assumed that Santa Monica's great period of growth occurred after the freeway. This came up when I was talking to Messrs. Trives and Gabriel, and they emphatically corrected me. Santa Monica's population, they said, had already grown to near its present size by 1950. I shouldn't have doubted the two sages, but I checked the census data. Santa Monica's population grew over the decades as follows:

1930: 37,146	1970: 88,289
1940: 53,500	1980: 88,314
1950: 71,595	1990: 86,905
1960: 83,249	2000: 84,084

Santa Monica essentially reached its current population, which has been declining for twenty years, in 1960, before the freeway. Not only that, by 1950 the city had reached roughly 85 percent of its peak population. If "sleepy beach town" equals, say, less than half of today's population (and no Arcadia Hotel, no piers, no Pacific Ocean Park), one would have to be about eighty today to have any recollection of when Santa Monica was one. Alternatively, if you think Santa Monica grew as a bedroom suburb, think again. Santa Monica reached its current population not because of the freeway and commuting, but because of jobs.

Santa Monica's population has been stagnant, more or less, for half a century. While no-growth rhetoric declares Santa Monica "built-out," nearby communities have grown to population densities averaging 30 percent higher than ours. In this context, it's a denial of history to complain about any City policies that have encouraged growth.

The artifacts the Historical Society collects—scraps of cardboard or newsprint or even just memories like Marty Payne's—are more ephemeral than landmarked buildings, but collectively they can provide, if preserved, catalogued, and studied, a more complete picture of history. The City Council recently indicated its willingness to make a special appropriation to fund preservation and cataloguing of a trove of documents relating to Santa Monica's history recently donated to the Historical Society. This will be money well spent.

The council also agreed to provide a 5,000-square-foot facility for the society in the new library. The society is undertaking a capital campaign to fund a five-million-dollar endowment to furnish and operate the new facility. Everyone should pitch in to help.

In the spring of 2004, I took two occasions to write about national issues. The following column was probably my strangest ever; it's about the gay marriage controversy that was then raging after the Massachusetts Supreme Judicial Court legalized gay marriage in the Bay State and Mayor Gavin Newsom had started marrying gays in San Francisco.

MARCH 1, 2004

One of my obscure interests is the history of the nineteenth century unification of Italy, the *Risorgimento*. It was a great, decades-long story of diplomacy, idealism (often betrayed), and soldiers wearing plumed helmets. The architect of reunification was Camillo Cavour, the prime minister of Piedmont under King Victor Emanuel II. One of Cavour's great diplomatic coups was the secret deal he reached with Emperor Napoleon III of France in 1858. They agreed that if Cavour could provoke a war between Piedmont and Austria in such a way that Austria appeared to be the aggressor, France would send an army to help the Italians, Piedmont would obtain various northern Italian territories from Austria, and, for France's aid, Piedmont would cede Nice and Savoy to France.

It was all hush-hush, but, as if to seal the deal publicly, Napoleon wanted a marriage first to be made between Victor Emanuel's fifteen-year-old daughter, Princess Clotilde, and the Emperor's thirty-six-year-old cousin, Prince Napoleon-Jerome. The latter had an unfortunate reputation, and Cavour had to sell the idea to his king.

There exists a fascinating letter from Cavour to Victor Emanuel in which he tries to persuade the king that it would not be beneath the dignity of his ancient House of Savoy for his daughter to marry one of the *arriviste* French royals, and that, notwithstanding what the king may have heard about Napoleon-Jerome, the lad had a good heart. Victor Emanuel ultimately agreed with Cavour, and so did Princess Clotilde, who was pious and considered it her duty to do what was best for her royal family.

Clotilde and Napoleon-Jerome married in January 1859 about a week after he formally proposed (through an intermediary, a French general). Within a few months Cavour had manipulated Austria into invading Piedmont. France sent its army and the rest is history. Before I forget, Clotilde and Napoleon-Jerome were married in church. The marriage was sacred.

Which brings me to my point, which is to say, "Gavin Newsom for President in 2024."

Marriage is like football; the rules change over time. It wasn't long ago that both the forward pass and divorce were illegal in most places. Most Americans today would consider sinful and sordid what was sacred to Cavour and Victor Emanuel and presumably

1959
The City closes Muscle Beach after a sex scandal involving weight lifters and two underage girls.

to the priest who performed the Clotilde and Napoleon-Jerome nuptials. Divorce, which used to be viewed as the enemy of marriage, is for most Americans, obsessed with free will and with carrying out their desires, what makes marriage sacred. I.e., that my wife and I could get divorced gives meaning to our staying together.

But as much as I tend to take a rather catholic (small c) view of the evolution of institutions, I have to say that up until the recent events in San Francisco, I opposed gay marriage. My opposition was political in part. I was afraid, as were most gay politicians, that pushing marriage for gays was going to feed, unnecessarily and futilely, and counter-productively, the right-wing culture war machine. I was a "civil unions" guy. Although my fears were political, my rationalization was grammatical, or etymological. I objected to using an adjective, "gay," to take the meaning from a good noun, "marriage."

It's like tea. First there was tea: the leaves of the tea plant, *Theaceae Camellia sinensis*. There was black tea and green tea, and oolong tea and Earl Gray, but it was all tea. Then came herbal infusions. These became popular and people called them "herb teas." The word tea lost its meaning, leading to the double-noun phenomenon, whereby a noun becomes an adjective of the same noun for the purpose of confirming the original meaning. You know what I mean: when you offer someone a hot beverage, after you offer coffee, you say, "herb tea, or tea tea."

I told myself I didn't like the idea of gay marriage because I didn't want to have to distinguish between "gay marriage" and "marriage marriage." As I said, I was a civil unions guy.

But you know what? That was then, pre-Gavin, and now is now, post-Gavin, because at some point the political and even, heaven forbid, the etymological, must yield to the emotional, and I get absolutely misty over civil rights. Seeing so many happy mono-gendered couples pledging their monogamy is enough to persuade me that the best use of the word marriage is to describe a state of love and commitment rather than any particular constellation of genitalia.

I suspect I am not alone. The joy radiating from San Francisco is palpable.

It takes two-thirds of the House and the Senate to amend the Constitution, and there's no poll out there saying that two-thirds of Americans want to amend the Fourteenth Amendment preemptively to exclude gays from the Equal Protection Clause. I predict that President Bush's amendment will find a place on the Congressional shelf next to his Mars exploration plan.

As for me, I will no longer begrudge a double noun. Black, green, chamomile, red zinger, lemon ginger: it's all tea.

On the anniversary of the invasion of Iraq, I wrote a column about the war. What is so depressing, writing these notes in 2009, is how long the war has lasted, and now much damage it caused.

MARCH 29, 2004

It's not often that Americans have the opportunity to commemorate the first anniversary of invading another country on a preemptive basis, so forgive me if I use the occasion of the first anniversary of the start of the Iraq War to write about something other than Santa Monica. But then I could not resist the urge a year ago to write about the invasion itself.

I would like to say that revisiting the issue would at least provide the opportunity to see if I am good at predicting the future, but the fact is that if you reread my column from March 19, 2003, you'll find that when it came to prognosticating, I cheated, or, rather, to put a nicer spin on it, I hedged my bets.

I said that if the Iraqis welcomed the Americans with open arms, prospects for success would be good. But if Iraqis resisted, or merely met our troops with resentment, then the prospects would be bleaker, and our last troops might end up leaving Iraq from the roof of our embassy.

As it happened, the Iraqi reaction was all over the map (in fact, more determined by the map than anyone then expected), and no one, myself included, is any closer to predicting the outcome now. Most Iraqis appear unhappy with the security situation, but happy that Saddam is gone from power and happy with their greater liberties. Other Iraqis, a minority, are resisting the occupation in ways that are disturbingly reminiscent of Vietnam in the early days of American involvement.

The problem is that there is not one Iraq but at least three. When I say "most Iraqis" above I am referring to the Shi'ites and the Kurds, and even for them it's lucky they live hundreds of miles apart. The "minority" who resist are the Sunni Arabs, who are a majority in the center of the country. The American occupation of Iraq could be the most wise and benevolent occupation in the history of occupations, but there is nothing we can do to make Shi'ites, Kurds, and Sunni Arabs like each other. Nor is it likely that they will give America much credit for keeping them away from the others' throats.

Even assuming that the Arab and Islamic worlds were ready to ride the wave of history to modern democracy (a big assumption), the administration's hopes for a stable and democratic Iraq are riding against other, even stronger historical tides, those of nationalism and self-determination based on ever smaller affinity groups. Let's put it this way: Turkey, Iran, Iraq, and Syria could save everyone a lot of trouble if they would let the Kurds form their own state.

As the revelations of Paul O'Neill and Richard Clarke make clear, the Bush administration was obsessed with Iraq. The fact that the British over several decades of influence could not create a stable country within Iraq's inherently unstable borders was not enough history to make them doubt that we could do so in a year or two with the help of such paragons as Ahmad Chalabi.

Even if one is willing to give the administration the benefit of the doubt and accept in good faith the "neocon" rationale for invading—to use a democratic Iraq as the lynchpin for solving all the problems of the Middle East—one must conclude that they did not factor into their analysis the relative probabilities of good and bad outcomes. (Where was the Rand Corp. when we needed them?) Now it's become apparent that one bad outcome has been the effect of the Iraq War on the war against terrorism.

I watched nearly every minute of Richard Clarke's testimony before the 9/11 Commission. The whole of the testimony is much more revealing and important than any excerpts you may have seen or heard, and I urge anyone who didn't see the whole thing either to listen to it (you can find it on the Web) or to read a transcript. While Clarke's testimony is gaining most attention for its political impact, because he has illuminated even better than Paul O'Neill just how stubborn and ignorant the Bush team was (and by their reaction to him, still is), the greater importance is historical.

Clarke's testimony (and presumably his book, which I have just begun to read) is the first blow-by-blow policy account of how the world has changed from one defined by the revolutions and wars of the twentieth century and the Cold War, essentially internecine struggles between competing western ideologies, to one defined by the clash between modernized and modernizing cultures on one hand, and reactionary traditionalists on the other.

Although at the moment I am happy along with everyone else on the left to revel in Clarke's unveiling of right-wing hypocrisy and incompetence, Clarke raises disturbing and challenging issues for anyone who during the Cold War opposed America's excessive or aggressive use of its powers, or the imperialism of our materialism. To put it mildly, Clarke was a hawk when it came to fighting terrorists. Before others in government were willing or saw the need to, he wanted to kidnap or kill terrorists unknown to most people, lob missiles at Al Qaeda training camps in Afghanistan, arm the Northern Alliance to fight the Taliban, and take other similar actions.

Today, if Clarke had had his way, would we look at such actions as having been preemptive and wrong, or, with 20-20 hindsight after 9/11, defensive and right? Keep in mind that the people who attempted to kill fifty thousand in the Twin Towers and who are no doubt looking for their next chance to do so or worse, are the same people who would globalize the market for burkas and institute a worldwide theocracy. They are not fresh-faced leftists seeking justice for *campesinos* or higher wages at the garment factory.

The politics are exciting, but the Clarke story is much less about politics than it is about the big decisions this country needs to make about how to secure its future.

I n a column the next month I was able to connect the local to the national and ponder how the big show in Washington wasn't much different than the little show in Santa Monica.

APRIL 19, 2004

I wouldn't be writing this column if I didn't love local politics, but last Tuesday evening's City Council hearing gave a good example why I do.

Let me put the meeting in context. In Washington, the 9/11 Commission has been conducting its explosive hearings on what went wrong in the fight on terrorism. I got hooked watching Richard Clarke's testimony a couple of weeks ago (I also read his book; talk about depressing), and I couldn't help but watch all of Condoleeza Rice's testimony, too.

You may be surprised to learn that the people running the big show in Washington, both the politicians and their staffs, don't seem that different from the people who run the little show here in Santa Monica. I don't mean that as an indiscriminate knock on D.C. or City Hall. What I do mean is that governing is only as difficult as predicting the future, there are competing interests all over the place, the competence of the people in government runs the gamut from zero to extraordinary, and most of us folks in the gallery don't have the foggiest.

Tuesday the City Council had on its agenda two proposals to revise building standards in most of the multi-family districts in the city. I hardly expected by the end of the evening I would be pondering big philosophical issues about democracy. But that's what happened.

As the *Lookout* has reported, most of the meeting was taken up with discussion of staff's proposal to eliminate review by the Architectural Review Board of projects that satisfy defined design criteria. That the issue was fraught with political significance was highlighted by an unusual introduction to the staff report that City Manager Susan McCarthy gave prior to the planning department's presentation. Obviously to counter accusations that staff had conjured up the proposals in secret, Ms. McCarthy detailed the history of public hearings the department had held on the proposals.

I thought she was auditioning for the White House Chief of Staff position in the next administration.

On one side of the ARB review issue, you had staff and some council members saying that we don't need design review for relatively small projects that satisfy specific design criteria, and that we should plan "by code and not by process." They argued that having every project go through the ARB created backlogs at both the ARB and the Planning

Commission that stretched the approval process beyond reasonable limits, so that projects, even small ones, routinely took two or three years to receive approval.

On the other side, you had fifteen speakers (by my count) and some council members saying that to eliminate this "public review" would be undemocratic and contrary to what Council Member Ken Genser called, "the political culture of the community."

Sitting in the audience I couldn't help but try to put to use that Poli Sci degree I got thirty years ago. What is democracy? Or what are its crucial elements?

Is the essence of democracy the right to appear at a public hearing and give your two cents on an issue, presumably two cents that relate to your personal interests? If exasperated after listening to two or three hours of public testimony on a contentious issue, take a moment and realize that this notion has a good pedigree. It's the sentiment, more or less, in the petition/redress/grievances part of the First Amendment.

Or is democracy more a matter of electing legislators who pass laws to improve life for the community as a whole, and then following those laws? The staff's "code not process" argument echoed a "laws not men" formulation that has had some popularity since 1776.

Or is democracy more a function of protecting rights? This is the idea that says we can never have perfect democracy, but we can have a civil society. But what are rights? A property owner has her property rights, she says, but a neighbor says, as did one speaker at the hearing Tuesday, that he has the right to have his neighborhood stay the same as when he moved into it.

Who is right, and what's the democratic thing to do?

No answer here, but for stimulating the intellectual juices, if you get tired of watching present and past heads of the CIA, the FBI, the NSC, the Justice Department, et al., play "who's on first," then tune into the Santa Monica City Council.

I'm not kidding.

In between the national and the local is the regional, and maps show that Californians are always on the move.

APRIL 26, 2004

A conceit of writing a column is that there are readers willing to accommodate the columnist's obsessions, provided that he or she can make them amusing enough. Thank you, and I try, but I know that like those of most of my friends and family, your eyes would glaze over if I cornered you at a party and started talking about everything that fascinates me. So it was with an ever-increasing sense of joy and wonder that I spent two-and-a-half days this past week in the company—dare I say, the bosom—of the California Studies Association at their sixteenth annual conference.

To be together with people who are fascinated simultaneously with how a new ride at Disneyland will affect the continued viability of California's *noir* literary and filmic culture and how far bus benches should sit from the curb, was so heavenly that I began to appreciate the rapture that enveloped California's early settlers as they looked upon paradise.

I participated on a panel at the conference about possible changes in the dominant paradigm of the "California Dream": the single-family, detached house in a development surrounding a shopping center. The idea is that because of a dramatic drop in the percentage of households with children and the ever-increasing social costs of sprawl, the time might be ripe for a paradigm shift toward a preference for city dwelling. The panel focused on downtown Santa Monica as a case study. Two panelists were Santa Monica's most active market-rate and affordable housing developers, Craig Jones, who has built most of the apartments downtown, and Joan Ling of Community Corp. They explained what they were building, who their customers were, and what they wanted.

We also heard from Christian Peralta, who works at Livable Places, a nonprofit developer of in-fill housing that focuses largely on providing first-time homebuyers with alternatives to buying houses on the sprawling fringe. The fifth panelist was D.J. Waldie, author of the remarkable book, *Holy Land: A Suburban Memoir. Holy Land* is about Mr. Waldie's hometown of Lakewood; it combines memory and history. For me the book was a revelation. It stood all my anti-suburban prejudices on their head.

Lakewood was the first example of developers building the full program of detached houses surrounding a shopping center. *Holy Land* describes the heroic achievement of housing of 17,500 working-class families and explains the durability of the existing paradigm. Mr. Waldie gave our panel a historical context. He pointed out that Lakewood, as planned in the late '40s and built in the early '50s, was the result of a fifty-year long

1966
Completion of the Santa Monica Freeway: Construction of the free-
way through the Pico Neighborhood displaces thousands of African-
Americans, Latinos and Japanese-Americans.

"conversation" about how best to house working people, and that any changes in that paradigm would need to result from a continuation of that conversation.

One thing that is clear is that any such conversation about housing involves a lot more than how many bathrooms there are and how many bedrooms. Along that line, one of the fascinating presentations I heard at the conference was that of Professor James Allen of the Geography Department of Cal State Northridge. Professor Allen presented a series of maps that showed the pace of demographic change in the region, based on census-tract-by-census-tract analysis of the 2000 census.

What the maps show is that Southern Californians are constantly on the move in search of better places to live, and that these movements follow certain patterns based on ethnicity. People tend to start from enclaves of their racial or ethnic group (whites having been the first to congregate and then to move), and then move outward to new enclaves with better housing. In general, however, there are more enclaves people move to than people move from, and the places people move to tend to be more diverse than the places they moved from.

The communities that have been here the longest tend to be the most dispersed. Only 22 percent of whites live in census tracts where more than 80 percent of the population is white; in Chicago or New York, 60 percent do. Although in the public mind, all African-Americans live in South Los Angeles and neighboring communities, in fact they are now scattered throughout the region. Blacks represent only 8 percent of the population as a whole, but there are only four census tracts in the whole region that have none, and very few that are less than one percent black.

As has been widely reported, the Latino population in Southern California now is the largest single group—40 percent as compared to 39 percent Anglo/white. Latino immigration has, of course, been dramatic. Another speaker at the conference, Gregory Rodriguez, a contributing editor to the *L.A. Times*, reported that today two-thirds of adult Latinos are foreign born; the figure in 1970 was 11 percent. While that explains why so much Spanish is spoken here, the process of North Americanization is inexorable: two-thirds of the grandchildren of immigrant Latinos speak only English.

Why is it that in a culture that places a lot of value on neighborhood and community, people feel the need to abandon the old places to create new lives elsewhere? In other societies, immigrants and new workers moving to the city from the countryside form the new neighborhoods and aspire to work their way into the center. Even in Southern California there are old neighborhoods that defy the trend and attract investment.

I may have heard the answer, or part of it, at another panel, one about building and maintaining the infrastructure that neighborhoods depend on. Speakers included Kathi Littman, a consultant who has played an important role in the L.A. Unified School

District's dramatic program of building and rebuilding schools, and Jonathan Kevles, an official at the L.A. Community Redevelopment Agency (CRA). While it is apparent that through the work of a new generation of technocrats like Ms. Littman and Mr. Kevles, governmental agencies are finding ways to work together to make fruitful investments in local communities, I was amazed to learn from Ms. Littman's remarks that until recently planning departments at the state and local level, and public developers like the CRA, did not consider schools to be part of infrastructure.

So while the CRA was dumping millions and millions of dollars into parking lots in downtown L.A. and Hollywood, none of the power brokers trying to protect their investments had the foresight to ask why families were fleeing Los Angeles for the outskirts, depressing property values and discouraging private investment along the way. What the CRA, government officials, property owners, or any other interested policy maker could have learned from talking to any suburban realtor, the first answer any new suburbanite gives for why he or she moved to the suburbs is, "the schools."

What if it turns out that our older cities have not been a revolving door for the poor of each generation because of an innate desire for one's own front lawn to mow, but because the people of California through their government(s) made a conscious decision not to invest in old schools and old neighborhoods?

As Mr. Waldie said, it's a conversation.

Many readers were happy that in May I was able to resume the saga of the Barbanell/Bass fence when the Planning Commission finally had the fence on its agenda.

MAY 10, 2004

I couldn't help it. Ignoring my usual 10:30 curfew, I had to stay up until the bitter non-end, until two in the morning, to watch the Planning Commission not decide what to do about Stephanie Barbanell and Jerry Bass's six-foot fence and fourteen-foot hedge on Seaview Terrace. But the lost sleep was worth it. I have a new hero: Planning Commissioner Julie Lopez Dad.

I'm ready to eat crow. Students of the battles of Seaview Terrace—and I understand that with part of the money the City is giving the School District under their new deal (Hurrah!) the district is establishing a Civics curriculum based on Seaview—may remember that when I first reported in November that the Barbanell/Basses wanted a variance for their overlarge fence and hedge, I reported on a meeting I chanced upon between them and Commissioner Dad.

Shamelessly (shamefully?) employing the columnist's stock in trade—blithe cynicism—I suspected that Commissioner Dad was giving advice to the Barbanell/Basses in advance of their upcoming hearing before the Zoning Administrator. Well, maybe she was, but based on what she said at the Planning Commission hearing on the appeal of the Z.A.'s denial of the variance, Commissioner Dad would have told Ms. Barbanell and Mr. Bass to "tear down that fence!"

To my shock and awe, at the hearing Commissioner Dad strongly articulated and defended the public interest behind the City's pro-civility, pro-pedestrian front-yard setback laws and by doing so prevented the commission from setting a precedent that would have subverted the City's efforts to build a more livable and open city.

So what happened? Not much, in a certain sense. The seven commissioners deadlocked without a majority of four able to agree on anything, and at two a.m. continued the matter. Two commissioners, Ms. Dad and Terry O'Day, were ready to reject the variance outright, as the commission has rejected all such attempts to wall-in front yards in the past. Commissioners Arlene Hopkins, Barbara Brown and Jay Johnson, not only would not vote to deny the variance, but took the position, amazing for public officials in a "progressive" community, that the City should abrogate the rights of the public to traverse Seaview Terrace and allow the residents to create a gated community. It's hard to imagine a more striking betrayal of the public interest by three self-proclaimed social and environmental progressives.

1972
June 5: City Manager Perry Scott and developers unveil plans to build
a 35-acre artificial island in Santa Monica Bay. The development
would include a 1,500-room, 29-story hotel and a 60,000 square foot
convention center.

The remaining two commissioners, Gwynne Pugh and Chair Darrell Clarke, were in the middle. Both appropriately acknowledged the public interest in maintaining an open and pedestrian-friendly environment on Seaview Terrace along with access to the beach, and neither was willing to bend reality to "find" the facts necessary to grant the variance the Barbanell/Basses wanted. (E.g., they rejected the Barbanell/Bass's argument that the fence is justified because they use their front yard as their back yard.) However, given what they perceived to be unique security problems near the beach, Commissioners Pugh and Clarke tried to craft a compromise that would give the Barbanell/Basses some leeway to build a fence higher than forty-two inches in the front yard setback, but with conditions designed to preserve the openness of the walk street.

A legal digression. The law is tough on variances, probably tougher than it should be. It requires that the City "find" that the subject property has qualities that make it different from nearby properties with the same zoning. Property owners are not entitled to variances to fix problems that affect an area generally. There is one exception under which the City can give a variance without finding unique circumstances, but that provision is limited to cases where a variance would create a public benefit.

Trying to find a compromise, Commissioner Pugh offered two possibilities. One was to allow a six-foot "transparent" wrought iron fence along the edge of the sidewalk (the location of the current fence), with shrubbery no higher than 42 inches. But a problem

Charming little garden behind forty-two-inch wall on Seaview Terrace

1972

June 13: City Council approves the plans for Santa Monica Island on a 6-0 vote (project opponent Clo Hoover is absent) despite opposition from residents and the Sierra Club.

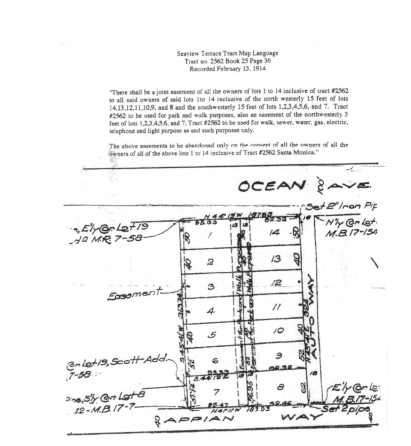

Seaview Terrace Tract Map Language
Tract no. 2562 Book 25 Page 36
Recorded February 13, 1914

"There shall be a joint easement of all the owners of lots 1 to 14 inclusive of tract #2562 to all said owners of said lots 1 to 14 inclusive of the north westerly 15 feet of lots 14,13,12,11,10,9, and 8 and the southwesterly 15 feet of lots 1,2,3,4,5,6, and 7. Tract #2562 to be used for park and walk purposes, also an easement of the northwesterly 3 feet of lots 1,2,3,4,5,6, and 7, Tract #2562 to be used for walk, sewer, water, gas, electric, telephone and light purpose and such purposes only.

The above easements to be abandoned only on the consent of all the owners of all the owners of all of the above lots 1 to 14 inclusive of Tract #2562 Santa Monica."

Original Seaview Terrace Subdivision Map with Tract Map Language

with this "yard behind bars" approach arose when Pugh and Clarke realized they could not make the required findings to justify it, because the security concerns the Barbanell/Basses cited as reasons for their fence and hedge are not unique to their property.

This was where Commissioner Dad made her heroic stand. She pointed out that if the Barbanell/Basses were successful in justifying a security fence based on neighborhood security fears, the precedent could then be used all over the city, wherever any property

261

September 8: The Save Santa Monica Bay Committee files suit to block development of Santa Monica Island.

November: California voters pass Prop. 20, establishing the Coastal Commission to protect the coast; City Manager Perry Scott admits this will doom the Santa Monica Island project. Santa Monica also gives Democrat George McGovern a small majority.

---

owner claimed that his or her neighborhood had a special security problem. (If you listen to people who testify before the commission and the City Council that would mean everywhere.)

Commissioner Pugh's second suggestion was more inventive. He noted that the one unique circumstance of the Barbanell/Bass property is that their house is set back the full depth of the setback, about twenty-six feet from the edge of the walkway. The rest of the block has been built out, typically to about eight feet from the walkway. Fact is, given the narrowness of the walk street, the required setback, thirty feet from the centerline of the walkway, is too wide. The charm of the walk street comes from the little gardens in front of the tight-knit buildings.

Commissioner Pugh's idea was to allow the Barbanell/Basses to build a higher than normally allowed fence that would more or less continue the façade line between the two adjacent structures. This would give the Barbanell/Basses the security they say they need, yet the front of the property would be visually open to the public to the same extent as other properties on the street. The interesting thing about this proposal is that it echoed the history of the site. In the original subdivision plan for Seaview Terrace [reproduced on page 261] a center strip running fifteen feet on either side of the centerline, i.e., to about ten feet from the edge of the current walkway, was dedicated for "Park and Walk Purposes."

In other words, when Seaview Terrace was still private, deed restrictions prohibited property owners from building where the Barbanell/Basses currently have their fence. Regardless whether Commissioner Pugh was aware of this history when he made his proposal, which would have, in effect, restored the old covenant in place of the City's setback requirement, it had a certain amount of sense. Given the unique location of the Barbanell/Bass house, the commission might have been able to make the necessary findings, and it looked like Commissioners Pugh and Clarke would have rounded up at least two more votes from Commissioners O'Day and Johnson.

But the compromise didn't happen. Barry Rosenbaum, the City Attorney's liaison to the planning department, opined that if the commission wanted to grant a variance different from the one requested, the commission needed to hear from the applicants as to whether they would want the variance.

Fair enough. A bad idea, maybe, in this case, but fair enough. Did the Barbanell/Basses accept this reasonable compromise that gave them what they said their family needed in the way of enhanced security, and only required them to "give up" the same narrow strip of front yard that all their neighbors now kept open?

While you ponder that, let's take a time-out for irony, reflection, and reiteration of overriding theme. The reason I started writing about the Barbanell/Basses and their desire for a variance to keep their ugly fence and hedge was because it was ironic that these two activists who had opposed so many other applications for variances now wanted to bend what is a rather strict law and get their own. The fact is, it's too hard in this city to get a variance or any other discretionary permit, politically because of people like the Barbanell/Basses, and I look forward to the next time they oppose a reasonable request for a variance to reduce parking requirements or to obtain a conditional use permit to serve alcoholic beverages.

Back to the hearing. Around 1:30 in the morning, when Chair Clarke asked Ms. Barbanell if she would accept Commissioner Pugh's proposal, she told the commission that she was so upset she was having heart palpitations. (I had the feeling she had expected a different outcome.) She told them she was unhappy, that they didn't understand that her family needed to enclose the entire yard. The answer was no.

So there the commission was. Stumped and stymied in the wee hours. Commissioner Hopkins asked for a continuance so that she could try to craft findings to justify the fence and hedge. Ultimately, Commissioners Clarke and Pugh agreed to the delay, even though it was clear that the Barbanell/Basses did not have the four votes necessary to overturn the Zoning Administrator's ruling, which should have been the end of it. Commissioners Dad and O'Day voted against the continuance, Commissioner O'Day noting that it was the commission's job to make decisions. My new hero, Commissioner Dad, pointed out that the evening's record would show that the findings Commissioner Hopkins wanted could not be made.

Notwithstanding Seaview Terrace, the big issue in Santa Monica in May 2004 was a ballot measure a group calling itself Community for Excellent Public Schools (CEPS) was promoting to require the City to give the Santa Monica Malibu Unified School District much more money each year: six million dollars to start, and then a percentage of future revenues. This led to much heated rhetoric, and negotiations between City Manager Susan McCarthy and the Superintendent of Schools John Deasy. These negotiations resulted in an agreement, alluded to in the previous column, to set the City's contribution to the schools at a higher level and make it permanent, so that the schools could rely on it. The City Council had to approve the agreement, and that led to a stormy meeting where the agreement barely passed.

MAY 17, 2004

That was some rant City Council Member Pam O'Connor went into Tuesday night about the school funding agreement. Ms. O'Connor is normally one of my favorite council members, and she ultimately did the right thing and voted for the agreement, but along the way she sounded like the worst kind of right-wing public education basher. Because Mayor Richard Bloom and Council Member Ken Genser did the job with eloquent remarks about public process and politics, I won't spend much time parsing the words ("schoolyard bullies," "pit bulls," "thugs," "slash-and-burn" politics, etc.) that Ms. O'Connor and Council Member Mike Feinstein used to describe the school funding activists who made guaranteeing a steady stream of City funding for the schools a hot political issue.

But it was weird having those words ringing in my ears three nights later when I attended Jackson Browne's "For the Arts" benefit concert at Barnum Hall and weirder still Saturday afternoon when I enjoyed the school district's arts festival at the Pier. I mean, there I was, shoulder to shoulder with bullies and thugs, yet it seemed that all people cared about was children.

Going back to the council meeting, it was perhaps weirdest of all to hear Ms. O'Connor and Mr. Feinstein insult residents who organized themselves for collective action, when they both owe their political careers to Santa Monicans for Renters Rights and Mr. Feinstein is a Green Party member who presumably lives to organize "folks" (as he likes to call the public) for political action.

If politics offend you, find a cooler kitchen.

And although Mr. Feinstein's point that the City Council has been generous in the past was well taken, he should understand that the voters didn't elect him so that he could abstain when his feelings were hurt. Notwithstanding past generosity, people don't

February 27: The City Council reverses itself and votes 6-0 not to
demolish the Pier and establishes a citizens committee to draw up
plans for preserving it.

---

like to beg and no one else liked his proposal for the district to swap land for money. His non-vote last week was reminiscent of his not taking a position two years ago on Santa Monica College's Prop. U.

Sticks and stones and all that, but Ms. O'Connor hit an ugly bottom with her charges that the school district is a "dark hole" and otherwise irresponsible and unaccountable when it comes to finances, the Brown Act, and anything else she could imagine. In her view, the City couldn't trust the district with the City's money.

Hmmm. Would it be thuggish to mention the tens of millions of dollars of cost overruns for the Public Safety Facility, or the fact that the City is spending more tens of millions to build a new library that except for the parking isn't much bigger than the old one? Would I be a bully to point out that after a couple of bond issues, our school facilities look pretty good, but it took a decade for the City just to decide what to do with Virginia Avenue Park?

Would it be slash-and-burn politics to remind everyone that the City has financial problems in the first place because Council Members O'Connor and Feinstein and their colleagues recklessly increased routine operations spending by nearly 25 percent (and more than $20 million) in two years (2000-2002), mostly for purposes that most residents would say are less important than educating children?

All in all, Council Members O'Connor and Feinstein embarrassed themselves more than making any charges against either school officials or the CEPS activists that stick, but the rhetoric they used was poisonous and took all the joy out of what should have been a celebration of local politics at its best—an engaged populace, intelligent public administration, broad-thinking elected officials.

One more thing. Mayor Bloom congratulated everyone for getting the school funding agreement passed and said that it was a good thing, "particularly for the children of this community." I respectfully disagree. We middle-aged types have no cause to be noble. Funding education is "particularly" good for us grown-ups who want the next generation to be productive enough to pay our Social Security, who are safer when young adults have jobs rather than rap sheets, and who want our real estate investments to appreciate.

• • •

I have been writing this column for almost four years—more than 180 columns. But when I meet readers for the first time, the column about 90 percent of them remember is the one I wrote after David Attias ran his car down that crowded street in Isla Vista. And

1974
Santa Monica buys the privately owned Santa Monica Amusement
Pier (formerly, the Looff Pier) and the adjacent land on the shore as
part of the plan to save the Pier.

there are many other readers who regularly inquire about the welfare of David, who is a patient at Patton State Hospital, where he was committed for treatment of his mental illness.

I bring this up because I received a note from David's mother, Santa Monica resident Diana Attias, informing me that NAMI, the National Alliance for the Mentally Ill, is conducting its inaugural Los Angeles County walkathon on Saturday, May 22. The 5K "NAMIWALKS FOR THE MIND OF AMERICA" will take place at the Santa Fe Dam Recreation Area in Irwindale. For more information, or to make a donation, either call (213) 351-2874, or click on www.namiwalkslac.org.

It shouldn't take a case like David's, or the sight of so many mentally ill people on our streets, for us to realize that mental illness is as much as part of human life as mental health. Those of us who have our sanity have no right to believe we did something to deserve it, and we should do as much as we can to help not only the mentally ill, but also those who work to understand mental illness' causes and devise its cures.

Ultimately the Planning Commission met again to consider the Barbanell/ Bass fence. I was pleased that because of my column the commissioners now had in their hands the original tract map. This time, after more discussion, Ms. Barbanell accepted the compromise plan after losing a vote on the variance.

MAY 24, 2004

I don't have much add to the *Lookout's* coverage of the Planning Commission's decision on the Stephanie Barbanell/Jerry Bass fence and hedge on Seaview Terrace ("Fence Saga Likely Ends," May 21, 2004), since reporter Olin Ericksen recounted the heart of the story, namely how Ms. Barbanell managed to pull the commission's collective chain over the course of two meetings.

I wouldn't want to play poker with Stephanie Barbanell or, for that matter, bargain for a pile of old LPs at a garage sale. There she was, defiant. She only had three votes to grant her appeal when she needed four; she was on the brink of getting nothing; but there she stood, refusing to grovel and accept the bone of compromise four commissioners were painfully trying to devise. That was two weeks ago. Then last week, there she was again, still bold, still fearless, refusing to budge. That is, refusing to budge until Commissioner Arlene Hopkins's motion to grant her variance lost on a five-to-one vote.

Oh well. What are a few hours of our lives give or take?

I may from time to time criticize various planning commissioners for one failing or another, but I have to admit they have "turn the other cheek" down cold.

I can't let this issue go, however, without saying something about the dialectic Commissioner Hopkins had with herself about historical preservation. I wish I could link to a little video clip so everyone could see it. Ms. Hopkins wanted to grant the Barbanell/ Basses' original request for a variance because she thought it was unfair that the City was claiming a public easement over Seaview Terrace, and preventing the residents from gating their community. In her view this was leading to a "degradation of the historic character" of the walk street.

For Ms. Hopkins (and it's worth noting that Commissioner Jay Johnson also wanted to gate the street) it was a matter of "historic preservation," yet the only significant historical aspect to Seaview Terrace is its public access. The buildings there are a mishmash of historical inauthenticities. The one undeniable historic quality worth preserving is that back in 1914 the original developer required the lot buyers to agree to keep a thirty-foot wide strip down the center open for walk and park purposes.

1974
Fire destroys the ruins of Pacific Ocean Park.

What the Planning Commission did last week by requiring the Barbanell/Basses to tear down the last remaining fence and clear the bulk of that easement is probably the most substantial action it has taken for historic preservation in a long time.

[Note: Unfortunately, it turned out that the Planning Commission's action did not mean that the fence and the hedge would come down. As the Seaview Terrace fence law enforcement saga had dragged on for more than a year, over in a different part of town, the tony streets north of Montana Avenue, a controversy had erupted and a political movement had formed over enforcement of the hedge law. This movement ultimately resulted in the election of Kennedy cousin Bobby Shriver to the City Council. But in between the Planning Commission's vote to have the Barbanell/Basses remove their fence and hedge, and the date the commission could formally adopt a "Statement of Official Action" that would mean the end of the fence, the City Council passed a moratorium on enforcement of the fence and hedge law, to last until the council passed a new ordinance. Saved by delay, the fence and hedge, though tidied up and trimmed, still stand.]

O ne indicator of the truth of Tip O'Neill's adage, "all politics is local," is the sheer busyness of local government. It's not always for the best, but part-time local officials are, on an hour-of-being-in-session-by-hour-of-being-in-session basis, the hardest working people in government.

JUNE 7, 2004

As a student (and sometimes practitioner) of disingenuousness in all its subtleties and permutations, I have begun to look forward each spring to the City Council's study sessions on the budget. It's an occasion where aficionados of the self-effacing and philosophical pause can observe masters of the quizzical yet caring look react to the unintended consequences of their years of trying to relieve Santa Monicans of all their complaints and anxieties.

This year the statistic that jumped out at me was not the 110,000 phone calls the planning department answered, but an item from the Office of the City Attorney; namely, that in 2003 the City Council enacted forty-one new ordinances.

On average, that's one every nine days. Looked at another way, that's forty-one ordinances for a city of 84,000, or one ordinance for every 2,049 people. In 2002 the City Council enacted only thirty-two ordinances, or one every 11.4 days, or one for every 2,625 residents. That's a 22 percent decrease in the number of residents per new ordinance. At that rate, and assuming the City's population remains the same (as it has for forty years), in only thirty-one years we will achieve the apotheosis of Squeaky Wheel Government: a perfect ratio of one new ordinance for each resident.

I'm not one of those people who bashes government for governing, but given that (i) the council met thirty-three times in 2003, and (ii) Santa Monica isn't facing any genuine crises that might in a less-favored locale seriously be considered emergencies, isn't it worrisome that on average, seven council members can't have a meeting without passing 1.25 ordinances?

I mean, let's take it easy. Save some laws for next year.

In the meantime, the wheels keep squeaking. The issue of the moment is fences and hedges. In response to complaints from well-heeled and well-shrubbed residents whose hedges are under attack by City inspectors (acting on complaints from neighbors), tomorrow night the City Council will consider whether to review the current law, which allows fences and hedges in front yards up to forty-two inches, and along side and rear yards up to eight feet.

As usual, there's a certain amount of Santa Monica hysteria going on, this time partly a function of some famous names and partly a function of the form order to comply that the City sends to alleged violators. The City routinely threatens violators that failure to correct a violation "will result" in penalties "up to $25,000 per day." The problem with this is that the finality of the "will result" part is not true for any violation, since no penalties are assessed until there has been appropriate due process, and the $25,000 part is not true when it comes to fences and hedges.

The $25,000-per-day penalty only exists for life-threatening conditions, like an over-hanging crane. More routine infractions like overly tall hedges top out at $2,499 per day. (In fact, no one at the City I spoke to could recall a hedge or fence case going so far as to require fines.) Everyone should calm down and the City should revise its compliance orders to explain the law and the process better, including the alleged violator's rights, and incidentally make the City look less like a bully, but again it's worth pointing out that staff has only articulated the unintended consequences of the City Council's obsession with code enforcement.

As readers of my Seaview Terrace columns know, I'm a true believer when it comes to keeping front yards open to view, although I will note that the City's regular practice, at least as I recall from when I was on the Planning Commission, has been to allow "adjustments" up to 48 inches. But as someone who has lived here in two single-story houses that taller buildings overlooked, I question the purpose of the current limits on side and rear hedges. The current eight-foot limit seems designed for neighborhoods of one-story, single family homes, but that's not how most Santa Monicans live.

For aesthetic reasons, no fence or wall should be higher than eight feet. But where buildings are higher than one story and separated by side and rear yards, it makes sense for privacy, aesthetic and even ecological purposes to allow, if not encourage, plantings that separate adjacent properties, provided, of course, that neighbors are not adversely affected.

While ideally property owners can use trees to accomplish this separation, sometimes in a narrow space a hedge works better. In that case, it's hard to see the harm in a hedge that is no higher than the permitted height of a building. The law should have enough flexibility to allow the City to approve tall hedges without finding the unique circumstances a full-blown variance requires.

Uh-oh. Sounds like another ordinance.

During the summer of 2004, other than the hedge issue, politics seemed to slow down in Santa Monica. I had some time to reflect on the town and its place in the world.

JUNE 28, 2004

My office is just a block off the Third Street Promenade, and I'm on the Promenade for at least a few moments nearly every day, running an errand, or just taking a walk. Last week the uptick in activity was palpable, as schools let out and the high season for tourists kicked in. Speaking of kicks, I always get one when I see people taking snapshots of themselves in front of the triceratops fountain across from Santa Monica Place. Last Friday I took these pictures all in the span of ten minutes.

It's humbling to think that people would travel thousands of miles to Santa Monica and memorialize their visit to our dinosaur topiaries. Usually they take multiple shots to ensure that everyone gets "in the picture." I see the dinos everyday, and I wonder what the point is. Do Florentines feel the same way about tourists who photograph themselves in front of the replica of Michelangelo's *David* in front of the Palazzo Vecchio? Sorry, that implies a snide comparison between their art and ours, which isn't the point I want to make. Maybe a better comparison would be to the fountain of a wild boar the Florentines have in their public market; tourists not only photograph themselves in front of that, but also rub the boar's nose.

Do the Florentines shake their heads?

Tourists photographing themselves.

April 10: Santa Monica voters replace three City Council members
who had supported tearing down the Pier and building Santa Monica
Island with council members pledged to protect the coast and the
bay and save the Pier.

I'm flattered that Santa Monica is a "tourist Mecca." I get a charge seeing all those tourists walking around, smiling even when the marine layer is at its gloomiest. A lot of Santa Monicans complain about the tourists, as if they expect something different in a town that's been a resort for most of its existence, but how can one not be charmed by people who take pictures of themselves with Santa Monica Place—a mall—in the background?

1975
Santa Monicans vote 10,540 to 5,823 to preserve the Pier; the City
hires local architect Frank Gehry to design a facelift for it.

A couple weeks ago after I wrote about the fences and hedges controversy, I received an email from a Santa Monica homeowner who didn't like the prospect of passersby looking into her living room window. She was ready to sell out and leave town; it wasn't just the prospect of the hedge inspectors showing up, she said, but because "Santa Monica is in essence part of LA and it has become too crowded and generally unfriendly overall."

"Unfriendly overall?" How many Santa Monicans believe that? I will not make too much of the irony of worrying about unfriendliness from behind a tall hedge, but perhaps if this woman's concerns are common, more Santa Monicans should get out and mingle with the smiling tourists. Something good might rub off.

We who live here become so caught up in our day-to-day complaints, that like the Moliere character who was shocked to find out that all his life he'd been speaking prose, what's prosaic to us is poetry to others.

S anta Monica's Muscle Beach had a huge impact on American culture. It's
  impossible to imagine today's fitness craze without it.

JULY 5, 2004

A week ago Sunday I attended the opening of an exhibit about the history of Santa
Monica's Muscle Beach at the Santa Monica Historical Society Museum. The event was
a reunion of many participants in Muscle Beach's fabled past. More than a few were in
their nineties, but they all looked more likely than me to do a handstand.

Those attending included the fearless acrobat Paula Unger Boelsems (in photos you
often see her flying through the air, or high up in a human pyramid), who led the discussion, as well as Glenn Sundby (who not only once walked down the 898 steps of the

Acrobat Paula Unger Boelsems recalls Muscle Beach's colorful past.

Washington Monument on his hands, but also became an important force in international gymnastics) and his sister Dolores Foster (who performed with him for many years

1975
McDonnell Douglas Corporation, the successor to Douglas Aircraft
Company, closes its Santa Monica plant.

on Broadway and in vaudeville), Moe Most (the strong bottom man on many of the pyramids Muscle Beach was famous for), the elegant Dolores Abro, and Armand Tanny (brother of Vic, and famous in his own right, especially in the weight-lifting world).

The acrobats and bodybuilders who worked out and performed on Muscle Beach in the '30s, '40s, and '50s had a huge impact on American culture, as much as any other performers. It is hard to imagine today's obsession with fitness without the contributions of people like Vic Tanny, Joe Gold, Harold Zinkin (inventor of the universal weight machine), Jack LaLanne, Pudgy and Les Stockton, George Eiferman, and many others who had associations with Muscle Beach. The irony is that in 1959, just before President Kennedy would make physical fitness a national phenomenon, the burghers of Santa Monica used a convenient sex scandal, involving a handful of weight lifters, some from out of town, as an excuse to close down Muscle Beach.

Although Santa Monica had historically been more tolerant of eccentricity than the rest of Southern California, a place where the urban sea met the sea itself, population growth and change in the '40s and '50s, and the prevailing '50s ethos of prudish conformity, changed the political climate. The nearly nude, muscular men and women of Muscle Beach were disquieting to residents who wanted to believe that they lived in an idealized suburb, not a factory town adjacent to a world famous resort and honky-tonk.

It didn't help that bodybuilders attracted gay men; the *Evening Outlook* charged that Muscle Beach had become "a favorite haven of the sexual athletes and queers of Southern California," a place for "athletes and their followers of all three sexes." (I'm lifting these quotes from the excellent history of Muscle Beach written by Marla Matzer Rose: *Muscle Beach: Where the Best Bodies in the World Started a Fitness Revolution*, which is available at the Historical Society Museum.) It probably also didn't help that the strong and fearless women of Muscle Beach projected an unabashedly feminine yet pre-feminist image not consistent with '50s female docility.

A few years ago the City restored some semblance of Muscle Beach by improving the equipment and providing a space for tumbling, but there was no attempt, by rebuilding the old performance platform or by providing viewing stands, to restore the exhibitionist or entertainment side of Muscle Beach that was integral to what the beachfront was in the days before urban renewal and oppressive family values.

The City has brought back some sense of the Pier's history with the Thursday evening concerts and with Pacific Park, although with the latter the City Council wouldn't allow a roller coaster big enough to amuse teenagers.

The new Muscle Beach lacks flair of old.

Glenn Sundby announced at the museum that he has formed a Santa Monica Muscle Beach Foundation with the aim of turning Muscle Beach into a California historical site, with not only a monument, but also a new performance platform that would be the setting for exhibitions and competitions in gymnastics, acrobatics, cheerleading, juggling, Special Olympics, and a renewal of the once popular "Mr. and Miss (Ms.?) Muscle Beach" contests.

More power to Mr. Sundby, but it's hard to imagine anything succeeding in Santa Monica these days that might attract more tourists. We're beyond fearing the homosexual menace and no one these days will complain about the beefcake and cheesecake, but imagine the howls about the traffic.

I'm proud that physical fitness started at Muscle Beach and I'm proud that within twenty years after the City shut Muscle Beach down, a few blocks away a bunch of local kids created skateboarding as the world now knows it, and a hugely popular pop culture to go along with it. Hey, I'm proud that while bodybuilders were pumping iron

c. 1975
Local skateboarders, based at the Zephyr Surf Shop on Main Street
in Ocean Park (a.k.a., "Dogtown"), win the first national skateboarding championship. They ultimately invent "extreme sports" by
skateboarding in empty swimming pools.

on Muscle Beach, a few blocks east, at Rand, Herman Kahn was devising "Mutually Assured Destruction."

I'm even more proud that not long before the Dogtown skateboarders had discovered the Bicknell hill, Daniel Ellsberg copied the Pentagon Papers here.

I like living in a city that is famous. I like having neighbors who do great things. I'm proud that Brecht and Diebenkorn lived and worked here. That Douglas built planes here. That Gehry built his house here. I'm proud that in fiction Santa Monica was Philip Marlowe's Bay City and that in real life Tony Cornero sailed the *Rex* off our shore. I'm proud that in the '60s and '70s the Civic Auditorium hosted the Oscars and rock 'n' roll, instead of antique shows.

I'm even proud that Britney Spears buys pets here.

I could go on. And on. There are other beaches in Southern California, and other beach towns, but Santa Monica has a history. We were never a sleepy beach town, we were never a suburb. We're famous, and that's why the tourists come and why I like it here, too.

An important history implies an important future. This year is a political year. The candidates are positioning themselves. The next City Council will oversee the writing of new land-use and circulation elements of our general plan. When the candidates debate, there will be a lot of questions about the homeless, and traffic, and school funding, and preferential parking. But what I would most like to know from them is what they believe our common destiny is.

What's the next big thing that's going to come from Santa Monica?

Y ou can always count on politics making people do or say stupid things. The Chamber of Commerce had decided to endorse candidates to run against SMRR.

JULY 12, 2004

"Have you noticed that downtown Santa Monica smells like urine?" —From a "public service" message the Santa Monica Chamber of Commerce Issues Committee sent thousands of Santa Monicans last week.

My in-laws own a successful chain of furniture stores in western Pennsylvania and Ohio, and I asked my brother-in-law, who runs the business, if he ever considered promoting the business by telling prospective customers that his stores smelled like urine. Not being up to date on modern West Coast marketing techniques, he said no.

Typical private dumpster: Where's the outrage?

1976
Santa Monica City Council creates a Landmarks Commission and
enacts a landmarks preservation ordinance.

About 90 percent of Santa Monicans regularly come downtown, but that's obviously creating too much traffic. So the Chamber of Commerce is cleverly trying to persuade more customers to stay away.

Enough with the jokes. I'm not a Pollyanna. I do occasionally see men relieve themselves against downtown alley walls (just one more way for Santa Monica to remind me of Italy), but what I smell every morning when I ride my bike in the alley between the Broadway Deli building and the parking structure on Fourth north of Broadway is garbage. The distinctive odor bacteria create when we allow them to flourish in our waste emanates from overflowing private dumpsters and the liquid that leaks from the private garbage haulers that service the businesses on the Promenade. Businesses that are, perhaps, members of the Chamber of Commerce?

The first anniversary of the Farmers Market tragedy when ten people had died put me into a philosophical mood.

JULY 19, 2004

Friday I attended the memorial service at First Presbyterian Church on the anniversary of the Farmers Market accident. I was in Italy and asleep when the accident occurred, and I learned about it when I awoke the next day and turned on my computer. I immediately thought about a friend, Bill. Bill and I take a bike ride up the beach every Wednesday at lunch. After the ride, Bill always goes to the Farmers Market and I return to my office. We usually finish riding about 1:30, so I knew it was likely that Bill was at the market when the accident occurred.

With some anxiety, I emailed to see if he was okay. He wrote back that he was, but that he had been there. He had seen the car in time to get himself up onto a vendor's table. The car missed him by about three feet.

A few weeks later I returned to Santa Monica and we resumed our weekly ride. I asked Bill about his close call. Bill said, on further reflection, that he had not truly been in danger. He said that the car was coming straight down the street, and he was already off to the side, near the vendor's table, so that the car would not have hit him even if he had not jumped onto the table. I told Bill I thought he was in danger, by any normal notion of danger. To myself I thought that Bill's thinking was a model example of human courage when faced with this business of living.

A friend told me about his friend who suffered two broken legs at the market but considered himself lucky—and I guess he was. I guess we're all lucky we live here, and not in the Sudan. When my wife returned to the market later in July, a vendor told her that the fact that he survived made him more optimistic about his future, that it was a sign that things were going to get better for him.

At the memorial service, Rabbi Neil Comess-Daniels pointed out that when God created the heavens and the earth, God only said it was "good." Not perfect, not wonderful. This hit home Friday. As I walked to the service at First Pres., I reached my wife on my cell phone. She had just heard from her brother-in-law that her sister's operation that morning in New York for stomach cancer had gone unexpectedly well; the doctors had found less spread of cancer than they had feared, and had been able to save much of her stomach. Everyone was happy.

Also on Friday, I was thinking about a friend here with multiple sclerosis. I planned to visit her that afternoon at St. Johns. She was there after breaking a leg, in intense pain. Yet whenever I spoke to her she cheered me up. I had to wonder what a strange world we live in that we can tolerate with hope all the terrible things that are the consequence of mortality.

Good, not perfect.

Having reached this far, you know that one of my themes is the imperfection of my own liberal ideology. Once again I found myself challenged when our local state representative in Sacramento pushed a plan to let hybrid cars with solo drivers into car pool lanes.

JULY 26, 2004

My wife is an academic and one advantage of that is that I meet some interesting people—people who actually know something. One such person I met through my wife is the linguist, Geoffrey Nunberg, who you may have heard on NPR's program, *Fresh Air*, or whose columns on language and culture you may have read in the *New York Times'* Sunday "Week in Review." Nunberg has a book out, a collection of pieces from *Fresh Air* and newspapers, called *Going Nucular: Language, Politics, and Culture in Confrontational Times*, and he was recently in Hollywood for a reading and book-signing at Book Soup.

One of the many linguistic developments Nunberg has reported on is how the meaning of the word "liberal" has evolved from being a word that neutrally described a set of political views or those who hold them (which views themselves were subject to change over time), to a word that identifies, in a negative manner, a particular subset of people who not only hold those views but also allegedly possess certain other characteristics.

"Liberal" has become, for many at least, a "negative brand" connoting people who are Democrats who have a certain ethnicity (white) and certain preferences in what they consume (e.g., expensive coffee drinks, expensive bread, expensive cheese, expensive imported automobiles). While this use of liberal is the invention of right-wingers out to demonize their ideological enemies, and doesn't have much to do with the facts (it turns out Republicans consume most of the nation's imports of brie), the word has taken on this new meaning in mainstream usage as well.

Nunberg has found, for instance, that while the phrases "middle-class liberals" and "middle-class Democrats" occur with equal frequency in major newspapers, the phrase "working-class liberal" is extremely rare, while "working-class Democrat" is common. So is, for that matter, "working-class conservative," and while it's easy to say "black conservative," "black liberal" hardly comes trippingly off the tongue.

As one who is a white Democrat, has liberal views, eats La Brea bread, drinks espresso and drives a French car, I am mightily annoyed that I've been negatively branded by the

1979
Santa Monicans for Renters Rights collects signatures to put a new rental control charter amendment, Prop.
A, on the April municipal ballot; Prop. A passes 56 to 44 percent. Two council members endorsed by SMRR
are also elected.

1980
Santa Monica population: 88,314

likes of Limbaugh and O'Reilly. But I'm even more annoyed when my political soul mates go ahead and do things that play into or even justify the stereotype.

For instance, our own Democratic and very environmentally minded member of the Assembly, Fran Pavley, has proposed a bill to allow single drivers of Priuses and other hybrid cars to use car-pool lanes, and, in Los Angeles, good liberals Mayor Kenneth Hahn and Council Member Eric Garcetti have proposed allowing hybrid owners to park free at parking meters. Can you imagine any law that could better fit the image of self-righteous, Westside, very comfortable but full of outrage, "liberals" than a law that entitles them to flaunt and benefit from the innate goodness that comes from driving an expensive car that gets—oh, how wonderful—45 miles per gallon?

I won't go into how wasteful it has been to spend hundreds of millions if not billions of dollars on car-pool lanes instead of mass transit, nor how more than anything else free parking encourages driving. Nonetheless, it is doubly wasteful to crowd those lanes, which should be used by buses and shuttles, with single-passenger cars, or to allow wealthy owners of hybrids, high up on the consumption chain, to park on L.A. streets for free.

According to an article last week in the *L.A. Times*, Pavley's bill has passed the Assembly, as well as a panel in the State Senate. Both the Governor and his frequent nemesis, Treasurer Phil Angelides, support it. The only obstacles to its passage in the Senate are suddenly vocal and outraged transit experts and federal regulations that limit federal funding for car-pool lanes to those that are limited to—car pools. But under lobbying from Toyota and other manufacturers, Congress is considering abolishing that.

To deal with the charge that allowing hybrids in car-pool lanes will congest them and make them even more useless than usual, Pavley's bill limits the privilege to drive solo in car-pool lanes to the first 75,000 hybrids on the road. Imagine—isn't that convenient? Or even more outrageous? Let's get this straight, to stimulate sales of cars that already have waiting lists, Pavley wants to give only the first 75,000 selfless environmentalists the special sticker that will allow them to use the car-pool lanes.

What about the poor slobs who can't afford to buy one this year? And for that matter, what about urbanites who drive less? My old Peugeot may only get sixteen miles to the gallon, but by living near my job in a congested (yet convenient) city, I only drive 3,000 miles a year. I use half as much gas as one of Pavley's Thousand Oaks constituents who drives 18,000 miles a year in a Prius.

When do I get my sticker?

In 2004, instead of visiting my parents in Italy, my son and I joined a week-long backpacking trip, "off the grid," with friends in the Sierras. When I returned, the City Council race was shaping up. The big news items were that Bobby Shriver, a Kennedy cousin and the governor's brother-in-law, was running, and that SMRR was not going to endorse Michael Feinstein—payback for his running a Green Party candidate against the SMRR slate in 2002.

AUGUST 16, 2004

I had the rare experience during my week backpacking in the Sierra Nevada of perfectly realizing a fantasy. I caught fish in a lake high in the mountains and then cooked them up in a frying pan and ate them with friends. Besides achieving the fish fantasy, I will best remember my week in the Evolution Valley of Inyo National Forest for the combination of physical beauty and emptiness. Usually, when you see natural beauty like that, you are surrounded by other tourists, but there are strict limits on the number of visitors who can enter the wilderness area.

It was also strange to be off the grid, not knowing the latest presidential polls, or how the Phillies were managing to break my heart this year, or how many candidates there were for the City Council. Instead, except for one's own thoughts, conversations with your fellow travelers, and the wind, there was just a rushing silence: the hushed week flew by.

Muriel Lake

1983
Winter storms destroy much of Santa Monica Pier; City creates Pier
Restoration Corporation to oversee reconstruction.

It was better to be off the grid than to return to Santa Monica and learn that nineteen hopefuls had submitted signatures to quality for the City Council ballot.

Tag team debates?

With so many running, Santa Monicans for Renters Rights would seem to have the advantage. Its opposition looks to be scattered, divided among the Chamber of Commerce endorsees and the Bill Bauer-Kathryn Morea-David Cole "Team for Change" slate. SMRR has its own uncertainties, however, to deal with. For one, the wild-card candidacy of Bobby Shriver is hard to handicap. Depending on how he runs his campaign—will he choose to focus on his unhappy homeowner issue of hedges or his broader liberal credentials?—Shriver could either further divide the opposition and perhaps take Herb Katz's seat, or leap over the opposition and take a SMRR seat.

That vulnerable SMRR seat presents an inherent difficulty for SMRR, because by not endorsing Michael Feinstein, SMRR will need to depose an incumbent (Feinstein) to keep its 5-2 majority intact. I could only attend about an hour of the SMRR convention two weeks ago. I didn't witness the counting of the votes, and missed the shock that greeted the revelation that none of the SMRR incumbents received an endorsement on the first ballot, but I did hear the calls for unity before the vote.

Council Members and candidates Ken Genser and Richard Bloom professed their loyalty to the SMRR cause, but two years ago they slammed SMRR candidate Abby Arnold at the convention and gave her no support during the election. Feinstein had the honesty to say that there were occasions when he wouldn't support everyone on the slate—as was the case in 2002 when he bolted SMRR to support fellow Green Josefina Aranda, the reckless act that caused SMRR, rightly from a political view, to refuse him its endorsement this year.

SMRR leaders Denny Zane, Nancy Greenstein, and Judy Abdo emphasized the importance of loyalty and fretted over the evils of "bullet voting," but when the votes were counted, Maria Loya, the newcomer candidate from the Pico Neighborhood, had forty some bullet votes and an endorsement, and Mayor Bloom didn't even have a majority. In fact, even without her bullet votes, Loya had more votes than Bloom, whose opposition years ago to the Ralph's Market on Olympic Boulevard still rankles Pico residents more concerned about economic growth and shopping opportunities than traffic congestion.

On the second ballot the Pico residents led by School Board Member Oscar De La Torre came around and supported SMRR old-guarders Genser and Bloom, but it was plain that if they had wanted to, for instance if Abby Arnold had been running again, SMRR's new blood could have forced SMRR to drop its endorsement of either or both Genser or Bloom.

Candidates endorsed by Santa Monicans for Renters Rights win a
majority on the City Council; SMRR member Ruth Yannatta Goldway
becomes mayor.

Instead of trying to figure out why Latinos and African-Americans from the Pico
Neighborhood might choose not to endorse the likes of Bloom, Genser, and Feinstein,
the SMRR insiders I've talked to either express indignation that the Pico residents came
to the organization with their own agenda and candidates, or dismiss their bullet voting
as simply "tactics." The insiders don't consider it possible that the Pico residents might
rightfully believe that for all the years SMRR has been in power, for all the nice words,
SMRR has cared little for the issues—traditional liberal issues like jobs, education, and
housing—that matter to them.

What have Bloom, Genser, and Feinstein done to create jobs in Santa Monica? On
the whole, have they encouraged or hindered the building of enough apartments to keep
up with demand? What's been their attitude toward Santa Monica College, the best way
out of poverty and into the middle class for people of color, and immigrants and their
children?

Consider the Lantana studio development. NIMBYs living near Lantana, including
SMRR stalwarts like Michael Tarbet, blocked Lantana's expansion for several years over
hyped-up traffic issues. Now it looks like the project will go forward, with Lantana having to pay a small fortune for traffic barriers and curb extensions that may not be needed.
In the meantime, the new leadership of the Pico Neighborhood Association got involved.
What did they want from Lantana? A jobs center. Was this on the list of "public benefits"
planning staff proposed in response to direction from no-growth SMRR planning commissioners and city council members? No.

It's hypocritical for SMRR leadership to bemoan people organizing to get the SMRR
endorsement when the incumbent City Council mandarins use SMRR for their own purposes. Sure, anyone who gets the SMRR endorsement will vote a certain way when it
comes to anything to do with the interests of existing renters, or certain social services,
but otherwise, as for content, what does the SMRR endorsement mean?

SMRR talks a lot about its platform, but in the real world it has little control over
what its council members do. Some will vote for Target, some against; some will vote for
fluoridation, some against; some will vote for keeping Kelly Olsen on the Planning Commission, some against; etc.

The SMRR convention takes place at Olympic High, the former site of Muir Elementary. People gather outside on the playground. The image I have of SMRR is of one of
those big, bouncy, red rubber balls; the hollow ones that kids easily bat from one side of
the playground to the other.

O kay, not all politics is local. There was going to be another election in November 2004. I was grasping at straws.

AUGUST 23, 2004

I drive an old car, a 1986 Peugeot, that at 94,000 miles is starting to have troubles. Peugeot hasn't sold cars in the U.S. for years, and although parts are not hard to get, I have no business driving the old machine beyond AAA towing range of my mechanic at Lincoln and Broadway. Due to last minute circumstances, however, I ended up using the car to drive my son and me on our recent camping trip to the eastern Sierra.

Arriving at the trailhead for our hike into the Sierra, about half an hour from Bishop, the power steering failed. All the power steering fluid had drained out from a leak. I had no option but to leave the car parked on the mountain.

A week later the expedition returned. The car manual said not to drive without power steering fluid, but I drove down the hill to Bishop and nothing terrible happened. The question I had was who would service a Peugeot in Bishop. I got referred to an outfit called Sierra German Auto and drove into their parking lot. Inside I told a mechanic that so-and-so had said that they worked on Peugeots.

"He lied," he said. Nonetheless, I pleaded that maybe he could take a look at the car and perhaps the only problem was a bad hose that he could replace. The mechanic—his name was Tim—obligingly said he would, or, rather that the other mechanic, Kenny, would, because Tim had to run an errand. Tim told my son and me that we would have to wait in the waiting area in the office.

The walls of the office were covered with photos of Tim racing a souped-up Volkswagen beetle on dirt tracks in Nevada and California, along with a good collection of trophies. There was also a bulletin board, on which was posted one document, a long email: an anti-Clinton diatribe of the "spawn of Satan" variety. Hmmm. Reading it, I wondered if Kenny, before he had put my Peugeot on the hoist, had seen my back bumper with the two bumper stickers: "Re-Elect Gore in 2004" (a souvenir from attending the counter-inauguration in downtown L.A. in 2001) and "Kerry-Edwards."

There I was in Red State California. My son later told me he had seen on Tim's car a bumper sticker reading "Vietnam Veterans Against John Kerry," but he hadn't mentioned it. Well, without overly dramatizing my political paranoia, Kenny turned out to be a resourceful mechanic. A part was cracked, but he said he could use a hose-clamp to make a temporary repair good enough to get us back to Santa Monica. He told us to return in an hour or so, at 4:30, which we did.

1983
In the April municipal election, opposition candidates to SMRR
sweep the City Council election including a defeat of Mayor Ruth Yannatta Goldway; SMRR's majority is reduced to 4-3.

By then, Tim was back and both Tim and Kenny seemed uncommonly interested in my car. They asked how I could keep it running, given that Peugeot no longer sells cars here. I told them that it wasn't a problem in L.A. because Peugeot had kept its parts network up in the hopes that they company would return to the U.S. market. I mentioned that Peugeot was still quite big around the world, and maybe they would.

At this point Tim said, "Oh, yeah, I know they're big in the Third World, cause they sell a lot of cars in Iraq and Iran."

I have to say that this rhetorical arrow whizzed completely by me, and I babbled something about the fabled Peugeot slant-four engine, but my son told me later that he considered blurting out, "Dad, didn't I tell you to take the Chevy!"

The repair held, and we made it back to Santa Monica in the heart of Blue State California.

I have friends whose son is an Army M.P. who was recently deployed in Iraq, and I wanted to send him a package of goodies. I learned that the soldiers like reading matter and hard candies, so I packed up a few books and several pounds of candy in a Priority Mail box and took it to the Main P.O. on Fifth Street to complete the customs form. Some weeks ago I read in one of the Santa Monica papers that a postal clerk had said that they saw little military mail here. Wondering if that were the case, I asked the clerk if she had been handling a lot of packages going to A.P.O. addresses.

The clerk, by the way, was an Asian immigrant, and she replied, in a thick accent that did not hide her irony, "In Santa Monica?" "No," she continued, "everyone is running from the army here." But then, before I could say anything, she added, "just like the Bushes. None of their children or nephews joined."

I suppose it's no surprise that there is not a lot of military mail originating in Santa Monica, but I was taken back by the clerk's bitter aside about the First Family. This immigrant didn't identify with Santa Monica's anti-military gestalt, but she saw right through the platitudes of the right wing as well.

I have been obsessed as many are with the presidential election, as the stakes appear higher than in decades. As a Democrat, I have tried to be neither optimistic about Kerry's chances (after all, I'm a Phillies fan, and 75 days is a long time in both politics and baseball), nor pessimistic, since so far Kerry has been able to withstand whatever the Bush campaign has thrown at him.

We'll see if Kerry can fend off the latest ghost-of-Lee-Atwater smears, those involving the "Swift Boat Veterans." If he can, I suspect it will be less because of Kerry and more because Bush and Cheney and company have done what no amount of flag-waving by Democrats could ever have done: By their venality they have broken the hold Republicans have had for years over patriotism and its symbols.

Bush is in trouble if a postal clerk is annoyed that his nephews aren't in the service.

U sually, local news is crowded out by national news, but in the case of our Assembly Member Fran Pavley's bill to give car-pool lane privileges to certain hybrid cars, the local went national.

AUGUST 30, 2004

Our Assembly Member Fran Pavley's bill to allow solo drivers of certain hybrid cars to use car-pool lanes passed the California Senate this week and awaits the Governor's signature. Not only did the bill pass, but the *New York Times* wrote about it, under this headline: "Detroit Fights California Bid to Open Car Pool Lanes to Fuel-Conscious Import."

As you can tell by the headline, the *Times* reported on the story that the U.S. auto industry objects to giving privileges to drivers of Japanese cars. William C. Ford, Chairman of Ford, and the United Auto Workers' Ford Department have written to Governor Schwarzenegger asking him to veto the legislation not because it's an unnecessary and meaningless feel-good measure designed to benefit eco-chic supporters of Ms. Pavley, as suggested in this column (although the *Times* does name many of them), but because the law limits the car-pool lane privilege to cars that get at least forty-five miles per gallon.

So far only Japanese companies make such vehicles; Ford is about to start selling a 32-mpg hybrid S.U.V. This goes to show that no matter how absurd and self-congratulatory high-maintenance American environmentalists can get, high-maintenance American corporations will always top them in the whining department.

Mr. Ford wrote Schwarzenegger that Pavley's bill "puts our workers and stockholders at a competitive disadvantage precisely when Ford is entering the hybrid market with a family-oriented, no compromise S.U.V." A "family-oriented, no compromise S.U.V." I love it. A family decides that anything less than two tons of top-heavy truck to haul the kids and their soccer balls would be a compromise, Ford sticks in a hybrid engine, and then they should get car pool privileges—for when they're driving solo!

But then this is the slope you start slipping on when you grant public benefits— the use of car pool lanes that the government built with hundreds of millions of tax dollars—to individuals in their private cars because of a particular environmental virtue test devised by and for the virtuous.

I spoke to Susan Little, Ms. Pavley's consultant for transportation issues, who worked on the bill. She told me that the bill has a sunset clause after three years, and that Ms. Pavley had no intention of granting the first 75,000 buyers of qualifying hybrids a permanent privilege. But Ms. Little also told me that 75,000 cars happened to be the estimate of the number of hybrids that would be sold in California during the life of the bill.

1984
SMRR sponsors a charter amendment to change the date of municipal elections to November of even-numbered years, to increase
voter participation, particularly by renters, in local elections; the
amendment passes on the June ballot.

In other words, the bill, the express purpose of which was to encourage more people to buy hybrids, will, based on the proponents' own numbers, have no effect except to confer a benefit on 75,000 people who were going to buy hybrids anyway. State Treasurer Phil Angelides, who owns a Prius and who recommended the legislation to Ms. Pavley along with environmental activist Laurie David, another Prius-owner, is quoted in the *Times* as telling Mr. Ford that what he should do is spend "his time figuring out how to out-compete the Japanese."

I suggest that Mr. Angelides, who I used to think would make a good governor, and Ms. Pavley spend their time figuring out how we can get significant public benefits from the car pool lanes before giving those benefits away.

S anta Monica received national attention during the 2004 election because
we had a celebrity candidate for the City Council: Bobby Shriver, son of
Eunice Kennedy and Sargent Shriver, brother-in-law of Governor Arnold
Schwarzenegger, etc. Although unfailingly liberal, Shriver represented an
attitude that had not received much attention before; the attitude that maybe
City Hall tried to do too much.

SEPTEMBER 13, 2004

If imitation is the sincerest form of flattery, then city council candidate Bobby Shriver
is floating around Santa Monica bathed in the glow of appreciation. Three council
incumbents, Ken Genser, Richard Bloom and Michael Feinstein, all running for reelection, have shown him the sincerest flattery by rushing to introduce measures to accelerate
and pre-judge the council's review of the City's hedge laws.

That is, if flattery by its very nature can be sincere: *Flatter*: "to praise excessively
esp. from motives of self-interest"; *Flattery*: "the act or practice of flattering" (*Webster's
Ninth New Collegiate Dictionary*).

Something, or, rather, someone, has unnerved the usually cool, calm, and collected
manner council incumbents typically affect; after all, it's been many years since an incumbent has lost a bid for reelection. In particular, candidates Santa Monicans for Renters'
Rights (SMRR) endorse usually campaign with a lot more confidence, stressing SMRR's
largely positive platform and their own records of responding to every whine and whim-
per from aggrieved constituents.

And all this anxiety over hedges? Hedge-angst seems to me to be one of those homeowner issues without a lot of political bounce, because there aren't many voters who
care. Remember the proposition to restrict the power of the Landmarks Commission
over single-family houses? It was the hottest thing and then ... fizzle. Only 30 or 40
percent of Santa Monicans live in single-family houses, and as with landmarking, even
those who do care about hedge heights are divided on the main point of disagreement,
the height of front yard hedges and how the law should be enforced.

So what's the big deal?

I was only able to attend one day of the Chamber of Commerce's interviews with
candidates, but it was the day that both Shriver and Genser appeared. Regarding Shriver,
the interesting point was that in seeking the chamber's endorsement, he didn't shy away
from the pro-social services positions that go with his background. As for the homeless,
for instance, he avoided bashing and empathized empathy and threatment, indicating
that he wants to keep his lines of communication open to Santa Monica's liberal majority.

1984

Four SMRR incumbent City Council members stand for reelection
on the new November municipal ballot. One loses, and SMRR is
reduced to a three-member minority on the Council

He seemed to be basing his campaign on an attack that was simultaneously both pointed and vague on the "attitude" of City Hall.

Genser emphasized, among other things, that he was always available to listen to constituents, including business and property owners, to try to get the City's bureaucracy to work. But that might be the root of the incumbents' problem.

After years of squeaky-wheel government, which has meant reams of new laws and procedures, and millions spent and many hired in the cause of "code enforcement," policies that appeal to a small group of complainers are starting to annoy a larger group of usually quiet residents who don't like receiving heavy-handed letters threatening them with daily $25,000 fines and who can't get their second-story additions approved.

One issue where I thought City Hall tried to do too much was with land-marking. It's one thing to landmark a building for what it was, it's another to landmark it for the nostalgia it represents.

SEPTEMBER 20, 2004

Santa Monica has a new landmark, a little bungalow at 921 Nineteenth Street.

This is big news. Guidebooks will be rewritten. Architecture students from Europe and Japan will find their way to Nineteenth Street, followed by tourists. Postcards will be printed. What will the neighbors think when the tour buses are parked up and down the street?

921 Nineteenth Street

Before getting to the bungalow, however, the Landmarks Commission initiated action to designate the Bay Cities Guaranty Building at 225 Santa Monica Boulevard (a.k.a the Clock Tower Building) a landmark. How ironic that in the twenty-nine years of its existence the commission never got around to designating as a landmark a building that truly is a landmark, a classic Art Deco tower from 1929 with an iconic clock, yet has

1984

Santa Monica adopts new land use and circulation elements of its
General Plan; the new plan calls for a pedestrian-friendly city, but
gives priority to visitor-serving and office development over housing.
By 2000, Santa Monica had added about 1,000 hotel rooms and
eight million square feet of office development with no increase in
population.

found plenty of time to sanctify little faux this and that houses. Do thirteen-story office buildings offend the prevailing nostalgia for Santa Monica as a leafy suburb?

Might the commission have an agenda besides preserving what deserves to be preserved?

After dealing with the Clock Tower Building (which new owners have restored beautifully without help from the commission), the commission devoted an hour of discussion to a garage door in the Third Street Historic District. This was no ordinary garage door. Although it will be barely visible from the street, this garage door will be the door to a new garage that Bea Nemlaha, one of the originators of the historic district, wants to build to replace an original historic garage that is, according to Ms. Nemlaha's testimony, beyond repair.

Historic garage door, as seen from street

Ms. Nemlaha testified that in designing the new garage she and her architect, Ralph Mechur, had followed the Secretary of the Interior's guidelines for renovations in historic districts. The Secretary, apparently not a proponent of faux historicism, instructs renovators not to build in such a way that anyone might confuse the new construction with what is historical. Mr. Mechur had designed a more or less modern structure, with a roof deck, but he called for traditional materials.

In case you can't imagine what happened next, go read something by Kafka. As bad luck would have it for Ms. Nemlaha, only four commissioners who could vote on the matter were present; two commissioners were absent, and Chair Roger Genser had to recuse himself because he owns nearby property. Ms. Nemlaha needed four out of four votes to approve her garage. This can be difficult, but she made it clear that she was willing to do whatever the commission wanted her to do.

1989
The redesigned Third Street Mall, now called the Third Street Promenade, opens with three multiplex movie theaters and becomes an
overnight success. Twenty years later it is one of the major shopping
and tourist destinations in the region.

Unfortunately, the commissioners couldn't make up their minds. Or, rather, they could sometimes make up their own minds, but they could never agree; they gave at least four different opinions, and ultimately tried to punt the whole thing over to staff, who said, no thanks, not unless you're going to tell us what to do. The upshot is that Ms. Nemlaha and Mr. Mechur have to figure out what it all means and return with a revised plan.

The garage door was a good warm-up for the bungalow on Nineteenth Street and its "craftsman-style elements." (Those were planning staff's words; architectural historians sometimes refer to "craftsman-style elements" as "Arts & Crafts Movement program-related activities.") What struck me from watching the commissioners deliberate was how casual they were. They were making a decision to freeze forever in time a building and a site, and their level of discourse was along the lines of "it's a gem," or "it's lovely," or it's "exquisite."

Commissioner Ruthann Lehrer, an architectural historian, tried to put the matter on a more scholarly plane, and called the house an example of the "late phase" of craftsman bungalows.

"Late craftsman?" What does that mean?

Try this: Google "late craftsman" (in quotes) along with "architecture." You get all of about eight hits. Not that the term has much meaning, but if you look at those eight hits and try to find out what "late craftsman" means, you find that it simply refers, if anything, to houses built, in the ten of thousands, mostly from pattern books after World War I; i.e., after Gustav Stickley's *The Craftsman* magazine ceased publication and after the Arts & Crafts style ceased to be its own architectural movement, having evolved into various forms of modernism.

Since Stickley published in *The Craftsman* Southern California architects as diverse as Greene & Greene and Irving Gill, it's not surprising that many different aesthetics can fall under the category of "craftsman;" but that doesn't mean that any old house that combines a little bit of this with a little bit of poorly proportioned that should be a craftsman landmark.

Fact is, the commission wasn't landmarking the building for what it was, but for what it represented, and that was an old Santa Monica they had nostalgia for: specifically, the old Santa Monica of single-family houses. What most impressed the commissioners, in fact, was that one family, the original family who had built the house, had lived in the house for seventy-four years. For that alone, Commissioner John Berley wanted to call the house a landmark.

Buildings with sociological significance rather than architectural distinction are eligible to be landmarked, but only if the significance is special. Vast areas of Santa Monica are still zoned single-family residential, and we have many houses that reflect the era of 921 Nineteenth Street. The house itself is in a neighborhood, Mid-Wilshire, that is already mostly apartment buildings. When I rode my bicycle through the neighborhood one Sunday morning to see the house on Nineteenth Street, I saw neighbors jogging, pushing strollers, walking. Mid-Wilshire is one of the more dense, but also one of the more desirable neighborhoods in the city.

The commissioners, however, made it clear that to them, the neighborhood has gone down since developers started replacing little bungalows with apartments and condominiums. The architecture of today's apartments and condos may not be distinguished, but then neither was the architecture of the original neighborhood, notwithstanding Ms. Lehrer's retrospective appreciation for "late phase" craftsman.

Now 921 Nineteenth Street is a precedent. If it's a landmark, then dozens of similar houses in Santa Monica, if not more, are landmarks. In effect, the commission has down-zoned a significant portion of Santa Monica's multi-family districts.

Has anyone notified the state housing department?

What the commissioners are protecting are not physical landmarks, as is their charge under the ordinance, but their own prejudices and fear of change.

One more thing. The commissioners also included the garage at 921 Nineteenth Street in the landmark designation, preventing the owners from developing any part of the property. Here's a picture of Santa Monica's latest landmark:

Santa Monica's latest landmark

[Note: The owners of 921 Nineteenth Street appealed its landmark designation to the City Council, which in July 2005 reversed the Landmarks Commission ruling on a 5-2 vote. The owners cited my column in their brief, which caused Council Member Ken Genser, who voted to uphold the landmarking, to ask them if they considered me an expert on architectural preservation. Presumably he didn't.]

The national election was in full swing. I should have kept my mouth shut and stuck to local issues, but everyone else was writing about it, and I couldn't help myself.

OCTOBER 4, 2004

What impressed me about Thursday night's debate between Bush and Kerry was that although you expect the candidates to prepare for a debate, to "rehearse" if you will, it was clear that to Bush this meant practicing his red meat lines from the stump, but for Kerry it was a chance actually to "study up." It wasn't Kerry's ability to put aside the doubts about whether he's had a consistent view about Iraq that won the debate, but his broadening of the discussion, bringing up issues and places that are just as important as catching Osama bin Laden or Iraq. Issues and places like nuclear proliferation, North Korea, Iran, and the fissile material in Russia.

When it came to North Korea, I confess that I had not paid particular attention to the subtleties of the six-party or bilateral talks question. But after the debate I learned that Bush was flat wrong when he said that if we talked directly to North Korea, we would wreck the multilateral talks. It turns out that all the other friendly countries in those talks, particularly the Chinese, have been pleading with us to reopen direct talks with North Korea, at the same time that the six-party talks continue. It was the equivalent of Gerald Ford not knowing that Poland was not independent of the Soviet Union.

With all the news from Iraq, will the electorate take a broader look at the international situation? The conventional wisdom is that chaos in Iraq is good for Kerry, but the bombings and the deaths of our soldiers in Iraq, however, just make Americans angrier. Bush is the candidate for those who want to lash out, but cooler heads know that you don't defeat a guerilla uprising with air-to-ground missiles. If Iraq were peaceful, this election would be about the economy, healthcare, and international issues that Bush has ignored.

Kerry would be winning in a walk.

* * *

Two weeks ago I attended the Rail-Volution conference in Hollywood. Rail-Volution is the premier get-together for people interested in "building livable communities with transit." This year's was the tenth annual conference.

Santa Monica played a big part. Mayor Richard Bloom gave the keynote speech at one of the lunchtime plenary sessions, on "Community Building, Transit, and Global

1994

January 17: the Northridge Earthquake destroys much of Santa Monica; causing $250 million in damage, making uninhabitable 2,300 dwellings. Henshey's Department Store at Fourth and Santa Monica is one of the "red-tagged" buildings and ultimately torn down.

Sustainability," staff members such as Sustainable Program Coordinator Dean Kubani participated in workshops, and the city was the destination for one of the conference's mobile workshops. Sandy Grant, from the City's Task Force for the Environment, was omnipresent.

I attended workshops with names like "Thinking Outside the Box to Make Housing Affordable" or "Sustainable Mobility as a Means to Sustainable Development." I took a tour of Pasadena. I met people from all over the country, from Santa Clarita to Norfolk, Virginia. I thought I would meet more big-city types, but it seemed that everyone was from the suburbs, or in mid-sized cities, and they were all interested in solutions to traffic congestion that might also enhance their quality of life.

At these conferences one can meet people who actually know something. One such person I met at a Rail-Volution party was Richard Stanger. In the early '90s, Mr. Stanger became the first executive director, and in effect the "father," of Metrolink, Southern California's commuter rail service that now has 512 miles of routes. Metrolink serves roughly 40,000 passengers each weekday, a 9 percent increase over 2003; while that is only 2 percent of all transit users in the region, Metrolink provides 13 percent of all transit passenger-miles in the region. The reason is that the average Metrolink passenger's trip is long, 36.4 miles.

Most important for all those people (you know who you are) who say they could never use transit themselves, and are stuck in their cars, in only about ten years Metrolink has reduced traffic on parallel freeways by 2.9 percent; that's a significant number when you consider that even small increases on already crowded roads can drastically slow traffic and make driving less reliable.

I got to talking with Mr. Stanger, who is now a consultant. One thing on his mind was a recent (September 8) L.A. Times story on the 2004 "Urban Mobility Report" issued by the Texas Transportation Institute (TTI). Every year, TTI releases a report quantifying the level of traffic congestion, and its costs, in eighty-five metropolitan areas. Newspapers love the TTI reports because they provide the occasion for scary headlines, the gist being that we are pushing the pedal to the metal toward traffic doom. The heading of TTI's press release announcing this year's report was "Annual Study Shows Cities Losing the Race Against Traffic Gridlock Growth

Predictably, the headline of the Times' article was "Inland Empire Traffic is 5th Worst; Population growth and more trucks raise the region's U.S. ranking." That was the headline, but the real news in the report, certainly in the "man bites dog" category (but which the Times buried deep in the article), was that average annual per peak period commuter congestion delay in the Los Angeles-Long Beach-Santa Ana region decreased nearly 25 percent between 1990 and 2002 (from 123 hours to 93), and the average annual delay in the Inland Empire remained largely stable between 1992 and 2002 (55 hours in 1992, 57 in 2002).

Huh? Traffic is getting better? (Or at least not worse?)

Before we go crazy, what does TTI measure? TTI uses several measures, but perhaps the best known is its calculation of the amount of time the average driver during peak traffic hours loses because of congestion. TTI determines "annual delay per peak traveler" by contrasting the actual length of commutes with how long they would take in an idealized universe without congestion.

For instance, TTI says the non-congested speed on a freeway should be 60 miles per hour. If you commute 20 miles over a freeway, and congestion reduces the freeway speed to 30 mph, the trip will take you 40 minutes instead of 20. Multiply those lost 20 minutes by the number of workdays in a year, and you get your annual figure for delay.

Keep in mind there are a number of variables. Your delay will go up or down not only because of changes in traffic speed (i.e., because of congestion), but also because of the length of your trip. A shorter commute will mean less time lost to congestion. For instance, according to census data, the average commute in Riverside is a couple of minutes longer than the average commute in Los Angeles, yet the amount of time lost to congestion in L.A. is 63 percent more; obviously, the average distance of a commute must be less in L.A.

So what caused the reduction in traffic misery in the L.A. region?

What piqued Richard Stanger's curiosity was that the decline in time lost to congestion in L.A. and the stabilization inland coincided with the region's beginning to invest in rail. The region clearly crossed a crucial threshold in the early '90s. In 1982 L.A. commuters lost an average of forty-seven hours to traffic congestion. That number then hit its peak of 123 in 1990. The figure has been declining, with ups and downs, ever since. The same goes for the Inland Empire. In 1982 drivers there lost a negligible nine hours a year to congestion. In 1992 that number was fifty-five, a more than 500 percent increase. But between 1992 and 2002, the number only increased two hours, to fifty-seven.

Metrolink, light rail, and the Red Line subway have all gone into service since 1990 when per traveler delay peaked. Nearly 300,000 people now use these systems every working day, and as discussed above, many of them travel long distances. The investment in rail is paying off; the TTI report concludes that if it weren't for all forms of transit in the L.A. region, the total number of additional hours lost to congestion would be about 20 percent higher.

But as important as the investment in rail has been, and as promising as it is, it probably does not explain the entire decline in average hours lost to traffic delay. I spoke to David Schrank, one of the authors of the TTI report, who said that traffic in L.A. is such

1998
Copley Newspapers closes the Outlook after 111 years of continuous
publication.

a complicated subject that, frankly, it defies analysis. For instance, the best explanation of the decline in peak period traffic delay might be that congestion is so bad in the peak periods, that people are adjusting their schedules to drive at other times. This lowers the peak period delay by spreading delay around.

My theory is that the decline in average delay has something to do with increasing density. Population in the five-county Southern California region increased 13.6 percent in the '90s, from 14.5 million to 16.5 million. The most dramatic percentage increases have been in the Inland Empire; the population of Riverside and San Bernardino Counties increased by 660,000 people, or 26 percent. But the biggest increases in numbers of people occurred in the more highly developed core counties of Los Angeles and Orange; 1.1 million people, or 58 percent of the total five-county increase.

So what causes traffic congestion, sprawl or density? You swap dairy farms for people in Riverside and San Bernardino, and the average annual congestion delay increases from nine hours to fifty-seven in two decades, mostly in the first decade when population made the first jump from rural to urban. Then jobs start moving to where the people are (i.e., more density, more development), commute distances decline, and so does average delay per commute. You add many more people to already urbanized counties, and average traffic delay increases more slowly and then declines.

It gets back to the TTI formula. TTI measures the impact of congestion on the average individual commuter. That means TTI divides total number of hours lost, which is a function of speed and distance, by the number of commuters. If you increase population, you increase the denominator. And if you shorten commutes, you decrease the numerator. What does density do? Obviously, it increases the number of travelers. But it also decreases the average length of commute, because "things are closer to each other."

The effect is cumulative. If your car trip is shorter, because density has made the destination closer, i.e., more convenient, then not only do you lose less time to congestion, but also, by not driving those additional miles, you reduce congestion for everyone else who is driving.

So let's make things closer.

The local election was around the corner, a local gangster had fired four-teen shots at a high school student riding his bicycle home from school (fortunately no one was hit), and not one political flyer mentions the word "gang." Isn't killing kids a political matter? The City convened a meeting.

OCTOBER 11, 2004

The auditorium at Edison Elementary was full. In many of the seats sat city council members and members of the school board, but on the dais were four civil servants: the city manager, the police chief, the superintendent of schools, and the principal of Edison. They were stoic. But as I watched them catch the flak, I wondered if they ever wondered if it was part of their job descriptions to deal with the anger and fear that can only emerge with the relief that comes from the miracle, as several speakers described it, that in the middle of the afternoon a gangster shot fourteen bullets at a high school student return-ing home on his bike but missed with every one.

I was waiting for a politician at least to give the rhetorical equivalent of a big hug, but all I got was the hired hands trying to explain why years of everyone "doing their best" still left us with a situation where some young people want to kill each other.

Excuse me, but kids killing kids is a political matter, not a budgetary issue.

As I write this, I have arrayed before me the political mailers I've received so far this year: an eight-page mailer from Herb Katz, a four-page mailer from SMRR, two mailers from Michael Feinstein, and a three-page letter from Bobby Shriver. The word "gang" never appears. Nor is the word mentioned in the SMRR platform. I haven't found it in any of the Chamber of Commerce political sites either.

It's the traffic, stupid.

After the meeting I spoke with member of the Board of Education Oscar de la Torre, who told me that in all of the Pico Neighborhood there are perhaps three dozen or so serious gang members, of whom only five or six are violent. De la Torre wasn't dismiss-ing the threat; on the contrary, his point was that even a few such dangerous people cause a lot of pain.

They drive to Mar Vista to kill people, and the Mar Vistans come here to kill us. Since 1989 some two dozen youths have lost their lives on Pico streets due to gang violence.

What strikes me is the "asymmetricality," to borrow a phrase from current thinking about warfare. As asymmetrical war in Iraq bogs down the U.S. military, certainly asym-metrical gang war is bogging down us.

Think of it. Twelve thousand people live in the Pico Neighborhood, 85,000 in Santa Monica, we spend $100 million on schools, tens of millions on police, millions on recre-

---

ation and youth services, and somehow no one has the imagination to reach half a dozen lost souls?

To tell them they are somebody? Or to make them somebody?

[On that note, this collection of columns will end; before readers find out just how badly I predicted the outcome of the national election. (I was, however, reasonably prescient about the local one.) I hope that these essays, absorbed as they are in the details, nonetheless collectively persuade one that the vigor in American politics is, or can be, local.]

Time Line Sources

Basten, Fred E., *Santa Monica Bay: The First 100 Years*; Santa Monica: Graphics Press (1974).

Capek, Stella M., & John I. Gilderbloom, *Community versus Commodity: Tenants and the American City*; Albany, N.Y.: The State University of New York Press (1992).

Kann, Mark E., *Middle Class Radicalism in Santa Monica*; Philadelphia: Temple University Press (1986).

Rose, Marla Matzer, *Muscle Beach: Where the Best Bodies in the World Started a Fitness Revolution*; New York: St. Martin's Griffin (2001).

Scott, Paula A., *Santa Monica: A History on the Edge*; Charleston, S.C.: Arcadia Publishing (2004).

Storrs, Les, *Santa Monica: Portrait of a City, Yesterday and Today*; Santa Monica: Santa Monica Bank (1975).

Wolf, Marvin J. & Katherine Mader, *Santa Monica: Jewel of the Sunset Bay*; Chatsworth, Calif.: Windsor Publications (1989).

Photographs from the Santa Monica Public Library Image Archive; permission to use them is gratefully acknowledged.

Index

316

321